The Best of Dreamcatcher Journeys

Fuel for the Traveling Soul

Beverly Lane Lorenz
Photography by Jim Lorenz

iUniverse, Inc.
New York Bloomington

The Best of Dreamcatcher Journeys
Fuel for the Traveling Soul

iUniverse books may be ordered through booksellers or by contacting:

iUniverse
1663 Liberty Drive
Bloomington, IN 47403
www.iuniverse.com
1-800-Authors (1-800-288-4677)

ISBN: 978-1-4502-1580-0 (sc)
ISBN: 978-1-4502-1581-7 (ebk)

Printed in the United States of America

iUniverse rev. date: 3/16/2010

ALSO BY BEVERLY LANE LORENZ

Unequal Justice

Dedication

This book is dedicated to Ol' Tex who made this dream a reality and a way of life.

He is the smile on my face and the song in my heart.

He brings joy not only to the travels but to the life we live on a daily basis.

Ol' Tex is known by many names.

You probably call him Jim Lorenz.

Contents

Foreword

Welcome Journeyer

If you have ever dreamed of traveling, or would like to, this book is for you.
It is for the adventurous as well as the restless.
It is for those who want to live life to the fullest and enjoy life everyday.
It is for the light-hearted as well as the serious.
It is for those who want to enjoy the breath-taking beauty America has to offer.
It is for those who appreciate beauty in all things.
It is for the sophisticated as well as the naïve.
It is for the experienced traveler as well as the novice.
This is a book everyone can enjoy.

About the Dreamers
. . . and how it all came about!

Once upon a time…they were traditional, career oriented, professional people who fell in love and married. They enjoyed successful but separate careers. Jim worked as an executive in the oil industry. His last assignment before retiring was accounts manager for all of the commercial oil business on the East Coast. Beverly enjoyed a successful career as a professor of speech and mass communications at a notable university.

During the week, the Dreamers went their separate ways. Jim often traveled for business while Beverly commuted to work and "held down the fort." They had a date each Friday evening and looked forward to the weekends when they shared the events of the past week with each other. It was a good life.

The Dreamers had no children of their own and the few relatives they had, lived at a distance. They moved many times during their marriage due to career opportunities, but their strongest ties were to Maryland where they had lived and worked for the longest periods of time. Yet, they really were not locked into any particular place.

Not only were they Dreamers, they were planners. They planned for their future so that they could financially secure their retirement years. They often talked about moving to Europe, buying a yacht to call home, and sailing the Caribbean. This would give them opportunity and access to the ancient architects and artists they studied and appreciated.

One summer while they were vacationing in Ocean City, Beverly became ill and spent most of a long weekend in the room they had rented at Phillips-by-the-Sea. Upon return to the mainland, her doctor determined that she had "Polymorphous Light Eruption." Simply said, it was an allergic reaction to sunlight. They already knew that fair-complexioned Jim had to be protected from sun exposure.

"How can we even think of spending day after day on the water in the sun?"

Not discouraged, Jim came up with a new idea. "Why not buy an RV and travel? After all, a motor coach is really a 'land yacht.'"

The dream was born. Over the next several years, the Dreamers researched, went to dealers, shows, campgrounds, and interviewed people in the industry. The more they learned, the better they liked the idea.

In time, the Dreamers sold their home and moved to a rented townhouse 3 months before they actually retired. The corporate buy-out offer came shortly after their move to the unit. Jim was 54 years old when they began the journey. Bev's birth certificate might have read a teensy bit earlier but she hides it beautifully!

Looking Back

We'd do it all over again—*in a heart beat!* We'd go farther and, without a doubt, we would stay out there much longer. The only caveat would be a specific plan going in for possible medical contingencies. We were fortunate that we did not experience the need while living on the road. Yet, it was this very *concern* that ultimately compelled us to stop when we did. Yes, we would have designed a plan that would cover those particular unknowns that eventually haunted us and drove us off the road.

Would we go back? Hardly a day goes by that we don't think about it!!!

Introduction

The ***Journey*** began with a dream—a dream so big and far removed from our traditional, mainstream life that family, friends, and neighbors thought we were…well, to put it kindly, ***crazy!***

Perhaps they were right in some respects. Yet, I had always 'marched to the beat of my own drummer' and got myself in a bind any time I tried to follow the herd. But in fairness, full credit for this idea has to be given to my partner who had always lived the "straight and narrow," except, of course, for choosing me. This was when he definitely went off that path!

There was much to be learned before even we were convinced that living full-time in a motor coach was a valid option. Therefore, our study and search began a few years prior to actually doing it. It was our unconventional history together which fueled our receptiveness to explore new ideas. It was our open-mindedness which afforded us philosophical as well as reality driven discussions. It was our research that ultimately generated our excitement and the necessary enthusiastic energy it would take to follow through. Once we were on this road, there were no regrets or no turning back.

We began to share our dream with friends. After the initial shock, they began asking some good questions. The theme of the questioning was basically this: *What will you do with all your stuff??*

The answer began to become clearer and clearer within weeks of this same type of response from nearly everyone we knew. All our possessions, a lifetime of accumulation, in a word was . . . *stuff!* It turned out that this very question was the key to our success in getting rid of "all our stuff." In truth, that is all it was. ***STUFF***! Just stuff.

Somewhere along the way, Jim asked me the question, "Do you want to have a home base?"

My immediate response was, "Of course. Absolutely. We need to have a *place* to call home."

His follow-up question was trickier. "Where do you want that home base to be?"

We had lived all over the country. We did not have children; there was just the two of us. We had no reason to be anywhere. It took me two weeks of hard thinking before I found the answer. *"I don't know."*

With that in mind, Jim said, "What if we travel for awhile and decide *where* when we get there."

Our working careers had taken us from East Coast to West. More often than not, corporate moves lent themselves to an average of 16 months in one place before moving to another destination. It got to a point that after a year anywhere, whenever I saw a moving van I would wonder longingly, "Where are they headed?"

One time, when we were following our moving van over the Rocky Mountains on a return East move from Salt Lake to Kansas City, I said, "I always wanted to travel. I just never expected that I'd be moving a house full of furniture—and vehicles, each time I went somewhere new!"

So, in a nutshell, in January, 1997, we sold our home—all three floors plus the beautiful one acre park-like property on which it set. All our *stuff* had been disposed of in some way or another except for a few necessary pieces we would move with us to a two story, rented townhouse on the outskirts of Baltimore. Here we worked and waited for the official word that would mean our life would begin anew.

Word came early that spring, and on May 1st, we watched as the last pieces, (our box spring and mattress), left the townhouse with a most grateful, newly graduated Maryland State Trooper. It would be the last of our possessions henceforth and forever known as *stuff*. We no longer needed it.

We rented a 4' x 6' foot U-haul trailer and hitched it to my little Cadillac Seville.

We loaded the trailer with the few items we would need on the motor coach—some clothes plus 3 or 4 small boxes of things we would continue to use in our new life—coffee maker, pans, toiletries. We then drove 3,000 miles across country from our home of the past ten years on Chesapeake Bay on the East coast of Maryland to Netarts Bay on the west coast of Oregon.

We want to share some of our experiences, the good, the bad, the funny, as well as some of the lessons. We've done all the hard work. We experienced the traumas, sorted through the nitty-gritty, and, hopefully, learned the lessons. We want you to sit back and appreciate this compilation, learn from our experiences, but most importantly, find the love of life that we share with you. ***Enjoy the ride!!!***

Chapter 1

Head 'em up and move 'em out!

Home in Oregon

We had rented Room #1 at Sea Lion Motel from the man who owned and operated HomeBase Oregon, our first mail-forwarding service. #1 turned out to be a large and generously furnished apartment. Basically, the unit would serve to be the motel owner's home except he had built a home nearby. The actual rent for this 2 bedroom furnished apartment complete with living room, dining area, full kitchen and bath overlooking Netarts Bay was $150 per week. There were public phone booths outside the Netarts Grocery which was located directly behind our bedroom.

It was somewhat difficult to wrap our minds around the people and the place considering the fast-paced, often perilous life we had been living on the East Coast. The natives were both interested and interesting. I was particularly struck by the genuineness of the people and the place. There was no pretentiousness because there was no need for it. Leading stories on the TV evening news in this area were about roses and festivals in the parks compared to the top three most gruesome murders in the city we had just left.

Extraordinary sights and sounds availed themselves to us. Sea lions, seals, and blue heron kept us company. Whales were frequently seen from the nearby shore where we dug blue clams to make our own chowder. Elk crossed the highway just a few feet from our living room.

For additional entertainment, we toured the local cheese factory in nearby Tillamook where we would go to purchase weekly supplies and anything else we needed from the local Fred Meyer store. We were not at a loss for company because by virtue of living there we were part of the community. We were welcomed into the local fish hatchery to feed the baby salmon. A coveted treat was an invitation to tour the privately owned Pearl Point Oyster Company where they grow larvae to seed oyster beds around the world.

This, of course, was but the first stage of our journey. We became residents of Oregon, bought our Jeep Grand Cherokee and renewed ourselves in the process. It was June 3, 1997 when the real adventure began. This was the day we took delivery of our brand spanking new forty foot, Class A, 1997 Monaco Dynasty Motor Coach and immediately christened it ***Dreamcatcher***.

Here Come the Bus! Here Come the Bus!!

We had never stayed in a tent, let alone a motor coach. The Coburg, Oregon Monaco factory provided us with a technician who would walk us through a five-hour, staccato-paced briefing of parts and procedures. (That's five hours of frenetically paced, complex, *new* information that we would need in order to survive! At once, it was both protracted and instantaneous depending on whether you looked at it from the perspective of need or stamina.) Then, of course, there was the perspective of our Tech who expected to spend about an hour or at most, two! In all his years of service, he had never met new owners of a Class A 40 foot motor home who had not "worked their way up" through the ranks from simple camper to Class C before buying a bus!

As is often customary, the company offers new coach owners both a place and the opportunity to stay in their new motor homes parked in front of the factory door in order to live-in and check out all of the equipment. This arrangement also serves to catch any of the potentially more serious mistakes made during manufacture. As the technician said, "There are over 100,000 moving parts in these rigs. If we can get all but 0.1% correct, we are happy."

You do the math. That left us with 100 things to break down; and, they all did that very first year! RVers are welcome to make appointments and bring their coaches back to the factory for these repairs if the trek back is possible and/or feasible. Therefore, the factory camping facility was filled with RVers who had returned with lists of repairs. At that time, Coburg was pretty much made up of the Monaco factory and homes of the workers.

Therefore, RVers waiting while service is done on their motor homes are eager to find anything to occupy them during the daytime while their rigs were in the shop. By default, ***we*** became their focus of attention. They called us the "honeymooners" mostly because it was more polite than other terms they could have used to describe totally ignorant novices.

Although our new acquaintances and responsibilities kept us up until after midnight, at 6 a.m. each morning, we got a serious wake-up knock on the front door of the rig from our persistent Tech who checked in to see if we had experienced any problems or had any concerns. We, in turn, had our list and we were ready!

The constant attention at Camp Monaco was well-meaning but draining. They *all* wanted to help. They shared their knowledge, their experiences, and their stories. Their interruptions became maddening as we tried to figure it all out. Exhausted, we decided to leave the Monaco factory campground (albeit prematurely). In three days, we bid everyone farewell and headed for the highway.

When we reached the Interstate with Jim at the helm, I was trying to figure out how this wide-bodied machine was ever going to fit in just one lane of the highway in front of us. Fortunately, there were two lanes going in each direction. As we came barreling down the ramp toward the Interstate, he began screaming, "***I can't do everything***. You are going to have to read the signs!" He was hanging onto the steering wheel for dear life with sheer terror in his eyes.

GERONIMO! We came down the ramp and hit the pavement running on all 8 cylinders and 6 wheels. (So far so good!) I read the signs ad nauseum.

We headed north to the campground in Woodburn where we would try to organize our life in plastic storage boxes. But first, we had to get in the gate, register with the campground host, and…*park the bus!!!*

For those of you who have not thought this through, there is more to this than meets the eye—at least for two complete novices. First, in order to maneuver, we had to unhook the Jeep which was in tow (not nearly as easy as it sounds). We had to get the motor coach into its assigned spot positioned in such a way that the sewer hose could be connected, the electric could be plugged in, and the Jeep safely stowed in its tight position somewhere adjacent to the coach within our rented space.

We had to hook the sewer, water, and electric to land services—for the very first time as well. In what seemed like days later, but in reality, only hours, we succeeded. We were two happy campers! We had done it. We were one of them.

We enjoyed the lifestyle for a day or so before we discovered we had a bad refrigerator or "refer" as our technician called it when we called him. What else could you do with a "bad refer" but head it back down the Interstate to the Monaco factory. Sounds easy enough, right? Wrong.

Now we have to unhook from all of our carefully hooked-up land connections. Power! Jacks! Sewer! Steps! And, we had to anchor everything inside that just might open, dump, or slide. (Let me note that this is a piece of cake for more experienced RVers—the ones we would soon become.) For total innocents, it was more than unnerving.

At the factory, they popped out the huge front windshield to remove the "old," defective refrigerator and replaced it with a brand new refer. We were both exhausted by the experience. The ordeal necessitated two round trips to Camp Monaco as it was affectionately called.

Heck, we needed the road experience anyway, right?

Now before you begin thinking we sunk the family fortune in some "wet-behind-the-ears" investment doomed for failure, let me set your straight. It was an adventure, a remarkable journey on many levels.

Although there were countless stories of our life and times once we left the secure and familiar womb of Woodburn RV Park, we've selected some of the best of tales—not necessarily the best of times. However, as we look back now, every day provided us with great opportunities and precious memories. And yes, perhaps they were ***the best of times***.

"On the Road Again"

The motor coach had a magnificent surround-sound system. We bought a CD recording of Willie Nelson's "On the Road Again" before we headed to Oregon. So, each time we headed out from wherever we had parked the Dreamcatcher, we played our theme song. It delights us to this very day.

When I began writing my tales, I needed to have names for my lead characters and Ol' Tex was easy enough to determine since my partner wore Cowboy boots, hats and shirts once he left his suit and tie world. His partner, so proper and lovely in appearance, had to be called "The Beautiful Bev." In our "periodic periodical" called **Dreamcatcher Journeys** which we published—well, periodically, (usually every 6 to 8 weeks), we were comfortable in crediting Jim as the Travel Coordinator, Bus Driver, and General Critic. The Beautiful Bev was, of course, Managing Editor, Writer, Columnist, and Navigator. DC Press published and mailed the publication from, where else? Wherever we were at the time.

When you have a brand-spanking new motor coach and are smack in the center of Oregon at Woodburn as we were, you have many outstanding choices. There's Highway 101 which parallels the entire coast of the Pacific Ocean, Desert High Country, another spectacular place to visit, and north, the Columbia River Gorge with all its wonders. Since we needed to end up in Moscow, Idaho for the LIFE ON WHEELS conference at the University of Idaho in about a month, we opted to head north for the Columbia River. There is no way to verbalize the magnificence of this area, so I'll try to state the facts of what's there.

Excitement and apprehension combined into a motivating energy as we unhooked the Dreamcatcher from its land-lines and our security within that area and Monaco.

Fasten Your Seatbelt

Columbia River Gorge – a preview of paradise

There is no way to verbalize the beauty of this area, so I'll try to state the facts of what's there.

Eight breathtaking and all very different waterfalls line Interstate I-84 on the south side while the Columbia River, along with the Bonneville Dam which provides power to the Pacific Northwest, are to the north. Magnificent Mt. Hood, capped with snow, stands majestically to the south and is a year round ski resort.

As part of the retirement dream, Ol' Tex was determined that his fishing would become a reality. As a matter of fact, there was never a doubt that if we were ever to settle in a traditional home again, we would be living on waterfront property where he could fish ever day.

For our first night on the "open road" away from the security of the Monaco factory area, we carefully selected a campground along the Columbia River. We cringed as we drove into Cascade Locks Campground. The heavily wooded, rock-studded grounds screamed, "POCK MARKS TO YOUR RIG!" Yet, we knew, beyond a shadow of a doubt, there was no way to turn around and get out of this big rig nightmare. As we scraped through the first dozen trees, we decided to grin and bear this *tenter's* paradise. It would be the first of many. But, we were there, we were off the highway, and it was time to take in the gorgeous sights and sounds that only the great Northwest can offer.

We begin with one of the most magnificent areas in all of North America, the Columbia River Gorge, an 80 mile geologic wonder that divides the states of Washington and Oregon.

Chapter 2

Tales from the Periodic Periodical

Let the Adventure Begin!

Columbia River Gorge – Phenomenal Beauty

We begin the adventure on the Columbia River which divides Oregon and Washington. There are many breathtaking waterfalls along the south side of Interstate Highway I-84, the historic highway which parallels the Columbia River. We had almost forgotten such raw beauty existed when we visited this area. It is truly overwhelming.

Columbia River Gorge has one of the largest concentrations of waterfalls in the world. Each waterfall is unique and can be accessed only by hiking to and from each different site. Multnomah is perhaps the most well known, but Bridal Veil, Horsetail and all of the others are worthy of your time and effort. Getting up close and personal to some of these spectacular sites requires some energy and agility. We were pleased to learn that we were not in bad shape for novice hikers and we were able to readily access each attraction.

The entire area is pristine and lush. As I said at the outset, the territory is overwhelming. There is a unique quiet "hush" in the midst of thundering waters. We carry the magnificence of the beauty with us in our hearts to this day.

Majestic Mount Hood beckoned at a distance and we tackled it in quite another way. Instead of testing our physical prowess, we put the Jeep in all-wheel drive and reached the Lodge in no time. It was a smart move in many ways. Number one, we had spare jackets in the trunk which we indeed needed, (even though it was nearly July), and number two, we'd still be climbing had we gone by foot. Remember, there is snow on Mt. Hood all year around.

It stands statuesquely pointing skyward with its white cape covering its shoulders even in June. Water from the melting snow races down over rock beds, fresh, clear, cold, sparkling in the sun light. Sometimes tears of joy can replace words; they did here as we soaked in the sights, the sounds, and the silence.

Shad Row on the Columbia River

Elbow to elbow they stood in every size and shape—*no, no—not the fish*! I refer to the fishermen who lined the narrow locks catching twenty-four to thirty-eight inch Shad---one right after the other. The fish, swimming up river to spawn, jumped onto their hooks. All but one hook, that is! Poor Ol' Tex stood along side the other fishermen—eagerly waiting while they were catching. It was pitiful. Really pitiful.

That same afternoon, we headed for the nearest bait shop to buy new bait. This would be the first of many bait shops we would see in our travels. *Talk about interesting!!*

The Official Counting

We went inside the Bonneville Locks and watched. "One little fishy, two little fishies, three…." The fish counters, real people, counted the number of fish swimming upstream during each spawning season. It was yet another interesting place to say the least. You could watch and count the actual fish in the river water through glass as they made their trek.

Beyond the Locks and up river, a sternwheeler, reminiscent of yesteryear, took visitors up and down the wide Columbia River for dinner or just a jaunt. Sternwheeler Days, an annual event, brought carnival and other festivities to the town park. The place itself was again delightfully reminiscent of by-gone days.

Dreamcatcher headed east to Walla Walla, Washington long before the Sternwheeler crowds arrived. Looking back, I believe we would have stayed. But, at the time, we were novices to the open road and to this part of the country. We would have savored the simplicity and richness of this culture that had long ago been lost to us. People here in this part of the country just seemed to appreciate the joy of being and each other. There is much to be said for this valuable existence.

Walla Walla - Walla Walla

"Walla Walla Sweets," "Walla Walla Sweets," sign after sign read. One soon got the distinct impression that sweet onions were the main attraction to Walla Walla, Washington. In actuality, it was, in fact, the *only* attraction.

The sound of silence permeated the entire area. It was so profound that it was a little frightening. Weighted down by this eeriness, we took a day and drove back to the Tri-cities where the Columbia and Snake Rivers meet in search of anything: noise, people, or just something to do. The search itself turned out to be the main event of that day.

The next morning, we eagerly unhooked our land conveniences and headed for Clarkston, Washington.

Joining Lewis & Clark for July 4th

Ah, the memories. I refer not to the evidence of these early explorers but to the ten *long* days we were parked at Hillview RV Park on Bridge Street at Clarkston, Washington.

The reason we stayed put for so long was that we wanted to keep off the highways for the holiday weekend. Insecure as we were in the beginning, we allowed plenty of time for the four-wheelers to get to wherever they were going and back again without threat to us and our 65 foot long rig and tow.

We did enjoy the evening's fireworks display from our big screen front windshield. Fireworks are legal in the Northwest. We watched families come and go during the holiday extravaganza.

The bridge at the end of the main drag of Bridge Street, the main route through the town, turned out to be the actual bridge at the state line which crossed over the Snake River to Lewiston, Idaho. During those long, hot days, we frequently visited the merchants, both local and chain. WalMart, Kmart, and Radio Shack became our main attraction since Hell's Gate and Hell's Canyon were accessible only by a boat or raft down the white water rapids of the Snake River. As they say in the Northwest, it was a 'spendy' adventure and we were not all that excited about testing our swimming skills.

Life On Wheels – RVers' Conference at University of Idaho

To Boondock or Not to Boondock . . .

Our apprehension of boondocking (dry camping without shore power, etc.) prevented us from taking full advantage or pre-conference week activities. We drove up to Moscow, Idaho in our tow vehicle--straight up, a six mile, seven percent grade. It was a half hour drive from where we were camped in Clarkston. We knew we would have to arrive at the conference early since we were signed up for the two day Professional Driving School which was to be given just prior to the main event.

When we pulled in, we were excited and thrilled to see our dear friend, Gaylord Maxwell, who was the originator and coordinator of Life On Wheels, standing in the parking lot of the Kibbie Dome. After an exchange of joy filled hugs and handshakes, he said, "Come on in," and we climbed into his home on wheels for a catch-up visit. Before we left campus that Monday, Gaylord had introduced us to many of the folks who would be our instructors over the next two weeks. Beyond that, they all would become friends for a lifetime.

Driving School

We "made the grade" to the University of Idaho (the six mile, seven percent grade, that is) and parked for the first ever dry-camping adventure. We would learn to adapt to this style of existence in the coming weeks and months as opportunity presented. It was hard to believe that mid-July could be so cold anywhere at night, but running generators at certain times in a large group is often restricted. It was here on campus.

We both took the difficult and physically demanding driving course during pre-conference week. To qualify for highway candidacy, each student had to be able to drive proficiently through an obstacle course of cones--backward as well as forward--and maneuver a series of tight turns---backward as well as forward. Traffic, equipment safety, and other considerations kept each driver fully engaged for two physically and mentally demanding eight hour days. Students drove their own rigs while instructors stood on the pad directing with official hand signals. Onlookers enjoyed watching this carousel of Class A's, Class C's, Fifth Wheels and Travel Trailers maneuver the precision course. The audience made the exercise all the more grueling for the participants.

Finals

The final exam was a trip from the campus pad, through campus, into town, up and down several steep grades on a narrow two lane road to neighboring Viola, Idaho. The return trip included what felt like an *extensive* tour of the city of Moscow and its busy streets.

Each student was evaluated, critiqued, AND, completely exhausted at the conclusion of this two-day, 8 am to 4:30 pm marathon. The words of instructor John Ward still echo in my mind when I find white knuckles gripping my steering wheel. "You're doing great," he said, "just great." So, too, do the words of one mean-looking university student who pulled up to me at a stop light. ***"Next time, lady, leave your sofa at home!"***

We left the school not only richer for the experience, but also as full-fledged alumni of the Dick Reed Professional Driving School. Each graduate had a diploma, official driving school alumnus pin, and an iridescent red road cone.

Dry Camping, sort of

We had our first lesson in what is called "dry camping" during our stay at the University. With much advice from earlier acquaintances, we had been told how to survive without hook-ups (electric, sewer, and water) for several days or, if you are really accomplished, weeks. RVs are self-contained units. The equipment on board will provide for comfort, convenience, and necessity. Pre-conference week offered the opportunity to try our skill at total dry-camping known as boondocking. We had no serious problem and only one minor discomfort when the temperature plummeted and we were reluctant to run either our diesel generator or gas furnace. Two layers of clothing, socks, and several blankets didn't even come close to replacing heat usually generated from the electric blanket which is always a part of our bedding.

During official conference week, we were hooked into 30 amp power (sort of). The reason I say "sort of" is because it fluctuated and therefore had to be watched. Also, since the power was from huge generators that made a great deal of noise, at 11:00 p.m. every night, they would turn off the generators leaving us with no power until the following morning when they started up the generators once again.

Once parked, no one was allowed to move unless there was an emergency. A hose was available to refill the fresh water tank if necessary. This left one potential problem. Yup! Water in means water out. Therefore, daily sewage service known to all as "honey wagons" eliminated the problem—at a price, of course. We opted for the gym showers.

Life On Wheels in Moscow, Idaho

Official conference week was held from July 13 - July 18. Qualified experts in the RV lifestyle taught classes on 80 different subjects during this informative and fun-filled five day conference. Classes began promptly at 8:00 a.m. each morning with the last bell at 4:30 p.m. (or later) each afternoon. Life On Wheels, by ALL accounts, was a whopping success.

The entire conference was held at the University of Idaho. Everything you would ever want to know about RVing, the lifestyle, Alaska, Mexico, Central America, North America, and Europe was available. There were classes on Digital Satellite Systems, Inverters, batteries, maintenance, etc. Additionally, you could take classes in photography, nutrition, writing, publishing, fitness, *the works*. These classes and more were available to over 700 students who lived on campus in some 260 plus rigs. Participants attended classes which ran an hour and a half each. We were given enough time to just barely make it to the next class therefore making days completely chocked full of information.

Evenings were filled with food, friendship, and special events such live music performances and theater. The highlight of dining was the salmon BBQ attended by every conference participant. Marinated salmon were smoked in the open on apple-wood racks Native American style.

After nearly two weeks together with fellow adventurers, saying "good-bye" was difficult and took a couple of days to do so.

Head 'em Up - Move 'em Out

With heads and hearts filled to capacity, Dreamcatcher headed south and west--- back through Lewiston, Clarkston, Walla Walla, and then back along the Columbia River Gorge. We had learned much and had 10 pounds of valuable literature to prove it. Friendships made during the two week program were intense and significant. They are our family now. As industry renown and RV Hall of fame super star Gaylord Maxwell put it, "You folks are the cream of the crop."

We exited I-84 at Yakama Bend on Route 12 and headed southward to desert high country. There is a dot on the Oregon map and next to it is the word, "Boardman." We found the dot and followed directions to Driftwood RV Park in the middle of "hot as Hades" nowhere. We emptied our tanks, did our laundry, and removed "bug-yuk" from both vehicles. The temperature was a "dry" 105 degrees in the shade. Talk about change in climate and scenery. The good news: an Olympic size, indoor swimming pool and a soothing Jacuzzi were available to weary travelers.

Umatilla and...

We retraced our tracks and returned to Umatilla to see what we could see. We found an indoor flea-market complete with fleas. It was so lonely and quiet in this desert town it was scary.

This experience brings me to an interesting observation. The only shopping available in places such as Umatilla, Boardman, Milton-Freeland, Moro and the like are second-hand (third and fourth in many cases) stores where merchandise is dusty, threadbare, or generally well used. If you are planning to visit some of these towns, think twice before deciding to kill time shopping.

As Dreamcatcher moseyed on down the highway, we began to see snow covered mountain peaks rise on the horizon. Winter snows melted and rushed through fields creating cool, clear streams with white water rapids which caressed the sides of the highway in contradiction to the surrounding landscape. We would spend the night in Bend, Oregon before heading to Crater Lake, "nature's theatre in the round."

Chapter 3

Here we go . . .

You're In the Army Now?

Now, *I know* that some of you already think I'm crazy by the sheer fact of being out there doing what I was doing. And, some of you wonder if there might not be a bit of a gambler in me, especially when you learn that I would go into a "beauty" shop, way out in the middle of high desert country, far from civilization as I knew it, and ask for a haircut! Well, that is exactly what I did.

Let me assure you, the shop came highly recommended. "They do a great job. I go there all the time!"

What I did *not* know at the time was that the clerk in the liquor store/post office who Ol' Tex had asked--was bald!!!

I left the Head Tech, as the shop was called, with the first military regulation haircut I had ever had. A month later, it was still standing at attention!

High Desert Museum

Not wanting to be recognized (as if I would be), I put on my safari hat and we went down the road a piece to the High Desert Museum just south of Bend, Oregon where we spent the afternoon enjoying the wonders of the wild.

High Desert Museum is a living museum of nature which provides visitors a walk-through observation of *live* animals in their habitats. A pioneer sheepherder's wagon and log cabins add interest to the porcupine, otter, and wild bird of prey exhibits. Desert snakes and other reptiles were exhibited---mostly in glass display habitats--*as far as I wanted to know.*

The Spirit of the West gallery portrayed life in the Northwest as it once was by offering visitors a "walk-through-time" tour in the Hall of Exploration and Settlement. With a longing look in his eyes, Ol' Tex lingered and looked. I reminded him that there was no running water, air conditioning, and TV. In moments, we were history!

Digital Dance

The bonding ritual of male RVers is an interesting phenomenon. And, any male RVer, worth his salt, has some working knowledge of the DSS (or Digital Satellite System for the reader who has not been plagued by this curse). It goes something like this.

After finding *ANY* excuse to get outside and away from doing one of a number of useful chores necessary for living this gypsy lifestyle, the male puffs up his ego and hauls out his tin dish from wherever he has it safely stowed during the voyage to the next stop. He parks this strange tinny sounding disk on a wobbly tripod, hangs his personally concocted anchor somewhere south of the center of gravity, and begins alternating his stares between the dish and the sky.

It takes less than two minutes for his nearest neighbor to come over and start the ritual. "How'dya like it?"

The dish possessor puffs up his ego and responds smugly with a positive nod.

"Whadaya get?"

The initial steps have been taken, and the dance begins. One at a time, the men in camp slowly move into the circle. Dancer number one forgets that he has someone inside who would rather be doing anything else but starring at a TV screen filled with strange messages and numbers while waiting to yell them out at the top of her voice as soon as the digital "dancer's" sky-watching produces an uncertain peak.

At this point, you can kiss the next two hours good-bye. The bonding ritual has begun and no one gives a hoot about the inside screen watcher. She is finally free to do whatever she wants.

Nature's Theater in the Round

Before leaving Oregon's desert high country, Dreamcatcher took us to Nature's spectacle of turmoil and tolerance. Crater Lake is a virtual theater in the round where the audience drives the 33 mile perimeter in total awe. Mirrored before you are snow-capped mountain peaks perfectly reflected into the water-filled caldera which is 1,932 feet deep and usually, very still. Perhaps the highest mountain in the United States at one time, Crater Lake is now the deepest lake. The richest, deepest, navy blue one could imagine is shown on its clear, absolutely still surface. Various shades of lush aqua marine appoint the perfect picture.

In contrast to this moist spectacle is the Pumice Desert created 6,800 years ago from Mt. Mazama when it coughed up great volumes of hot pumice and scoria. Unexpected desert flowers paint the stone laden landscape with various hues of purple, lavender, pink, fuchsia, white and yellow. One must admire and respect this thriving vegetation for its determination to survive here. Equally unexpected in these lava fields is the light, fresh aroma of heated pine. So delicious is the fragrance from the little red protuberances which grow on the tips of the cones, I wanted to pluck them and put them into my mouth and chew in an effort to harvest their pungent odor and allow it to permeate my being.

Diamond Lake Duplicity

A jewel in fact as well as in spirit, Diamond Lake, Oregon was a retreat to the sanctity and times of yesteryear. Life around this family oriented vacation spot was a throw-back to the 1940's and early 50's. We spent Saturday night at the Lodge where a dance floor was set-up out of doors so guests could participate in an evening of square dancing. Light bulbs on electrical wire were strung around the floor to provide light while providing an atmosphere of treasured times from my past. I was a child again as I watched families enjoy music and each other. No one seemed aware or cared that life and culture had changed so dramatically outside the State boundaries of Oregon.

Think about it. Then, search it out. Your life will be richer for your effort.

Rogue River Gorge

Just south of Diamond Lake is a little bitty town called Union Creek. This is where we came upon the rushing waters of the Rogue River at its infancy. There no longer was evidence of the melting lava flows as the cold, white water thundered through the crevasses of the Rogue Gorge filling small gateway pools at the rate of one Olympic sized swimming pool every minute.

It was a majestic and enchanting in sight and sound to meander among the pools, the rock formations, and the genuine raw beauty of this place.

We would experience the significant beauty and taming of the Rogue on our decent of the Cascade Volcanic front. This adventure in itself is as perilous today in a 40' motor coach as it was in a covered wagon in the days of the Old West. Although the map indicated it was a "truckers' route," it became immediately apparent, as Dreamcatcher careened down this mountainous highway, that "truckers' route" meant *one truck* at a time going *one direction* at a time--very slowly!!! We were most fortunate not to meet on-coming traffic. There simply was no room.

Pacific Coast - Northwest

Dreamcatcher enjoyed a few days of well-deserved R&R at Crescent City, California. We left the Dreamcatcher to cool its wheels while we hopped in the jeep to explore the majestic redwoods and paint-brush perfect sunsets.

The Red Wood Forest is all that it is boasted to be with minimal commercialization yet enough to make the trek through it enjoyable. We were delighted by the ambiance and took it all in.

It was hard to imagine that Crescent City had once been swept away in a Tsunami. This is a sea-faring village still today. The campground where we stayed celebrated the end of the crabbing season by having a crab feast for all guests. Californians are friendly and fun people and we enjoyed a fabulous feast.

DC Moseys Up the NW Coast

If you never had the opportunity, Highway 101 on the west coast of the United States is a "must see." A two-lane road, the highway runs directly adjacent to the Pacific Ocean. It has spectacular summits and breath-taking views both high and low.

Our first stop back in-state after our brief hiatus out of Oregon was Honey Bear at Golden Beach. What we thought was going to be a rather boring 3 days turned out to be one heck of a good time. As it turned out, Honey Bear Campground is home to Black Forest delicacies. You'll find them in any good deli around the country if not the world.

Talk about fun...all one needs to do is tell your hosts that you plan to join them for dinner so that they will know how much food to prepare. There is only one seating and dinner selection is made by the chef who is the owner of the entire operation. At six o'clock, guests are seated at large tables in the restaurant on the grounds. Live entertainment follows dinner each evening and is provided and performed by--whom else? Our delightful German host--the owner!

The people we met at evening dinner opened doors we didn't know were there for us to investigate and enjoy. They invited us to not only their world but their homes. When I think back, today, this world we uncovered was like a fantastic dream. Yet, it was real and we carry this spirit in our hearts today.

The Thrill of the Wild

We enjoyed the company of a local couple who befriended us at evening dinner. Since his early retirement from the Oregon State Troopers, Gary and Colleen had become full-time lobbyists for the Northwest forest industry. We shared Washington politics, places, and concerns for society while contrasting life on the east and west coasts. Due to commitments on both sides, we were unable to join them at their ranch while in the area. The couple did, however, convince us to take a trip deep into the wild Rogue wilderness area of Siskiyou National Forest. What a trip it was! Spectacle after spectacle delighted us as we bounced along rough terrain and roads often spiraling out of (my) control. Still, we climbed and climbed, and then we climbed some more.

We turned the Jeep around only after this passenger pleaded and begged for mercy during the last half hour of the climb. Ol' Tex was having the time of his life! Those of you who relish the thrill and excitement of the roller coaster would consider this trip through the frontier to the outpost called Agnes even more exciting—and nerve-wracking than any you've ever experienced.

Yahoo!!!

Coos Bay Here We Come

There's that ***eerie quiet*** again--so intense it is almost palpable.

Many New Age and spiritual devotees live in this area. It is an unassuming place and unencumbered. I would like to have met up with some of the authors I've read who call this area home. Had we not been scheduled, I most certainly would have done so.

Coos Bay is different than I had imagined. The stillness was well… ***eerie!***

Florence – A Scenic Must See

All too soon, we were on to Florence, a pretty little seashore town about midway up the coast of Oregon. This is where we had become completely enchanted by the northwest Pacific Coast.

It is also the place where we dedicated our life and weekend to JPL's coming of age...and, the birthday gift "to die for"…the digital satellite dish roof mount installation.

Sadly, this also means no more digital dances around a tripod—unless, of course, we were unfortunate enough to park under trees!

JPL Becomes An Old Man at Sea

It's official! Jimmy Paul Lorenz celebrated his 55th birthday on the Pacific Coast at Florence, Oregon. We had come "full circle" in our Oregon Odyssey. It was nearly time to head "home."

Monaco's Come Home Rally

A "rally" in the sense of recreational vehicles and travelers is a gathering together of like-minded people for several purposes. First, and foremost, it's fun. Beyond that, it is often for the purpose of learning and socializing. Vendors also are frequently available to present new products and/or present their wares. Frequently, there is fabulous entertainment.

Monaco's Come Home Rally, in a word, is *family.* And, in keeping with its name, it was a family that had come home--Monaco Motor Coach, Coburg, Oregon, the company that had produced the Dreamcatcher. This corporation, in its' earlier years anyway, treated its' customers as family. In this day and age, it is difficult to begin to remember that concept.

This was our first rally and although we had only recently become members of the family, it didn't take long for us to fit right in and enjoy the many advantages--and yes, the blessings of belonging.

It is not simple to espouse all the virtues of this clan, but allow me yet another word: *CARE--people caring about each other.*

There was a time when corporations in general had values. After years of my personally being pro corporation, the pendulum has swung in the opposite direction. Monaco renewed our respect and admiration for corporate entities. All employees from the CEO and President, through the rank and file, to owners genuinely care about and respect each other. We were all there.

Are You Having FUN?

Maybe the buzzword but obviously the number one concern and question, "Are you having fun?" From Corporate CEO to Technician, everyone wanted to know.

Days and nights were filled with food, fun, and frolicking. We were educated and introduced while strong bonds between attendees were developing. Plans were made for the future. Every possible rejoining was contemplated from hooking up with another couple down the pike to the Monaco pre-rally at El Paso, Texas. Here we will all meet for 3 days, 4 nights and then caravan on to the FMCA winter convention at Las Cruces, NM (2/26-3/7/98).

We are renewed. We are revitalized. *Bravo Monaco!* We'll see you all in El Paso. ***Viva Las Cruces!!***

A Study of Cooperation

Always in search of higher purpose, I try to recognize the spiritual gains in this life. I had become somewhat cognizant of the necessity of getting along well with one's traveling companion in this nomadic lifestyle. Yet, the RVing Community gives new meaning to the word *cooperation.*

It is moving to watch two people work together as frequent challenges present. The scope of this cooperative effort is enhanced to encompass the RV community. For example, on the final evening of the Monaco rally, we were returning from the main hall with our dinner companions and making plans to leave the following morning. The next thing I knew, we were all involved in a group effort helping one another prepare for a safe journey beyond the security of this conclave.

I watched in awe. Instantly, I realized the level of good we were achieving beyond the moment. There was an immeasurable spiritual presence. You could feel it.

These are treasured, meaningful experiences one finds difficult to put into words.

Cutting the Cord - (Heading East)

Dreamcatcher headed south on I-5 through Southern Oregon and on into Northern California before pointing East to Reno. We passed an Indian Pow Wow at McCloud and a Spiritual Ceremony smack dab in the middle of Shasta National Forest. It felt almost sacrilegious to go into Reno, to the Casinos--Harrah's, Eldorado, Riverboat, and the like. But we did so anyway doing penance, I like to think, at Circus Circus. I stood in silence and watched a young mother hold her son who was severely afflicted with cerebral palsy. She sat him on the edge of a circus booth and pulled his limp body to her. She clasped his little arm in her hand along with a dart. Together, *they* threw the dart at the balloons on the facing wall.

Sounding much like a loaded shotgun, the balloon popped and the frail child flinched and his small limp body reacted on cue for half and instant. I held my breath in silent prayer seeing how stingy they were with prizes. Without hesitation, the booth attendant handed the child a stuffed animal.

I cried. Perhaps this experience nurtured my soul's yearning for the redemption of society through love and kindness.

Rolling Into Reno

Not that we weren't up-tight enough rolling into Reno for the very first time, but to add to our experience, traveling the same highway and coming from out of nowhere, was a ***big, bad biker*** who went by the name of **T-Bone.** To top it off, **T-Bone** was having a *bad personality day*. He was not satisfied with giving our bus driver *the bird.* **T-Bone** hauled his hinny not more than 6 inches from front and center of our motor coach (which was traveling at 60 MPH) and dared my air-horn honking bus driver to run over him. Thank God for passenger brakes!

Now each time Jim sees a biker, he calls him "road kill." He claims he is still wiping "cheek grease" off the front of the motor coach.

The OLD WEST

Carson City, Virginia City, even the outskirts of Tahoe remind us that we are not all that far distanced from our country's frontier days.

Virginia City has maintained the same buildings and atmosphere. You can feel the ghosts of the gold miners walking the same streets as you. It may be a new world but all the old buildings, saloons, and cafes remain in their original form. Tex bought his handcrafted belt buckle from one of the local merchants. He is one happy cowboy--Tex, that is!

Puffer Belly Pontification

If you thought you'd heard it all when you read the one about the Digital Dance, when Ol' Tex met with guys in the RV Parks to tout the values of the satellite dish on the 3-legged mount, well, wait until you here about old Puffer Belly who installed and roof-mounted his own DSS (digital satellite system) and saved $1500 bucks!

Self-appointed expert and hero to his peers, he now struts from RV Park to RV Park crowing the rewards of expertise and, awe shucks, genius. Life is good.

Return to Roots

"Roots" in the truest sense is a term generally reserved for childhood beginnings. However, in the case of this writer and the bus driver, in partnership, we planted roots in many parts of the country throughout our life together. Therefore, as Dreamcatcher traveled eastward, "roots" were revisited as early as Sandy, Utah, a suburb of Salt Lake City in the south end of Salt Lake Valley. We lived in the Salt Lake Valley from November 1979 through November 1981.

Salt Lake City--"on my terms"

Our anticipation peaked as Dreamcatcher exited I-80 onto North Temple Street. It had been nearly 20 years since we followed the moving van east over Parleys' Summit and said good-bye to "twinkle town," my pet name for Salt Lake City. (The thin, hot atmosphere at this altitude causes the lights at night to seemingly dance across the valley.)

Nothing but fond memories remain: colorful flowers bursting from pots throughout the city, clean streets, manicured yards and gardens, a pristine city. Although the people were materialistic, (a contradiction to that which I idealized for their church-going, family-oriented way of life), it did not hurt the beauty of the area. Alcohol was prohibited, smoking was *really frowned upon*, and any form of caffeine, from coke to coffee, was taboo. It was a different world from where we had moved originally, (NYC & Philadelphia area), but certainly admirable, (idealistically speaking, that is).

Materialism here had mushroomed. Commercialism now runs roughshod over not only the city, but the entire valley. Every business enterprise, be it Wal-Mart, Fred Meyer, or simply ZCMI, has 3 to 5 branches and that did not include the east or west suburbs.

Clearly, this is not a bad thing in and of itself, but add to that all of the Burger Kings, McDonalds, Taco Bells and other fast food fantasies along with their cardboard and Styrofoam debris, and you've got commercial chaos.

The city I once called the "jello capital of the world," is now home to Greek, Mexican, Italian, and yes, even Asian foods. Prohibition, once the hallmark of the Beehive State, has been lifted. I saw young people drinking from "brown paper bags" in automobiles while racing aggressively from stop light to stop light. People smoke freely on the streets. And last but far from least, it seems there is more *pot* than flowers!

My heart sank farthest when on our way back to camp early on Saturday evening, a couple of squad cars pulled along side our Jeep. One car was marked "gang unit." The evening was further destroyed when we made a quick stop at a grocery and noted the *armed* security guard patrolling *inside* of the market no less.

Back in the day, so to speak, "the day" meaning protectionism of a way of family/church oriented life, I used to jokingly say, "I'll take a one-way ticket anywhere if you just get me out of here." Today, I'd take a one-way ticket back to that time.

All aboard? We're heading east to Oz.

Return to the Land of Oz

As Dreamcatcher bounded down the Interstate I-80 washboard, the hot, dry winds filled with dirt and dust announced our arrival in Kansas. It had been a long drive from Cheyenne through the heart of Denver. We were getting impatient to get off the highway by the time we arrived in world renowned Russell, Kansas, home to Senator Bob Dole who, at that time, was running for President.

We immediately inquired if Bob and Elizabeth were in town for the forthcoming holiday weekend. From the response we received, we were sure this would have been a *rare* occasion. Hmmmm…not how the message was portrayed during the political campaign.

Oh well, determined to keep this eagerly anticipated stop a memorable occurrence, we changed our duds and headed out at dusk for a tour of the town before having dinner at "Barb's Café." Surely you remember. Barb's Café was the one in the TV ad where everyone in Russell eats and Barb asks dear old Bob Dole for some I.D.

The place was so dead quiet that it was eerie--not a soul in sight throughout the sprawling town. Evidence of oil drilling businesses was apparent. However, at this hour, all remained eerily quiet and still. Not one eatery was in sight--let alone Barb's Cafe.

Tired and disillusioned, we made our way back to the Dreamcatcher and "nuked" our own dinner in the microwave oven. Tomorrow would be a new day and we would return to our former hometown, Kansas City.

Kansas City Here We Come

As we were leaving Flying J campground in Russell, it dawned upon me why there was a building in the RV Park identified only as *STORM SHELTER.*

During the two years when we lived in Kansas, I spent *a heck-of-a lotta* time in and out of our basement. We spent many a night on the sleeper sofa in the family room which was adjacent to our basement stairs. This area is the tornado capital of the country. It is well-armed with sirens which announce threats regularly during tornado season.

As Dreamcatcher moseyed on East on I-70, my eyes carefully surveyed the skies, ever grateful for daylight and sunshine.

Holiday Coming: Get Off the Road

During the time we lived in our motor home, we were always eager to get off the highways as holidays approached. Holidays were a time to leave road space to novices who had limited time to travel. We were guided by the fact that one was coming and we wanted to be safely in our spot long before the onset of heavy holiday traffic.

Tucked away in the safety of our campground, we spent Labor Day weekend filled with good friends, good foods, and good memories. Who could ask for a better way to spend a holiday?

We saw many old friends and returned to our old neighborhood of Seven Hills in Lenexa. Kansas City has maintained a positive approach to growth and seems to accommodate both people and industry in a visually pleasant environment. It was refreshing to see; it was heart-warming to remember our year and a half here.

A Dark Cloud Over Our Heads

On the morning we left Kansas City for Indiana, the sky opened and dumped the rain we had not seen all summer. Although it was a day not fit for man or beast, every man, woman, and child with access to I-70 across Missouri was on it. It was, after all, the first day of school for many. For the other bazillion travelers, I'm not sure why they were out there.

We were rolling. We had much to do, many folks to see, and after months of leisure, we were *scheduled.* If we wanted to spend Christmas in Florida with *the mouse*, we had a lot of miles to cover.

Back Home Again In Indiana

Dreamcatcher headed for Ft. Wayne, Indiana, childhood home of Jimmy P. Thank God we were reasonably rested with 2 days en route because it took 2 additional days to find a place to park. The Dreamcatcher was fast becoming a "mansion" on wheels as we traveled east. Where parks in the west welcomed forty-footers with open space, Ft. Wayne really didn't acknowledge motor coaches at all. In the end, we were unable to find a campground in the Ft. Wayne area that could accommodate us. We ended up in Michigan calling Yogi Bear's Jellystone at the Indiana/ Michigan boarder home for nary a week.

Most of the family came out to visit for an old fashioned family get-together on Saturday where they were introduced to Dreamcatcher and the joys of living life on wheels. Their eyes rolled up into their foreheads, but we didn't care. What anyone thought about our adventure didn't matter by then. We were living the dream.

The rest of the week we experienced a "busman's holiday" trekking back and forth 3 hours a day to the Waynedale homestead.

Good-byes and good memories readied us for moving on. We were headed east again.

New York, New York—my kind of town!

New York

Our "return to roots" visit to New York was short but very sweet. Family there was excited to see us and spend time learning the ways of road-warriors.

Returning to Upstate New York is melancholy and bittersweet. I personally miss every one of my ancestors and close, personal ties. When you come from a small village, pretty much everyone is a "personal tie" in one way or the other.

In addition to parents, grandparents, and a sibling, I enjoyed a large extended family. As a matter of fact, my farm roots came complete with an additional set of "parents"—and more!

Gone Yet Not Forgotten

While the landscape never seems to change, nothing remains the same. This is Upstate New York. My mind turns to memories of a distant past, my heart becomes filled with those I love, and, as my soul joins them in what once was. I cry real tears for what could have been. So many opportunities lost.

Leaves filled with color exuberantly greeted us in the Northeast as we made our way through grape and apple country heading south—destination Baltimore, Maryland. Patches of brilliance cheered us on while sections of muted fall colors eased us through the mountainous passes. We headed south through eastern New York and west through Pennsylvania. Our world and our hearts became more and more filled with color. Anticipation of returning to our old "stomping grounds" from where we began this odyssey 5 months ago filled us with excitement and tension. We could sense the vibes of folks we considered "family."

First stop on our agenda would be Andrée's Optical. Owner and optician, Andree` helped us out of the eyeglass dilemmas we had both encountered during our months away. Andree` had been a dear friend for years and owned her own optical business. In addition to eyeglasses, she also had accepted several packages with replacement parts which had been sent to us from Coburg, Oregon. (Today, we can't remember which number of this was part of those 100 defective parts they told us about at the Monaco factory!)

Maryland, Our Maryland

Before we did retire, we had been transferred to our beloved Maryland to live for a second time. We had never expected the opportunity nor did we anticipate the duration. We considered it "our home state" since we had so many wonderful memories and had actually lived there longer than anywhere. Our return with the Dreamcatcher was bittersweet: so many friends, so little time.

A whirlwind visit at best, there simply was not nearly enough time to spend with loved ones. In the end, we were glad to leave behind the idiosyncrasies of Morris Meadows campground where we stayed. Our schedule had us heading south in the reasonable safety of early Sunday morning when the Baltimore and D.C. beltways would not be buzzing with as much traffic as usual.

Living In The Moment

Excitement built as Dreamcatcher cruised into Elizabeth City, NC on State Road 158. The road was, perhaps, more challenging than the lady at the Tourist Information Booth had indicated. But we had come a long way and we were doing great. Seeing the sign, "Nags Head - East 158," the bus driver confidently eased the coach over into the turning lane to make a 120 degree turn.

Think about it! His sole passenger and professional driving school graduate looked in horror and whispered, "It's a bad one, Tex." He responded, "No sweat, I can do it."

I held my breath.

"MOVE THE GARBAGE CAN," he shrieked as he maneuvered forward our home on wheels.

"Slow it down," the ashen driving school grad responded as she popped out the door and immediately began hauling one king-sized can back behind...."Oh my God, NO!"

The "Nags Head-East 158" sign stood eye-to-eye with Tex. He hit the brakes, put the rig in neutral, and ran for the street shouting orders. (Did I mention we were in *very heavy traffic?*)

Fortunately, the police car that was coming toward us did not make the traffic light. As Tex bailed out of the motor coach and I ran for the jeep in tow, the officer engaged his beautiful set of bubble lights and began directing traffic while we unhooked the tow vehicle. In case you are not aware of this, you cannot, *under any circumstance,* back-up a motorcoach that has a vehicle in tow.

In a matter of several very *tense* moments, we drove our respective vehicles away from that ***"I can do it"*** corner.

It was gratifying to recognize how much we are "living in the moment." It was a dicey situation. With God's help and the kind young policeman, we handled it and went on to new experiences and other challenges.

Moral of the Story

Life is a journey; enjoy the ride!

Chapter 4

We are rolling now . . .

Nothing Could Be Finer?

Excuse me?

Dreamcatcher pretty much waded through North Carolina. At Hatteras Island on the Outer Banks, we saw the famed lighthouse and Kill Devil Hills at Kitty Hawk where Wilbur and Orville earned their wings. Rain or no rain, you can simply soak-in the history by the sheer fact of being here.

Damp and dismal, we moved further south to Emerald Isle--where it *seriously rained.* The wind blew so hard that Dreamcatcher rocked back and forth on its tires.

We did our best to ignore the weather conditions and did the 50 cent tour. The rains continued and we were ready to move on. We were scheduled now.

Holy Moly

Look at all the golf...courses, clubs, links, greens, communities, villages, plantations. South Carolina. This is *serious* golf country. North Myrtle!

Dreamcatcher cruised on into the famed Myrtle Beach where the ocean is the main event. The pace seemed somewhat frenetic even in off season. I looked for the famed southern hospitality and found it in a neighboring fellow RVer *from Pennsylvania.*

Choices for fresh seafood in Myrtle Beach are overwhelming. And, there are plenty of sights. Pick a spot, sit back, and just watch—mostly the people. It's hard to get really close to the famed beach unless you own or rent a piece.

Charleston, South Carolina

I always felt we should have been transferred to Charleston during Jim's career with Amoco Oil. Actually, it was more of an unspoken dream. Now, I better appreciate why.

First, it is adjacent to the ocean and *packed full of places to SHOP*. City markets and shops line the streets. Residences are straight out of a southern novel. Romance abounds; you feel it in the air. You can see it in the horse-drawn surreys which moved about easily with other city traffic. There is an undercurrent of hustle/bustle but on a pedestrian level. It was difficult to make the decision to move on when the time came. More nostalgia for what could have been. But, that time had passed, and we had "miles to go before we sleep."

Hilton Head

Interesting. That's one of those words one uses when one is not quite sure what to say about something--or someplace. The obvious, of course, is that Hilton Head is a golfer's paradise. It is a resort town, but only if you are staying at one of the resorts. Since it is surrounded by water, it is an excellent place for fishing and boating.

Commercial businesses are hidden behind attractive facades. Signage is respectably discrete. All in all, a pleasant place with one way in, and yes, one way out.

Think about that in regard to hurricanes. We did when several years later with first hand experience of 9 hurricanes the year prior, we moved to Hilton Head for a year.

Savannah, Georgia

Maybe it was the beautiful Savannah River, maybe it was the "laid back" atmosphere, or maybe it was the ghost I left here a long time ago, but Savannah felt like home—the first time I visited the city.

I was not at all surprised by the Spanish moss hanging from the trees; everything here had a subtle deja` vu. The streets, the town squares, the waterfront, the stories, the legends were accepted with an ease of familiarity as if I had been a part of them. Not in any recent past, but way back then, back when it was in its own real time, even before Flannery O'Connor. Perhaps even before the Civil War.

Savannah is a fabulous place to visit. It offers tourists many interesting sights along with lots of good food. It is comfortable.

In the Garden of Good and Evil

A best seller for several years, the story fit the city. We saw the haunts of the characters; we met their unsuspecting neighbors. And, as seamy as it appeared, it was the impetus that sent me back to my own novel writing. A year or maybe even two years ago, I left a group of people at the edge of their final crises and I wanted to know just what happens to them. I also know there are some interesting characters in my travels who will be invited into some future plots!

Legend of the Waving Girl

Her name was Florence Martus and for nearly fifty years she greeted every ship that entered the port of Savannah. It is said that as a very young girl, the love of her life, a young sailor, went off to sea. She promised to be faithful and wait patiently for his return. She greeted every ship by waving a white apron by day and a lantern by night. She had even trained her dog to wake her at night. There is a statue of Florence and her dog at the East end of River Street in remembrance of her spirit.

This wonderful, romantic story brought tears to my eyes until our second bus driver and tour guide remarked that it is also said by local folks that her elevator did not go all the way to the top. (This was one of those pieces of information I really never needed to know.)

Colloquialisms

Without a doubt, one of my favorite words which I heard and learned for the first time while living in Oregon was "spendy" which is used to describe something considered to be expensive or costly. We liked it so well that we immediately adopted it into our vocabularies.

Presently, adapting to the south, the expression "I'm fixin' to" has grabbed our attention. It is easy to use while we are here in the heart of the Deep South, but we are not certain of it permanency in our vocabularies. At any rate, we were fixin' to leave Savannah and head for Atlanta.

Don't Feed the...GATORS?????

We tooted into our first Coast to Coast park in Yemassee, South Carolina a couple of hours south of Charleston. (Coast to Coast is a network of private RV parks where members buy-in through an ownership program.)

After lunch, I decided to do a walk-about to see just what advantage there might be to a private park. Excited to see the lake which had to be the feature of this small, not unusual campground, I headed through the thicket, down a dirt path called, (what else?) Lake Avenue.

In the clearing was a small pond. It could not have been very deep. I walked further feeling disappointed by the fact it was so small, yet hoping I might have overlooked something.

I did.

What I missed was the *first* sign that said, "Don't feed the gators!" The second one caught my attention. In a flash, my Nikes went into <u>*reverse*</u> and I was ***"outta there."***

Later that evening, intrigued by my information, Tex took his fishing pole and headed for "gator" lake. He couldn't have been gone more than 15 minutes when he returned to the Dreamcatcher <u>*and me*</u> for support. "Come with me," he said excitedly, "I want to show you something."

His lovable grin was from ear to ear. This was one happy camper. I slipped into my reluctant Nikes and we followed him. As we headed down Lake Avenue, he told me of the two small alligators who chased his bait.

We approached the pond. A fish jumped out of the water as we looked for Tex's fishing buddies. Suddenly, from the opposite direction, we saw the water stir. My Nikes stood at attention. A gator, six feet long or more, was in hot pursuit of the jumping fish. My Nikes became very nervous. Tex was ecstatic and moved closer. My knees weakened. Tex's arms flailed frantically signaling me to move closer to the action.

I took a half dozen steps in his direction until my Nikes failed me. They would no longer move forward. Without warning, they went into reverse when my mind's eye envisioned other gators in search of their evening meal. I could feel them watching me from the pond. I continued to back down Lake Avenue. Tex continued to wave me forward, but my Nikes were determined.

Tex was happier than if he had caught a dozen fish. Reminiscing later that evening he grinned, "So, you saw your first alligator in the wild."

"No," I responded determinedly. ***"My last!"***

Campground Ratings

Trailer Life Campground/RV Park Directory is a source that we relied on nearly exclusively to identify and locate parks to stay in as we traveled from place to place. It is often with amazement we review the TL ratings after parking. There were so many times when I wondered which helped most to flush out a stellar 9/8/8 rating. Was it the junked house trailer? The gaudy adornment on the headstones in the small in-park cemetery? Perhaps it was the old truck or loose trash at the shower room doors. Then again, maybe it was the knee-high weeds?

Stone Mountain, on the other hand, is above and beyond *any* rating system. JP had been there before and knew of this park first hand. For certain, it is a 10/10/10…and then some!

Stone Mountain - Atlanta

This is an absolutely delightful place to stay. It seems to be a semi private, semi state-owned, people and entertainment oriented place. Golf, tennis, lakes, boating, fishing, swimming, playgrounds, trains, sky lift, cruise boat, conference center, antebellum plantation, grist mill, Road to Tara--the works!

In the center of this enormous park with trails, walkways, roads, and footpaths is a mountain consisting of one huge stone. Carved in the stone on one side is a memorial to the confederacy, specifically, Robert E. Lee.

On Saturday evening, hundreds upon hundreds of people gathered with blankets and picnic baskets to wait for a laser light show to be projected onto the memorial. At dark, the mountain lit up with lights, fireworks, and music causing people to sing, clap, and tap their toes to the rhythm of the beat. The ending was so moving that I cried and wondered why. Was it because so many people with different backgrounds and colors could enjoy an evening together without incident? Was it because for one night, there were no differences? I felt remarkably blessed to be able to be part of all of this.

Highland Games

People of Scottish descent from everywhere gathered for the Highland Games at Stone Mountain to celebrate their heritage. There were parades, dances, games, and competitions of every description. Food and frolicking were also a large part of this four day gathering of clans. Again, it was memorable and moving to meander about and feel at ease within the crowds.

Low Country Boil

In a word...umm, umm, *GOOD!* Crab, unpeeled shrimp, smoked sausage, corn on the cob, potatoes all boiled in water in one pot. If you have never enjoyed a low country boil, it's well worth a try. Good friends, good food, good people. It was difficult to say...good-bye to Atlanta.

Boiled Peanuts

Peanuts are not usually worthy of a whole story devoted just to them, but I want to tell you, I have discovered a treat beyond the joy of popcorn--*AND* more valuable as a food source. While not really a food group, they are an excellent and convenient source of protein. Fortunately, Ol' Tex had been introduced to these delectable morsels years earlier while on a business trip to the Deep South.

Our only problem seemed to be how we would locate a ready supplier once we left the Deep South. The good news we learned from a Cajun couple two doors away while at Stone Mountain. Boiled peanuts are popular in Louisiana. The bad news is if you decide to boil them yourself, it takes all day. To be safe, we bought a six month supply at Pine Mountain when we visited Callaway Gardens.

Callaway Gardens Golf Resort - South of Atlanta

"Nourishment for the soul. Consolation for the heart. Inspiration for the mind."

Our tour began on the wings of wonder with a walk through an enclosed tropical garden with thousands of butterflies. These winged flowers surrounded and kissed us as we floated through the tropical splendor of the Day Butterfly Center where butterflies from the far corners of the world enchanted us in a display of unparalleled beauty and mystery. These magnificent gifts from God begin life as an egg the size of a pinhead and unfold before one's very eyes eager to drink nectar and fill our lives with pleasure.

Beyond the butterfly conservatory are 14,000 acres of pure nature and world-class sports.

Safari

The sport that delighted us the most at Pine Mountain, (other than eating boiled peanuts by the pound), was feeding the giraffe, camel, zebra, buffalo, llama, and my personal favorite, the ostrich with his great, big eyes and tipsy feet. We boarded an old bus, windows removed for better viewing and feeding (if you were brave enough). As the bus made its way through the fields, the animals ran to catch up with us. Although we did not feed them, we enjoyed the antics of the tigers, lions, panthers, rhinos, bear, and about every other wild creature from around the world.

Many years ago, I did a research project where part of my field work required me to go off into the swamplands. Often it involved counting critters while I was there. In the late afternoon when my friend would call me from the clinic where she was employed, she would inquire, "How'd everything go on safari today?" knowing how much I enjoyed hip boots, crawly things, and collecting bugs for an in lab microscopic count.

This kind of safari was more to my liking.

Researchers at Heart

While we were visiting Georgia, it was a real treat for us to see cotton and peanuts actually growing. We eagerly went out into the fields and experienced the harvest. These two staples are a part of American history.

It was awesome! It was also time to head 'em up and move 'em out. It was time to head to the tropics!

Two Wrong Turns to Panama City Beach

Bad enough we missed the turn to take the belt around Dothan, Alabama, but, "Good Lord, no!" we missed the street that was to take us to the Magnolia Beach RV Park at water's edge in Panama City Beach.

"No problem," Tex says, "I'll just zip into the next parking lot and turn around."

Is this the same driver who nearly left me in North Carolina when he couldn't make the turn? The very same one who was ready to stay in Oregon rather than to take this baby out on the highway?

Later that night when no one was looking, I went out and measured the rig. Yep! Still 59 feet long—and then some--with Jeep Grand Cherokee in tow!

Under Attack

At Panama City Beach, we experienced our second pelting of...***NUTS***. This time I would have been convinced that we were under attack had it not been for a preview pelting at Stone Mountain.

Next, the earth shook with a 4.9 quake in the wee hours of the morning. (I thought those things happened in California, not Florida!) Then the rains came. And the tornados...and, we listened for hurricane warnings. Someone once asked, "Are you ever afraid staying in your motor home?"

"Na," I said. That was before I looked out of my bedroom window that morning and saw a huge Navy helicopter circling just above the water a few yards away.

I must admit, my heart "quickened" a couple of beats during our stay here on the Gulf of Mexico.

Confusion Say . . .

I cried when it rained and I had to stay inside until I met a man who lived in a tent.

Routine Care at Tallahassee

They may call it "routine maintenance," but arranging and getting a 40' motor coach into the Cummins dealer takes some doing, especially in Tallahassee where the foreman, Ben (Mr. Personality), decided to ignore us before, during, and after our appointment! I don't know what his problem was, but he was one strange dude!

The good news is that we got the job done in spite of the heavy traffic in downtown Tallahassee, the unmerciful rain, *and BEN.*

Tex, of course, didn't miss one single maneuver during this five hour test of endurance in and out of the garage bays. As I wiped the grease from his forehead and off the end of his nose, I could see one happy camper, glad to have *that* "project" *behind* him.

Mule Days (Muddy Day)

During our stay in Tallahassee, we drove up the road a piece to Mule Days at Calvary, Georgia. Storms had moved in the day and night before so maneuvering around the "mule fields" was a sport in itself. There were mules, crafts, food, people, more people, *and sugar cane!* One of the most fascinating features of this post Halloween annual event is the processing of sugar cane into syrup. The stalks are fed through presses where the liquid is collected and boiled into thick syrup. It is practically a sacrilege to leave without a bottle of the syrup and a bag of fried pork skins.

Hold Up North of Jacksonville

Now I know what you are thinking--robbery! So were we when we paid our money and then drove into the Hance's First In Florida RV

Park. This was one of those Trailer Life 9.5/10/9 ratings that drive us *crazy.*

Having just spent three hours on the road convincing ourselves that our *immediate surroundings* were far more important than what there is to "see and do" in the area, we were angry and appalled to find barely enough space to park the coach (let alone open the door). Our sewer and water bay door opened onto our neighbor's dinner table, the "lake" for fishing was a water run off/gator hole, and the sewage treatment plant was nestled in the park as was I-95--*practically.* If we opened our windows, we could enjoy the smell of the nearby paper mill which could also be confused with the smell of dead fish.

Like we have asked so many times, "Where do they get those ratings?" We decided to buy next year's Woodall's rating book at the Tampa RV Show in January.

Amelia Island & Plantation

The best part of our stay at Hance's First In Florida was it's proximity to Amelia Island. This was on Tex's list of places he had been and now wanted to show me.

Eager to once again see yet another championship course where Ol' Tex, the former corporate executive, had played golf, we parked and headed off into the sunset to see this grand resort. It was indeed grand—and, the end of a perfect day.

Gulf Coast Thanksgiving

We prepared to head further south.

Our very first Thanksgiving on the road was to be at Sun-N-Fun RV Resort, Sarasota, Florida. Normally, choosing proper attire was a major part of the event. That year, deciding which pair of shorts to where to dinner was not nearly as difficult.

Chapter 5

Move 'em out . . .

Opening a Can of Worms

Those of you who have ever had to deal with a motor coach sized refrigerator after having a home-sized 'frige and freezer will better appreciate my frustration in this situation.

First of all, there is no such thing as automatic defrost. So, frost was building and to make the defrost job a bit easier, I decided to "eat down" the tidbits tucked in the recesses of the darkest corners of the shelves. Imagine my horror the evening I discovered our main entree, thawed and waiting to be cooked for dinner was fish bait! *Who?* I wondered, would have the audacity to put dead *critters* into an already overcrowded refrigerator used to save the delectable treats such as lobster, shrimp and boiled peanuts???

Single and Looking

When you are "living on the road," you don't have time to dwell on things for long. The scene and circumstances are always changing. Take the night we stayed at Amelia Island, for example. In the campground, we parked next to a BOAT---literally!

SINGLE AND LOOKING! Seriously. Not just the guy, but the "rig" in which he lived was named ***SINGLE AND LOOKING.*** A handsome, ocean-going, 38 foot Chris-Craft! The boat, the boat! (I have a photo, honest!) The owner was using the boat as an RV for camping.

Buddy Gregg – Lakeland, Florida (Monaco Dealer/Service Ctr.)

The good news and bad news is that the technical service department at Buddy Gregg's is home to many very nice people; and, we got to know them well during our winter in Florida. *(Think about it.)*

Roosting In Florida for the Winter

Sun-N-Fun Resort in Sarasota was a buzz of activities from the moment we arrived until the moment we left. Heated pools, hot tubs, golf, tennis, lawn bowling, shuffle board, horse shoes, miniature golf, volley ball, billiards, exercise room, woodworking room, craft rooms, library and every activity under the sun--for fun. With 1600 to 1700 units, there were miles to walk on paved surfaces. There was also a lake for fishing.

We Survived

If ever there was a reason to give thanks, it's because we survived the preparation of Thanksgiving dinner in our motor home. That was all I could think of as I dried and put away the last dish. Had it been any more challenging for the pilgrims?

Actually, it would have been as simple as a piece of pumpkin pie had Tex not decided to make the cooking time more festive by defrosting the refrigerator, washing the floors, and putting down tile sealer--all during the same time we were preparing our first dining extravaganza (with all the trimmings) aboard the bus. Did I mention each of the extra-curricular jobs that took place during the holiday meal prep took *two* people?

Now you know why I used the word: *survived!!*

Black Friday at the Mall—And We Were There!

He would have liked to have blamed me, but it was in fact ***he*** who "crashed" the hard drive in the computer and wanted to go out to get it fixed right in the thick of the Friday, day-after-Thanksgiving, shopping! Now had I wanted to go, Ol' Tex would have dug in his cowboy heals and said, "Whoa!" Instead, old scrooge said, "Not bad at all." (Go figure!)

Live Cut Trees - 85 Degrees

It was a sight to see! Live, cut, evergreen trees tied to the tops of vehicles in hot sunshine and 85 degree weather. For sheer spectacle and entertainment that "day after," we parked in a Target lot and watched the needles fall. If only I had my camera to capture the "tree skeletons" as they drove home for the holiday!

I Love A Parade

In another life, I was in line to become the next Macy's Parade Coordinator. So 'ya gotta know' *"I love a parade."*

Scrooge's version of a Christmas parade was viewing the motorized floats stranded on the side of I-75 south between Bradenton and Sarasota the day after Thanksgiving.

Speaking of holiday parades, there's always light displays to make the season festive. We joined right in the festivities when our brake light and turn-signal display lights began working sporadically during the weeks that led up to the holidays that first year.

In an effort to get them repaired, the Service Department at Buddy Gregg, Lakeland, along with Technical Support from Monaco, Coburg had them flashing a bright red and amber when it was time for our move to Disney World. We really were sweating this one out as we maneuvered toward the busiest highway stretch in Florida. *Talk about keeping a sense of humor when your life is on the line.*

MISSING...2 Sense of Humors

We arrived at Tropical Palms Resort near Disney World after dark. Since we don't travel after dark, this was our first time ever—and hopefully, the last of night maneuvers. Maybe it was an omen of things to come.

It was here that Tex declared, "The other side of the story should be told!" I opted for telling "Just the facts simply the facts." You judge for yourself.

First, the Rains Came . ...

Came and came and came! For 7 days and 7 nights it rained--***hard***. We prepared to move to higher ground then realized we *were* on higher ground. The canal, the lake, the preserve and the grasslands kept rising.

Since all the fun activities were outdoors, we thought life had gone really bad. Then it got worse. The temperature plummeted. It turned cold, bitter cold, colder in Florida than in Upper Peninsula, Michigan!

It continued to rain. We bundled ourselves up and went out in search of the perfect gift for Mumzey, Ol' Tex's mother in Indiana. After all, it was close to Christmas. Too close.

Later that evening, we huddled in front of the TV to see how others were managing to keep the Ho, Ho, Ho in holiday. That was when we learned the ***REALLY BAD NEWS!***

Lioness Loose

Two miles away from where we were in Tropical Palms (or less), according to news reports, "An agitated and hungry African lion has escaped from Gatorland." Worse yet, it was heading for the Tropical Paradise Preserve that we were, at the time, calling home. With an umbrella in one hand, microphone in the other, and eyes darting in both directions, the terrified reporter continued. "Do not go near this large and dangerous animal. Officials hope she will return here for food!"

My immediate thoughts were, "Why would she bother in this land of food-a-plenty?"

Helicopters buzzed overhead while national media cruised the area. *Her lioness continued to roam around our yard...**for three days!***

They finally captured her three days later. Cautiously, we roamed the area until . . . oh no, in the name of . . . .

Murderer! Hostage! Police Standoff

Surely you saw him on television as well--the man who held the 2 and 4 year old children hostage for three days while keeping the police at bay did this unconscionable act just miles up the road. Murder! I stopped listening to this part of the news once I learned that there had been **several additional criminals** in Florida released early due to the "over-crowding of prisons."

E-x-c-u-s-e M-e*??* Over crowding prisons? *Has anyone looked at the streets and roads around here lately?????*

Black Bear

I'm not even going to try to explain about the big black bear in the tree. Now, we're talking some 500 to 600 pounds of burly beef sitting on a tree limb in the hustle and bustle of Orlando.

We simply looked, shrugged our shoulders, and walked away. By then, it was just a bear in a tree!

UBE - That's U-B-E

While we are still camped in the animal kingdom of Tropical Palms, I want to tell you about our pet Ubangie--who we think might have been from the Kyabe African Village. Or, at least, that's how we saw her as she ate rice cakes. She was so addicted to the delicacies that she would come to the front screen door and beg.

We thought we had lost our flying squirrel to the beautiful big bird that was hovering but low and behold, he simply joined the chorus of beggars: UBE, Big Bird and Cee (UBE's mate).

A Yuletide To Remember

Although we missed family and friends, we experienced a Christmas Eve and Christmas Day we will long remember.

The Dreamcatcher was decked-out in holiday splendor, a big red bow on its generator door, and a green mini tree with bright lights warming the dash. The angel on top played imaginary Christmas music while we continued to wait for the defunct Sony radio (which controls our sound system) to be returned from the Sony repair shop so that we could play the new Tabernacle Choir Christmas CDs we had purchased from our Mormon friends when we visited the Temple in Salt Lake

City. We had planned to spend Christmas Eve and Christmas Day at the Magic Kingdom with the Mouse, but unexpectedly we ended up spending both in the bliss of Dreamcatcher and our immediate surroundings. After two weeks of being practically alone in a 600 unit campground, fellow RVers began arriving in droves. Another blessing, our mail from Oregon and Texas arrived late afternoon and we joyfully settled in for an unexpected treat of news and cards from family and friends around the USA and Canada. We reveled in heartfelt messages of good will.

Since we were finally experiencing balmy and dry weather, our windows remained open letting in delicious smells, colorful sights, and muted sounds of fellow travelers. We had no desire to leave such contentedness. Our hearts and minds were filled with love and true Christmas spirit. Perhaps a Higher Power had sprinkled fairy dust over us for it truly was magical.

Love in Abundance

During our travels, I had been teaching North America geography lessons to a Baltimore elementary school. Much to our surprise and delight, a large brown envelope filled with love and good wishes arrived with notes, cards and letters from the students. Brightly painted holiday scenes and carefully lettered messages filled each and every hand-crafted exhibit.

Dreamcatcher came to life as we displayed the works of art throughout the coach. The next day when Tex went to shave, he was hard put to find the mirror. We decided he might look good in a beard. The messages from the children were too precious to take down.

Then the Real Rains Came

I had been reading the December issue of *Lifestyles* magazine that included Randy Puckett's savvy article, "Heading North for the Winter," and I found myself wondering how folks could find favor in snow and cold. This is when the rains and tornadoes returned with vengeance. The ground was completely saturated from the earlier storms, which meant the new 10 inches of water in 24 hours had nowhere to go.

Liberal rivers of water ran through the streets of the campground. Cars, trucks, and recreational vehicles were sinking in over their hubcaps. By morning, folks who had set up "guest tents," were hauling the inhabitants from water-logged bedrolls into the main houses before they grew algae. When the temperature plummeted this time and we huddled in front of the TV screen, I found a certain irony in looking back at the faces of "happy campers" in the sun and snow who were pictured on the cover of the *Lifestyles* winter edition.

Splendid China

There were a few days of sun in the "Sunshine State" and we spent one of these precious days in the nearby, man-made orient. China in miniature! From the Great Wall to the Imperial Palace in the Forbidden City, it was all there. The temple of Confucius, Leshan Grand Buddha Statue, Sun Yat Sen.'s Mausoleum, Shaolin Temple, plus eight theater and show areas.

It was a different atmosphere from the frenetic pace of the Kissimmee area and we enjoyed more than nine hours of oriental splendor. The day was capped by an evening performance called the Mysterious Kingdom of the Orient where talented Chinese performers brought to life the history, mystery and magic of their country in a live stage show presentation.

Se Hablas Ingle`s

Since we were only two of but a few people speaking American English in the Kissimmee area, we soon learned that some things required our best use of Spanish and sign language. I particularly enjoyed the grocery shopping challenge when we engaged in mime to acquire bananas for breakfast.

Reptile Education

Always eager to learn, Tex managed to get me into a live presentation of "Magical Snow Tiger Adventures" at the Temple of Light. Since the Snow Tiger portion of the program turned out to be only 5 minutes long at the end, much of the "filler" was...you guessed it! ***REPTILES***! Not only did they "show and tell" on the stage, but they brought all those slippery critters right out into the audience for "touchie-feelie."

Aside from several very large, colorful, and surly snakes (even an albino with no color whatsoever), we learned about alligators which appeared in several sizes both on stage and in the audience. (***Whoopee!***) I have to admit I did learn two things:

(1) The reason the signs throughout Florida say, "Please don't feed the gators," is because if you do, the next time they could mistake YOU for food.

(2) How fast do you have to run to out-run a gator? Only faster than the slowest guy in your party!

Kennedy Space Center

Our *crew pass* took us first to the space shuttle orbiter. We walked through then waited for the first bus to take us to the Apollo/Saturn V Center.

We saw the Vehicle Assembly Building, VAB they call it, on our way to the Launch Pad Observation Gantry. It was interesting to see the crawler which takes the space ship to the launch and its three and a half mile long tracks. It takes up to eight hours and a crew of twenty to drive this monster transport.

We boarded and re-boarded several times as we continued our journey. With the crew pass, one gets to see the launch pad and the International Space Station. At launch central, we had a choice of two IMAX presentations. We chose the show " *First City in Space*" since we had lived the other offering, *The Dream Is Alive. We are,* in fact, part of that history!

International Cooperation

I must admit that I was truly impressed by the galactic progress we are making through peaceful cooperative efforts among nations. Our children will be able to visit places beyond earth; and, our children's children could even be born there--IF we don't kill each other off on the streets, in the schools, post offices, or homes across America.

Let's put an end to the violence, and learn to live amicably on *this* planet--now. ***Here! Here!***

Route 192 - Bumper Cars

Tropical Palms, the campground we called "home for the holidays" is directly off SR-192, the major highway between the city of Kissimmee and Disney World. It is quite probably one of the most heavily traveled and populated roads in the State of Florida. Restaurants, attractions, hotels, and souvenir outlets line both sides of the four to six lane stretch.

Whether people believe they've been sprinkled with magic dust or are simply more interested in the sights that line the road is unclear, but there were more cars bumping into each other on Route 192 than at the amusement park. After December 19th, I cringed each time we would leave the campground figuring the odds were "bumper to bumper" against us.

High Level Security

Maybe I was out in the Northwest too long, but, at the time, I found it disquieting to note official signage that advised "Night Time Security" at rest areas along highways from the panhandle to the keys of Florida. Also, many communities were fenced, gated, and secured. Intelligence tells me this is to make folks feel better. In my mind, however, there remains a nagging question.

Spirit of the Road--in the East

The spirit of the road was best summed up in one bumper sticker we saw in Central Florida. It said: *Horn Broke! Watch For Finger.*

New Years - New Promises

Tired of fighting the crowds and traffic that the holidays brought with them, we hunkered in and tried to find joy in simple things--our first invasion of ants being an exception. It seems obscene to pay premium campground rates to engage in the busyness that kept us going through the remaining days in "paradise," but we learned and grew from our mistake.

We welcomed in 1998 from our motor coach and found promise in the fact that we had only to endure five (count 'em 5) more days and nights in this tropical paradise. We promised ourselves that *after* Ft. Meyers Beach, we would never again lock-in to a month or even two weeks at a time. If we like a place, we will just stay on.

We also promised ourselves we would accept what is rather than bemoan what could have been. And last, but certainly not least, we promised to head west and rekindle our spirits, a promise we eagerly anticipated.

Pursuit of Happiness

We've all been guaranteed happiness, haven't we? As the Constitution says, all we need do is pursue it. And, pursue we did. This is what we have found so far.

No Magic Kingdom or Planet Hollywood can replace the joy one feels when you look deep into the eyes of a stranger and greet him. When your souls connect, a miracle happens and both become one with the Universe. The gentleness of a warm breeze caressing your face far surpasses being careened in the shins by a baby stroller as you wait in line for the material rewards of commercial display. Silence and the solitude of deep, deep thought are gifts to savor.

And just what is happiness? Happiness is in knowing it is not a what but a when. Happiness is *when* you know this to be true. Happiness is when you no longer feel the need to search for it in material things and find joy in being. Happiness is when you know joy comes from within and that it is there for the knowing of these truths.

Chapter 6

Livin' the life a beach bum (or not!)

Truth be told . . .

Everyone believes that when you go to a place like Florida, a peninsula in the middle of a great body of water, you will be able to go to the beach any time you choose. Truth is, you can't get near the beach or the water if you don't own property on it. Of course, you might try to rent something for a large sum of money that might give you limited access, but it is not as easy as it looks.

Another interesting fact is that just because a place has "beach" in its name, it doesn't necessarily mean it is on the water.

We headed for Ft. Meyers *Beach.* We were scheduled.

Movin' On to Ft. Meyers

The move from Kissimmee to Ft. Meyers Beach was somewhat uneventful--much to Tex's surprise. Why do I use the vague term, "somewhat"?

Tex! He was absolutely and resolutely convinced that if I did not keep my corneas completely locked on the computer screen, we would end up somewhere south of Key West. Bleary-eyed and bursting from holding my opinion about his obsession with the GPS (global positioning system), I guided us through the secured gates of the Indian Creek community which we would call "home" for one month.

Indian Creek Park & Resort--SW Gulf Coast

"Balmy days, tropical nights, a snowbird's paradise."

It was sheer *gridlock*, an RVer's worst nightmare. When we pulled into Indian Creek Park, a community and RV resort, Park Ranger Bill came right out of the office and said, "Ya better pull that rig back around and park here, close to the building. I'm afraid some little old lady on a three wheeler may run right over you!"

For a moment, albeit the temptation was enormous and immediate, our eyes responded in harmony, "Excuse me, but have you noticed the size of this outfit? Don't you think it might be easier for *her* to move around us?"

But, Park Ranger Bill was in uniform and not only was he in charge, he looked official. He also looked as if he had been around the park for quite awhile. We were the new folks on the lot and if he thought we were in danger, then we'd better move the bus.

Park Ranger Bill was right on target. I later found out that if I wanted to get my morning walk in safely, it was necessary for me to be out and about before the crack of dawn and back inside before the three-wheeling traffic peaked shortly after sunrise. This is an active community; people have places to go, things to do from sun up to sunset--and beyond! And, either you go with the flow, or you just don't go.

Indian Creek Adventures

Indian Creek is filled with small lakes. I began to direct my sunset walks to the shores of two of the larger lakes. One evening, shortly after we arrived, I visited with one of the fishermen to get the scoop on fishing at the resort. Not only did he tell me the anticipated catch of the day, but he also advised me that there was a large gator in the adjacent lake.

I hurried back and got old Tex to come along and share my discovery. (Okay, fear.) Sure enough, there he was, the "fisher of men," six to eight feet long and moving.

Later, each time I passed this lake, I felt as if I was looking for the Lock Ness Monster! Those gators can move!!!

Tamiami Trail

There are two main routes south along the Gulf Coast of Florida: I-75 and Route 41 which is also known as the Tamiami Trail. Although many names have Indian roots, Tamiami was so named when folks here decided to build a highway from Tampa to Miami. Eager to explore the area south of Ft. Meyers, we opted to take the Tamiami Trail.

I had my heart set on seeing Naples. Tex's heart belonged to the Everglades. We took the Tamiami Trail south, zipped off and whipped through Naples. We ended up at Everglade City—all in one day! But that's not all. Let me tell you about it.

Metropolis to Moor Lands

Paradise found! Shortly after noon, we arrived at Naples and headed the Jeep into town. I "ooo—d" and "aaah-d" from the front seat as the vehicle (I'm tempted to use the word "careened") traveled up and down the streets. Tex would call my interpretation of this tour through town a gross exaggeration. (I call it an understatement.) In ten minutes or less, we had "done" Naples, and were back on the Tamiami Trail heading directly into the Everglades.

Instinct told me to lock my automatically locked doors as we cruised deeper and deeper into this lush wasteland. This is not only a contradiction in terms, but a contradiction in space. In an eerie sort of way, it was breathtakingly beautiful; in another, it was vacuous, lonely, and foreboding. As I looked from my window, I could sense we were heading toward a point of no return. I watched. Tex drove. Surely, it was too soon to die. I just wasn't ready.

We were on a two-lane road which had narrowed substantially once we left Naples. We came upon a lone sign: "Panther Crossing next 3 miles."

I slid further down in my seat. It was worse than I had expected.

Everglade City

In what seemed to be hours later, we came to a crossroads. The signpost indicated "Everglade City" and pointed due west. Out of the corner of my eye, I could see old Tex tighten the reigns and, sure enough, old paint headed in the direction of the arrow. There was no congestion, no signs of in-town traffic. All was quiet, perhaps too quiet. We were headed for the western front.

The outpost was on the Chokoloskee Causeway near the end of Route 29. Tex yanked on the reigns once again and we came to a complete stop at the Ranger Station. We had made it into the wilderness and were now about to board a boat and head out into the mysterious Mangrove Wilderness of Florida's Ten Thousand Islands.

Captain Crocodile Dundee

Our guide was an Australian adventurer wanna-be who, in reality, was a satirical humorist hippie born about 35 years earlier. After boarding us on his vessel, he provided us with days of entertainment crammed into two short hours.

I anxiously looked for my life jacket but Captain Crocodile explained, "We are in approximately six feet of water going out through the channel." He said that if he were to guide the boat just a little to the left or a little to the right, we would have to sit there until high tide because outside the channel, the water was a foot and a half deep. "Not much need for a life jacket," he said as if he had read my mind.

"Captain Crock," as I affectionately called him, expertly maneuvered us through the heart of the Ten Thousand Islands before reaching the Gulf of Mexico. Everyone on board nervously peered into the water. "No point looking for gators," he finally advised. "There aren't none except the occasional one every few years to make a liar outta me."

"Occasionally, we see a shark," he continued and I quickly drew in my hands. "But, not too often," he continued and I breathed again. "The birds are the attraction." Ospreys, American and snowy egrets, ibis, spoonbills, pelicans, frigate birds, and once in a while, a bald eagle. "Manatees and dolphins, not porpoise," he exclaimed, "are frequently part of the tour."

Not this day. But, there were birds and Mangrove trees. Millions upon millions of Mangrove trees with roots so big and thick that one would not want to think about hiking around the Islands for fear of being entangled and never, ever being able to get loose again.

Captain Crock told us of the Caloosa who had settled in this south Florida area long before the Indians. We saw the raised lands where they caught their food. No one knows what happened to the Caloosa people. They are gone now, said Crock, "Gone before the Indians settled here."

Captain Crock told us about Shark Valley and Alligator Alley. I could see Tex lean forward and hang on his every word while he told the story of the Italian tourists who rented the bikes, and well, I don't think you want to hear the rest of that story. But if you ever go to Italy and see a young man with hundreds of stitches, Captain Crock told us, "You better not ask his mama about the alligators in the Everglades that *rarely* attack. But should you decide to mess with any part of Mother Nature, alligators, snakes, panther, black bear, sharks, etc, while in the Everglades National Park, be prepared for the consequences. Uncle Sam will slap you with a fine for "molesting the wild life in a National Park [**period**]."

We cruised back into dock just before dusk, thanked Captain Crock, and headed back to the Jeep. It had been a full day. I was ready to get safely back on the Tamiami and head home. We headed instead, directly to Alligator Alley. Ol' Tex had the reigns. If you are wondering what happened, all I'll say is that I am still here to continue the saga of our misadventures in the swamps of Florida!

Sanibel Island

To our surprise, our earliest gator spotting in southern Florida was on Sanibel Island. Known for plentiful and exquisite shelling, the last thing we expected to see on this upscale tourist refuge were the two alligators we encountered in the J. N. Ding Darling National Wildlife Refuge. The park ranger had spotted them and had advised the information desk before we headed out on our personally guided safari.

Evidence of shells in days past was apparent throughout the refuge. Most had been crushed and formed part of the ground under our feet. The rest of the shells were to be found on private beaches, I imagine, since there was limited public access to the water.

We learned, "It's against the law to feed the alligators." Finding a place for mere humans to eat may not have been against the law, but certainly not easily accessible either!

Okeechobee

Don't you just love to say that word? What a work-out for the facial muscles!

Unlike Tamiami, I would guess that Okeechobee has Indian roots. You can find this enormous body of fresh water far out in the middle of southern Florida.

So that's what we did. Lake Okeechobee. We found it! We saw it! (Again, limited public access!) We left it!

Once you leave the area of Ft. Meyers and neighboring coastal towns, it becomes quite desolate compared to the hubbub of the Gulf cities. There are citrus groves, some sugar cane fields, a couple of migrant towns, but little else as you go deeper into the interior. While we were in the major town of Clewiston, we stopped into the local hardware/ electric store because Tex was looking for a "bonger" to put on the turn signals of the motor coach so that we would hear them when they are engaged. He shopped for parts while I became engaged in an exchange with a Spanish speaking young man.

Tex found his parts and came looking for me. I could see his tonsils when he found me in an animated discussion in the men's room of the small establishment with the young man whose knife was now drawn and pointing directly at me. He had been using the instrument to identify specific places on a map which happened to be displayed on the bathroom wall.

After that poignant moment, Gatorama looked like a cakewalk--to Tex!

Gatorama

Our next stop--and ***experience of a lifetime!*** Gatorama, an alligator lover's paradise.

Okay, I was reluctant at best, but to this day, I clock this in as one of the best stops on our Florida tour! There are alligators—lots and lots of alligators--every size, shape, and kind; plus crocodiles, every size, shape, and kind! And, you are there, *right there,* in the middle of them with only a thin, little board walk between you and them.

I was so overwhelmed with the sheer volume, that I pranced right out onto the boards in the middle of the lake with my camera in front of my face when the *"mother of all gators"* decided to break from her nap and take a closer look ***at me!*** As she ambled toward me, my knees weakened, and my camera dropped. "I have got to be out of my mind," I wanted to scream. Instead, I eked out a very weak "Holy...!"

Tex? My big white hunter was back on the other side of the pond addressing camera problems. He was oblivious to the entire situation.

Once I regained trust of "the boards" *and myself*, we excitedly navigated throughout the grounds. Most of the super-sized alligators and crocodiles were sunbathing on the banks of the small lake. Seeing them together, it was easy to identify crocodiles as the reptiles with tapered jaws whereas the alligators had broader, shorter snouts**. *Both have unmistakably big mouths and sharp teeth!***

We enjoyed seeing the "youngsters" in various stages of development. It was much like going through a reptilian elementary school—so to speak. At mid-afternoon, the younger groups were "podding," which in fact is stacking themselves on top of each other vying for top of the heap to nap and sun.

More than Reptiles

On this safari, we encountered several other interesting species eager to attract our attention: two ducks, four deer, three monkeys, a tiger, two raccoons, nearly thirty peacocks, (one NBC wanna be), twenty osprey, two ostrich, and one too many black snakes! Suddenly, the alligators didn't look nearly as threatening!

I was glad Ol' Tex had his way. When I look back on the Everglades, it is without a doubt one of the "must see" sights of the East. It clearly is a unique experience, one I would venture to do again.

Fashion

Do you ever wonder where those really neat, unique fashions come from when you know you've faithfully shopped every mall from Portland to Orlando and not found a one? I did! Then, to my surprise and delight, we discovered Fleamasters in Ft. Meyers! Well shut my mouth--I was so overwhelmed with the possibilities that I soon became too exhausted to make decisions. We wandered around aimlessly and ate shamelessly until it closed.

We returned. We shouldn't have! Open only Friday, Saturday, and Sunday (and we knew already how crowded it is on Sunday), we returned on Friday when everyone is at work forgetting, of course, that everyone in Florida is either retired or on vacation. It took nearly an hour to get into the place, four to five hours to pick up my special order and get back out. Okay, so we looked around and ate again! We earned the right!

Leaving Ft. Meyers

We prepared systematically and carefully, enjoying fully the anticipation of our long awaited move. One thing is for certain, the joy of the spirit of the road entails exactly that--being on the road! There may be a time and a place for Florida in our future, but Lordy, this was not it. (At the time, I had no idea how prophetic this statement would be.) Perhaps the lessons learned were worth the time spent.

We said good-bye to our neighbor and at daybreak, we rolled out of Indian Creek before the three-wheeling traffic got too heavy.

Deep In the Heart

We made a major move during our stay in Florida that year. Perhaps it was a precursor of greater things to come.

With a strong emotional attachment to Oregon, it was a psychological challenge to move our mail forwarding, or "legal residence," from Tillamook, Oregon to Livingston, Texas. Economically, it made sense.

So our new residence was finally "deep in the heart of Texas," therefore legitimizing the name "Tex." *And,* he was ONE HAPPY COWBOY!!! Ol' Tex tells me I need to lose the "dude" which I have affectionately called him for over 30 years. Now I'm wondering if this is why he finally embraced the idea of joining Escapees and "moving" to Texas.

Sorry Dude! *I calls 'em as I sees 'em!*

Chapter 7

All Aboard . . .

Hallelujah!!!

With the kind of excitement a Christmas morning can bring, we headed north out of Ft. Meyers to Lakeland. We had several driving challenges ahead of us, but we were heading *WEST* at last.

Our first stop on the journey was to see old friends at Buddy Gregg. This writer's long anticipated computer work station was ready and going to be installed in the Dreamcatcher. The joy was untenable.

Custom-made Computer Work Station - Ready to Roll

After some warm and lighthearted conversation, we were escorted back to the wood shop where Jim's architectural design had been born. Lin Winchester, master craftsman and cabinet maker (and not unlike a proud papa), guided us inside to see what I consider to be the 8th wonder of the world.

There the workstation stood in stained cherry woods, finished smooth as a baby's bottom and beaming a warm welcome. My new desk was complete with drawers and sliding trays—a beauty if ever there was one.

"What do you think?" he asked. It was too soon to respond. No one could ever understand the longing I had endured before getting to this moment. A year since I walked away from well over 4000 square feet of living space equipped with every convenience including three offices outfitted with every modern convenience. And here, in front of me, was a small piece of furniture which would save my sanity and open the door to my future.

"What did I think?" I had to respond. This kind and gentle man really cared that his efforts were pleasing to me.

"It's beautiful." Surely there was more I could say--*should* say. I could tell that my approval was important to him.

"It's bigger than I expected," I managed.

"Do you like it?" he persevered.

'Like it' is so insignificant when it means *everything* to you. "Oh, yes, I do 'like it'," an understatement if ever there was one!!!

Seasoned Veterans

Our three night stay in Lakeland afforded us time to enjoy several shopping expeditions and fine dining. One bought parts while the other bought clothes; together we consumed enough seafood, Mexican food, beef and fried foods to fuel an army. It was evident that this was a time of celebration. We had our computer work area, we were headed west and, last but far from least, we felt like seasoned veterans. No more belly aching, no more projects, no more gridlock. We had places to go and people to see. "And miles to go before we sleep."

Yes, miles to go before we sleep.

Spring Comes Early

As we joyfully sailed onto I-75 North from Route 4, we noted signs of spring in the new green and crimson pink of the foliage. It was February 8th and nearly time for the Strawberry Festival in Plant City (between Lakeland & Tampa). I delighted in each flowering tree and shrub, the delicate scent and beauty of flowers ignite my passion for living. It was exciting just knowing that we will experience spring in so many parts of America this year.

Memories

I read the sign at Black Angus Farms, "I never met a T-Bone I didn't like." I knew this would get a response from you-know-whom.

I could see Tex's feathers ruffle as he countered, "I could show him one!" Remember the biker in Reno who parked his hiney square in front of the generator slide and dared my cowboy to run over him? To this day we have never figured out what his problem was, but we will never forget him either. Interesting, isn't it? Some things are better forgotten.

Road Runner.....B-Beep

B-Beep! Pensacola, Mobile, Pascaluosa, Biloxi, Gulfport!! I'm out of breath with excitement and discovery.

Biloxi had changed from the quiet Gulf town with beaches and fishing fleets of yesteryear. They were still there, of course, but when we passed through in 1998, they are incidental to the Vegas-style casinos and buses filled with people.

It was reassuring to see famed Mary Mahoney's Old French House still in operation. Dining there was again a memorable experience. It was easy to understand why presidents, celebrities, and novelists enjoy it as much as we did.

For those readers unfamiliar with Mary Mahoney, you may recall several mentions in John Grisham's *The Runaway Jury* as well as *The Partners*. Because of Grisham, our heart beats quickened as we walked the familiar streets: Main Street with City Hall, Vieux Marche, and of course, the Harrison County Courthouse, the very same streets and places familiar to Grisham's fictitious characters.

We grazed our way through this area's fresh and plentiful seafood delicacies and other fine gourmet offerings. From here, we are headed straight into Cajun Country and Lord knows, it would be inhospitable to not try the Louisiana fare!

All Aboard!

New Orleans, Baton Rouge, Lafayette. B-Beep! Bump, Bump!

We had been warned; we just needed to confirm road conditions. We hit serious road construction as Dreamcatcher wove its way over the bridges of Baton Rouge and we peered out the big windows to look down the Mississippi River, enjoying the romance of the many paddle wheelers docked along her shores.

We crossed miles and miles of bayous on roads suspended on concrete pillars. I was relieved to note that these particular bridges appeared newer for I could never have held my breath for so long a stretch as the miles we covered. At Whiskey Bay, we peered eagerly out our picture windows but alas, no "rum runners" just more bayou country.

Cajun Country

Dreamcatcher and crew had to learn how to speak and eat Cajun. Tex did so much better with Cajun than Spanish I thought maybe we were missing the boat of where to winter in '98. I'm not certain if it was the hot Cajun spices, the suds to wash them down, or the general ambiance of the area:

Laissez le bon temp rouler. Let the good times roll!

Tex was one happy cowboy.

Home at High Noon

Finally, the day was upon us; we would be in Texas in 3 hours. We readied the Global Positioning Satellite System, prepared to stop at the first available welcome center, and sat at attention.

Our journey would put us in the heart of downtown Houston at *High Noon*. We were psyched. *Okay, we were scared!*

We pulled into the tourist center East of Beaumont and gathered several more maps. Tex was ready to face the enemy. I had my computer "crew" readied with navigational systems up and running. We proceeded.

All *would have* gone well ***if*** I-10 downtown Houston had not been under construction. But, it was! We made it through, but we didn't go back that day to enjoy the sights and sounds of Houston.

By the way, we would learn much later that I-10 in downtown Houston is *always* under construction. Some of the workers affectionately call it their 401 K plan!

Tornados Touch Down

We camped on the west side of the great city feeling relaxed and happy that the worst of the driving was behind us. We went out to explore and spotted a beautiful, big shopping mall not far from the campground. Threatening skies somehow convinced us it might be prudent to return home rather than shop my favorite petite department in the Dillard's store.

It was less than a half hour from that decision that the mall store was ripped apart by one of four funnel clouds moving through and touching down in our area of West Houston. To this day, I think of myself in one of those dressing rooms when . . . .

We were at our front door when the dark clouds opened and sent down pounding rain. Fierce winds accompanied the rain. Dreamcatcher rocked back and forth on all six tires for about an hour. We quickly turned on the digitals to see what was happening and, faster yet, decided to stow the dish antenna before it was torn from the roof. T-V without antenna provided local coverage of the nearby destruction as tornados continued to touch down.

We rode it out in the Dreamcatcher but checked to see if we would both fit with pillows in the space in front of the commode room---just in case, you understand. Fortunately, we did not have to test that plan out.

Livingston, Texas

From the get go, we had been feeling insecure about Houston. Then add the extras of road construction *and tornadoes,* and we were filled with trepidation. Therefore, we decided to leave the Dreamcatcher in the RV park and pursue our next adventure with the Jeep only. We headed east on the Sam Houston Tollway then North on Rt. 59 toward Livingston.

We felt a little like two misplaced souls in search of a home. We did not know what to expect or how we would feel when we got to **Rainbow's End** which is the name of the National Headquarters of the Escapees RV Club to which we belonged. It was also our new mail-forwarding service. Since there are some twenty-seven-thousand members, would that be all there is to Livingston? Or, was it a full-fledged Texas town with Escapees being a part of that town?

Indeed, there is more to Livingston, Texas than Escapees, and, we had to ask directions at a local gas station. Without fanfare, we drove the Jeep into Rainbow's End. It was lunch time, so we decided on a self-guided tour.

Rainbow's End

Rainbow's End is a park/campground with varying degrees of RVs--some full-sized homes with motor coaches outside, a section for transient member visitors, and an area near the CARE facility for members with disabilities to stay with loved ones and be near support. There is a clubhouse with full facilities: library, activity center complete with full kitchen, auditorium with stage, billiard room, ping pong room, swimming pool, laundry, registration office, and business office with mailroom. This was where we were shown our legal residence: 200 Rainbow Drive, Suite #10802--*a hanging file*! Like any new neighbor, we were warmly welcomed. Like an Escapee, we were hugged when we left.

Before leaving the compound, we stopped by the CARE facility where there is an "in charge" nurse. The facility is available to help and support members through difficult times. It addressed my great concern for the big "what if" question we all seem to have.

We were satisfied knowing all about our legal residence--Rainbow's End at Livingston. It was time to be rolling again. We returned to Houston to pick up the Dreamcatcher. There were promises to keep "*and miles to go before we sleep.*"

San Antonio

Route I-10 from Houston to San Antonio was pleasant but uneventful. As we approached the city limits with a fistful full of unique directions, I could see the "bus driver" tighten his grip on the reigns. This was particularly useful when he "jumped the gun" and exited before our turn-off to Admiralty Resort. With much spirited discussion, we wove our way through an office park and the adjacent WalMart parking lot a couple of times before regaining a proper sense of direction and composure. The Jeep followed.

Remember the Alamo!

San Antonio is a culturally diverse city with a complimentary mix of Spanish and American influence. Its American heritage supports a balance of European, Asian, Indian...well, every country and nationality one might expect in this historically significant frontier town. English was well-spoken by Spanish-speaking people; and, Spanish was well spoken by English-speaking people.

We had but one full day to explore the town. So, by arrangement through the campground, our guide picked us up at our motor home at 8 a.m. and chauffeured us downtown where we boarded a 45' tour bus that first took us to the Japanese Sunken Gardens, a unique experience especially considering our location.

We returned to the downtown area and boarded a boat. Our guide provided a detailed and most entertaining excursion of the San Antonio River which is bordered by the widely known and very popular *River Walk.*

After disembarking at the 135 store shopping mall, we hastily passed many interesting shops to get to the IMAX Theater where we saw the award winning film, *The Price of Freedom*, a stunning enactment of the events leading up to and capture of Mission San Antonio de Valero--the *Alamo!*

With eager cameras and great awe, we leisurely toured the Alamo grounds and ruins following lunch at the famed Meager Hotel where temperance agitator, Cary Nation, left her axe in the beautiful mahogany bar. (Go Cary!)

The afternoon was filled with Missions including a guided stop at the Queen of Missions, Mission San Jose y San Miguel de Aguayo founded in 1720.

The next stop on the tour was the famous Lone Star Brewery which brought smiles to faces and beer and root beer to everyone's lips. The old brewery housed an enormous collection of antlers, stuffed game and fish, and rattles from snakes, sights beyond one's wildest dreams.

German builders and business men were prominent among the early settlers, and our guide provided a rolling tour of this segment of San Antonio's multicultural heritage. The last stop on tour was the El Mercado, a market similar to any in the interior of Mexico. It was after 7 p.m. when our guide dropped us off at our motor coach door.

The rest of the city will have to wait until we remember and return to the Alamo!

Texas Hill Country

To get to our scheduled destination, El Paso, Texas, it was necessary to cross Texas Hill Country which is a uniquely different type of terrain with elevated desert land and fabulous trees which looked like bonsai only bigger, of course. It is a long, tiring drive, and we looked forward to spending the night in Ft. Stockton, a military post established in 1859.

History identifies an overland mail route and an ancient Comanche War Trail through here. It was popular with Indians long before white men arrived because of large springs nearby. The only thing of real significance now is the world's largest roadrunner, a 20' long and 11' tall bird called Paisano Pete.

And a Walmart's, of course!

The Other Side of the Hills

El Paso! The main impetus for the trip cross-country was to get to El Paso! We arrived three days before the "pre-rally" rally and were lucky to get full hook ups at Mission RV Park. Many weary travelers arriving after us were relegated to the campground's over-flow lot.

Mission is a turn around spot for caravans traveling south into Mexico. Additionally, we were only days away from not only the Monaco International Rally, but also only a week or so before the FMCA, Family Motor Coach Association's Winter Convention in Las Cruces, New Mexico. Therefore, many RV travelers were on the move and needing a place to stay in this area.

We explored this bordertown and often found it difficult to decide which side of the border we were on. Unlike San Antonio, where English as well as Spanish are spoken by most residents and shop owners, in El Paso, one got the feeling that Spanish was the primary language. Fortunately, we had no problem communicating--especially when it came to purchasing boots for Tex. (Love those Tony Lamas, cowboy!) This writer settled for fancy long winter undies and was very glad she did!

Before we had opportunity to cross the border into Juarez, Mexico, El Nino chased us back to the safety of the RV park and our motor home. We apprehensively peered out our windows as the winds blew the sand and dirt ferociously. We were rocking back and forth hard. We could not see either light of day or the lights at night. It would take weeks to get the sand and grit out of the motor coach, but that was only the beginning of our sand storm problems. Fortunately, the storm subsided before we were scheduled to head out to the rally.

This was the first encounter we had with a sand storm. Fortunately, we learned the lesson well: ***Do not mess with Mother Nature!*** Get off the road as soon as possible.

Rally Bound

Excited and rolling once again, we were headed onto I-10 from the approach when the bus driver rendered the volt meter to be in an inoperative mode. *"THE VOLT METER'S NOT WORKING! THE VOLT METER'S NOT WORKING!"* he screamed.

"WATCH THE ROAD! WATCH THE ROAD!!!" I shrieked.

This exchanged continued with added furor as we rolled across El Paso and on into Fort Bliss Army Air Defense post where we would begin an adventure of a lifetime. (It did not help for Ol' Tex to see a fellow Monaco owner, previously en route, being hauled up onto a gargantuan tow-truck along the way. *Talk about spendy!*)

Well, at least we made it off the highway before misadventures of our own coach began in earnest. But first, let me tell you about the lines.

A Line In the Sand?

Someone else said it best, so let me reiterate what was told to me. “Don't stand still too long or a line will form behind you!”

Sure enough. Everywhere we went at this gathering there were *lines!* There were lines to eat, drink, do, and undo. We learned too late that we had missed the first line to register for coach work. By the time we found another, it was already necessary to re-prioritize our limited "wishes" as they called them. I left Tex near the front of this line while I pursued the line to register. By the time I got there, it was already around, through and out the other side of the building. Mercy! This was not at all like the Monaco Come Home in Albany, Oregon! At any one time, there were some 500 to 600 coaches parked on the lot--some pre-registered, some not. Registration was necessary in order to proceed. Oh well, I could do this. ***I would do this!***

It took time, but finally, I was within pencil's grip of signing in when the registrar declared that I had not paid my dues! "But my dues were paid for a full year when we bought the coach last June," I lamented with a sinking feeling in the pit of my stomach.

She countered, of course. "See, right here," she pointed to her papers. "No dues, you don't register!" And, with an official shrug of the shoulders, *"I don't make the rules."*

"But, my husband has the money and..."

"NEXT."

Now let me tell you, ***if*** the volt meter, the coolant leaks, tire leaks, check engine light, and the other repairs did not need immediate attention, I would have turned Dreamcatcher around in the parking lot myself and headed out. But the fact of the matter was, **we couldn't leave**, or so we thought. *And, that in fact, was the good news.*

Once I got ahold of Tex and *the lousy ten bucks*, we completed the registration procedure without further incident. My heart sunk as I read the roster and somehow missed the names of some dear RV friends who I thought for certain would be on the attendee list. When I looked up from the list, they were in standing in front of me. Finding them put us back on track. They had an uncanny way of presenting all circumstances in a positive light.

Monaco brought its full mechanical repair and parts department to these rallies. Each owner was allowed a number of repairs that were put on his personal "wish list" and at a scheduled place and time, the company handled the requests during the rally. ***Sweet!***

Meeting the Editor

And speaking of "positive light," I am reminded of Randy Puckett, Editor of *Lifestyles Magazine*, the official Monaco publication. For those of you who have read this fine publication, I need not tell you what a talented and creative person Randy is. What I want to tell you is what a genuinely delightful and hard-working person he is as well. After a heart-warming visit with this enthusiasm-filled young man, I missed my former University students even more (if that was possible.)

The rally was a wonderful experience in the end. The registration incident was soon forgotten and necessary repairs were completed. That's the great part of the RV life. One is pretty much forced to live in the moment.

Caravanning to Las Cruces

The headlines probably read "endless stream" but in fact, there were 298 Monaco Motor Coaches, *all in a row,* which caravanned from the El Paso pre-rally to Las Cruces, New Mexico and the FMCA Winter Convention. It was a sight to behold—even 18 wheel truckers saluted us with that "go with God" middle finger to let us know they appreciated us!

During the day before our official departure, all who were planning to caravan dumped holding tanks and put fresh water onboard. We would continue to "dry camp" for nearly another week on the campus of the University of New Mexico at Las Cruces. We had been advised to head out to our rendezvous point between 6:00 and 8:00 a.m. on Tuesday. The caravan leader would begin our sojourn promptly at 8:50 a.m.

We readied ourselves the night before and rolled out of bed promptly at 6 a.m. By 6:30, we pulled back the drapes and prepared for battle and...lines! To our great dismay, we were practically alone in our navigation of the course to the outpost. Foolish thoughts like, "We must be early," crossed our minds, but we didn't care. We didn't want hassle.

Our hearts began to beat faster as we turned the corner and onto the approach of the rendezvous roadway. We stopped at the appointed spot and were handed our number. **238!** Would you believe? "238 of 300," the sign said. In a matter of seconds, we pulled in "nose to rear" of coach #237 and parked on the side of the road. We would have breakfast and wait for our Caravan Leader. We would also take turns getting out and looking at the spectacle.

18 Miles of Monacos--IN MOTION

It was a sight to behold--at least the truckers thought so!!! As far as the eye could see...Monaco Motor Coaches rolling along like one gigantic caterpillar. People stopped and starred. Pointed! Sheer wonderment. Any fears we had soon dissipated into unbridled fun. We were kids again. We laughed as we listened on the CB to truckers jawing vociferously about the laxness of "Smokey" when it came to these condos on wheels.

7,255 Motor Coaches Inundate University of New Mexico Campus

Our caravan remained a spectacle as we took our places one-by-one, side-by-side in a very large parking lot devoted to Monaco Motor Homes on the campus of the University of New Mexico. The other lots were filled by over 7,000 SOBs (Some Other Brands). Additional coaches parked at shopping malls and other facilities throughout town. There were more than 20,000 motor homers tooting around campus at any one given time. ***You had to be there!*** We were glad we were. And, it was amazing; in such a short time there were so many "old" friends.

First, Lloyd found us. He and Anne had headed out from El Paso the Monday afternoon before the caravan. They were settled in and watching when we all arrived. Next, we found a note from Di and Perry Barnes on the message board telling us where they were parked. After getting directions and hopping a tram, we found their coach and left them a note. Somehow, and quite simply, we arranged to get together and do dinner in town that very same evening.

On our way back from the initial find of the Barnes' coach, we stopped by the Student Union for a bit of lunch and ran smack dab into Betty and Paul Crawford, our neighbors and fellow classmates from the Life On Wheels Conference '97, Moscow.

We ventured around and before the second day was over, we walked right into Sheila Jansen. Later, we would get together with Ron and Sheila and eventually, we managed seats together with the Brays at the Helen Ready Concert, a feat in and of itself! (We managed to get in and sit with Anne and Lloyd at Glen Campbell Concert the night before by toting sandwiches and snacks. It was worth it! Because we were novices, we missed the Ballet Folklorico on opening night.)

Now if all this wasn't exciting and heart-warming enough, we met up with Linda and Steve Pedersen (Professional Driving School Friends from pre-conference, Life On Wheels) on Sunday morning before departing the convention. They found us in our coach. We visited for awhile and exchanged information since we were all planning to stay on in Las Cruces following the exodus from the university campus.

I tell you about these various and special people because it is important to know that when you are vagabonds and living on the road, you create family and make friends. Because of your particular circumstance of limited opportunities and time, there is no reason for false facades, pretentiousness, or other subtleties of traditional relationships. When you are together, you celebrate each other and the opportunity to be together.

Miracle or Snake Oil?

Although there is plenty of good entertainment, seminars, displays, parades, and foods for all reasons, a large part of the FMCA Convention is an opportunity for vendors of every kind to show and hack their wares. It is a symbiotic and stimulating relationship between convention goers and merchants.

One booth which caught my attention as well as that of several friends was the Wild Yam Cream, straight from Mexico and touted to be the miracle cure of the ages for women suffering from everything--PMS to hot flashes and/or heart attacks. Indeed, research of Dr. Le... well, it doesn't matter, but it was "cutting edge" and, yes, by rubbing this elixir on the soft skin of the female anatomy, well, there was no telling the benefits. It was a cure; no, it was a *miracle*. And, only $24 for a 2oz. jar. I was intrigued. I am also not an impulse shopper. "I'd have to think about it." But golly, I could sure use a "quick fix."

Several days later, while searching for other essentials, I spotted Wild Yam Cream on the shelf of a health food store. Hmmm…$10 cheaper. I bought it without hesitation! (So, too, did other RV friends who could not pass up this bargain either.)

I had been right the first time--*SNAKE OIL!!!*

Do you know anyone who could use a half a jar of Mexican Wild Yam Cream?

Another Week of Fun and Friendship in Las Cruces

A year prior to this reunion, it was hard to believe it would ever happen, but it really did. The Barnes and Lorenz coaches parked side by side at RV Doc's RV Park on Avenida de Mesilla. Gosh it felt good--like comin' home! The Barnes are the folks we met way back when we moved from East Coast to West. We were neighbors and daily companions for over a month at the mail-forwarding homestead on Netarts Bay at Tillamook, Oregon. They had moved up from California to wait for their Country Coach Motorhome to be built while we waited for our Monaco, the Dreamcatcher. It was time to celebrate our reunion.

We reunited with others here and shared new adventures and told the tales only seasoned road warriors could tell. Much had changed in less than a year.

Alas, it was time to move on.

Dreamcatcher Is "Unscheduled"

When writing the original periodic periodical, ***"Dreamcatcher Journeys,"*** we liked to include our schedule for the next several months so that recipients and subscribers would know where we would be and be able to contact and/or catch up with us. Occasionally, the best we could do was to print our *"unscheduled schedule"* so other vagabonds could be on the lookout for us.

At this point, we were able to find ourselves happily unscheduled but with plans that would include Vancouver, British Columbia at some point, and, a return to Coburg, Oregon for a mirror replacement for Dreamcatcher.

Our plans always included watching the weather and in the southwest, we were watching the snow levels on mountains as we prepared to head north for the summer months.

Our plans to head north to Sedona and on to Grand Canyon were postponed when it snowed heavily in Flagstaff, Arizona. Dreamcatcher opted to mosey on west before heading north.

Chapter 8

Beautiful Places – Lots of Spaces

Tombstone, Arizona

Dreamcatcher and crew cruised the New Mexico desert at the posted 70 mph speed limit right on into Arizona. It was difficult to leave friends behind, but we knew we would be seeing them again soon. We also were comforted in knowing that more friends were waiting for us in the Phoenix area. Consequently, we stopped for just one night at Benson, east of Tucson.

Drawn by the romance and excitement of yesteryear, we couldn't resist a side trip to Tombstone, Arizona and the OK Corral. We were not disappointed. The ambiance easily takes you back in time to the era in which it was so famous.

Surely, you remember **TOMBSTONE** and the ***shoot out*** at the **OK Corral**, don't you? If you ever decide to go there, be sure you don't miss the old graveyard. "Here lies...........hanged by mistake. He was right and we was wrong!" and many other intriguing epitaphs.

North to Sunflower Resort

Situated comfortably between Sun City and Sun City West on the West side of Phoenix, is an adult community unlike any other we had visited. It is remarkably clean and beautiful and packed with facilities: 2 swimming pools, 3 whirlpools, sauna, golf, horseshoes, tennis courts, social hall, ballroom, billiard room, craft and card rooms--every thing under the sun! But more than facilities, it is filled with the friendly, kind, and enthusiastic people. This is an RVing community par excellence!

Arizona

A lot of the southwest was virgin territory not only to the Dreamcatcher, but to me and Ol' Tex. So we parked the motor coach on the sidelines while we explored Arizona.

Sun City, Sun City West, Sun City Grand, Sunflower, and Happy Trails are adult communities on the West side of Phoenix. Each is buzzing with activities. Everything you would ever want to do is available for the active and interested.

So, this is where Tex decided he needed to outfit himself to become the big game fisherman. Yup! Right in the heart of the desert. ***SAY WHAT???*** (Hey, I just report the news from the road as it happens.)

Ol' Tex got himself a fine ocean-going Zodiac inflatable boat and an outboard motor. And, out on our *cement patio*, he inflated it and tried it out. Embarrassed, I hid inside the coach and watched the performance as I am certain the rest of the Sunflower neighborhood did. The experience took up most of a good day but he was a happy camper, *err sailor*, I mean.

"Catch anything?" you ask. He's still pinching the sand fleas out of his under shorts!

Orange Blossom Special

No, I'm not referring to Johnny Cash's golden oldie hit, but something equally impressive--the smell of orange blossoms! Sweeter than perfume, the pungent odor filled the air as well as our motor home. If you have never smelled orange blossoms, think of the most delicious potpourri you have encountered then imagine it enhanced ten-fold.

Happy Trails

Roy Rogers' legacy lives on in a community of motor home retreats called, (what else?), "Happy Trails." In the Sun City West area, this resort was convenient for us to explore with RV friends who stopped by for a visit. As part of their sales promotion, Happy Trails still rents out limited space on a weekly basis.

We quickly learned that the grounds are tightly secured and that the rentals are an opportunity to interest prospective buyers. We did the tour of the grounds and we saw what others had done with building structures on the lots. The four of us live in our motor coaches full-time and were awed by how much living space 399 feet provided. (Hard to believe now that we once filled 4,500 square feet. And, I mean filled!) But that was in another life.

North Ranch

Four of us piled into our Jeep and headed out beyond Wickenburg to the Escapee co-op at North Ranch which was beyond yet a smaller burg called Congress. North Ranch is high up in the desert hills. At the time of our visit, there was considerable building going on. We leisurely toured the grounds and facilities. It was food for thought since the co-op was still selling lots.

On our way back to Wickenberg, we detoured off the path to explore Merv Griffin's Ranch at Wickenberg. We explored this quiet vacation resort with rustic buildings which included a restaurant--a good choice for lunch. We opted instead to head for the Golden Nugget in town--an even better choice! (We were in the wilds of the west remember!)

Dan & Marilyn Nest in Engine Compartment

Quail watching was a pleasant pastime for us at Sunflower until the day old Tex discovered our favorite Gambel Quail couple building a nest in the engine compartment of the Jeep. "I don't care how you choose to spell potato," he told Dan. I'm going to tell you what I think about your choice for a home."

Maybe that's why the Quails decided to take another look at the big White House on Pennsylvania Avenue.

Border Cactus

There were several memorable experiences the day we visited Organ Pipe Cactus National Monument at the Arizona/Mexican Border. It was here that we saw and learned everything anyone would ever want to know about cacti: Saguaro, Pear, Organ Pipe, Mexican Jumping Beans, Teddy Bear, Ocotillo and many other fine prickles.

If you have not spent time there, the quiet desert is a peaceful and scenic place to enjoy just *being*.

Sedona - Red Rock Country

My legs felt weak from the awe-inspiring beauty of the area as we drove into the Red Rock Country of Sedona, Arizona. Jetting rock cliffs and rushing mountain streams in and around this desert town combine for breathtaking scenery. We drove into town to pick up a map. Unbelievable beauty lurked from every window and walkway.

Tex chose a self-guided tour of the undeveloped roads in Boynton Canyon nearly 8 miles outside of town. Although I longed for an opportunity to explore several other vortexes and experience the spiritual energies well-known to the area, they were not on my companion's priority list. I will admit, however, the Canyon was magnificent--and rugged.

Before leaving the area, we made a compromise stop at the Chapel of the Holy Cross between Sedona and the Village of Oak Creek. The view from the majestic Chapel is truly awe inspiring and we enjoyed a perfect setting for quiet time, reflection, and prayers. It was here that I recalled the somewhat poignant words of another spirit. "If the only words you ever pray are 'thank you,' it is enough."

In a stream of heartfelt tears, my prayer for that day was "thank you." Indeed, it was enough.

Colorado River at Parker, AZ and Earp, CA

Happier than a hog in swill and undaunted by 30 mph winds, Ol' Tex was a man who knew where he wanted to be. After parking the rig at Emerald Cove on the Colorado River, we hopped into the Jeep and headed for town under the guise of, "Let's go to the Tourist Information Center and find out what there is to see and do around here!"

Now for those of you who have traveled the southwest barren desert between Phoenix and Los Angeles, you pretty much know. For those of us who have not, "barren" is the key word.

So disregarding the obvious and being an optimist at heart, I believed he was interested in just that--checking out the potential "hot spots" while all the time Ol' Tex was looking for a contact to find out about a fishing license!

Tourist Information

A small, dusty, desert town, Parker serves as a wide spot in the road about 9 miles south of the Parker Dam just before crossing the Colorado River into Earp, California, a not nearly so wide spot in the road. A strange square building along the road was some sort of municipal structure housing the chamber of commerce among other things. We walked in and after several moments of feeling self-conscious and looking to find *anything that* might summons up a reason for our being there, Tex moseyed over to the Hispanic gal sitting at a desk in the center of the small entry room. "Hi," he said with boyish charm.

"Buenos dias," she responded. They were on common ground. He was eager to tell her about his boat so he broached this avenue of possible commonality--once again with more verve perhaps than necessary.

"How's the fishin' around here?" he asked although he swears this was not why we went to town. Just an exercise in the art of small talk, I'm to assume.

I soon lost interest and found myself trying to discern whether there might be a possibility of further exploration and adventure by blowing dust from a few meager pieces of paper I found housed in tiny racks on a side wall.

Eventually my enthusiasm waned once again and I tuned into the exchange Tex was having with his new friend. "Let me show you how to get to June's Place on this map," she said before we left the building. With that, the happy cowboy thanked the young woman profusely, and, with map in hand, we headed for the Jeep.

June's Place

With only a couple of streets in town, June's Place was not all that difficult to find. However, once we got a look at it, it was reassuring to be able to confirm that we were, in fact, at the right place. It was surrounded by years of neglect, trash, junk, and weeds as I recall so vividly.

Ol' Tex hopped out of the car as excited as if we had arrived at the Taj Mahal. "Think this is it?" he gleefully inquired. "Says June's place," I retorted cautiously getting out the car and following him to the door.

A loud, irritating buzzer sounded as we pushed against the screen door. This was the place: bait, tackle, and "fine" china consignment shop rolled into one. This was June's Place, an official fishing license establishment. The only thing holding the hovel up so far as I could see was a combination of dirt, spit, and wind.

The old codger behind the dusty, clutter-filled counter looked at Tex who was unnecessarily adjusting his britches as men will often do when preparing for serious discussion. "Hi," Tex grins at the stranger who stares impatiently back at him. "Come to buy me a fishin' license," he coos, eager to show he is "one of them."

"What kind ya want," the leather-skinned old man barks back. "Arizona or California?"

"I just got a new boat and motor and I'm gonna do some fishin' in the river. What kind do I need?"

"Well, if yur gonna fish in the river, yur gonna need a river stamp down as far as the reservation. You can't fish on the reservation without a reservation license so if yur plannin' on fishing below here," he points to a pencil line on a small local map, "yur gonna have to buy a reservation license."

By now, between the complexities of which side of the river and how far north and south on the waterway plus the potential for approximately 10 different fees, (maybe more), I'm ready to bolt! The complexity of the situation alone was enough to discourage the most avid sports enthusiast. But Ol' Tex had his new boat and new motor and nobody was going to discourage him. So the exchange of possibilities and prices began. I don't even want to remember the fees!

Finally, a deal was struck and now Tex was ready to discuss fishing. "Whaddaya catchin' around here?"

"Well, we catch allotta different fish."

"What are you catching now??"

The evasive old coot patronizingly kept calling Tex "sir" as he patiently waited for him to fork over the fees. But Old Tex was oblivious to June's demeanor. He was eager to share, fisherman-to-fisherman.

For his part, June saw no commonality and was tolerating him because of the money that would soon be coming his way.

Finally, we left the place, licenses and permits in hand, and a smile that stretched ear to ear. "Big bickies," I said using the British expression I had learned. "Cheap entertainment," countered the fisherman. The next week would tell who was closer to the truth.

The $4,000 Fish

Proud as a new papa and happier than I had seen him in years, Tex returned from his second boating expedition with a beautiful greenish-yellow, scaly character who gasped for air on my kitchen counter while the fisherman searched the cabinets for a ruler.

"Ya gotta write a story about my $4,000 fish!" he exclaimed excitedly.

"Yup, he's legal," he grinned measuring carefully as I watched. With an inch to spare he jubilantly continues. "You've got to write a story about this," he insisted. "This will be a really great story," he chirped as he lopped his trophy into the kitchen sink.

"You write the story," I retorted. "It's your fish. You'll do a much better job."

For me, the $4,000 said it all as I watched the poor little feller gasp and take his last few breaths in this stifling hot, dry, desert. ***No, no!! I'm talking about the fish!!!***

If I was to write the story, I guess I could say, "It will take two to make a decent dinner!"

Seeing the Sights

The weekend brought the Colorado River alive with a buzz of activity. Jet skis and speedboats raced back and forth. Tex thought this was a good time to park the boat and take the jeep off--*into the desert!*

Our first stop was Earp, a treasure-trove of really *dry* history. A sign on the post office told the story.

"After he escaped the shoot-out at the OK Corral in Arizona,
Wyatt Earp spent 2 decades of summers here at Earp."

This begs the question, "***WHY?***"

Travel At Your Own Risk

We crossed the Colorado River and saw Parker. This exhausted 2 more minutes before we headed north along the river. Before I realized what was happening, we were off the road and I was reading a sign that said: **Primitive Road--*Use At Your Own Risk*.**

Complete with hair-pin turns, washboard surface, dust, dirt, and rock, we drove back into this totally undeveloped land for about 5 miles. It seemed more. Around the next turn, we saw a church front--that's all, just the front. No sides. No top. No back. ***Just the front, complete with steeple.***

We parked our car in the church front parking lot and crossed a bridge into a small establishment of mostly building fronts. There was one establishment which was a complete building—front, back, sides, and roof! I reluctantly sat at a table outside while Tex went into the building and purchased a couple of drinks.

Surprisingly, there were several people sitting around tables both inside and outside, but the outside tables were better positioned to enjoy both the beauty of the land and the *live entertainment.* That's right, smack-dab in the middle of nowhere, there was live musical entertainment--and quite good, at that! This was where the not-so-young and the restless come to party.

So we did too!

POSTON MEMORIAL MONUMENT

With the Colorado River raging with speedboats and skidoos, we drove from the nothing place of Parker, AZ to out in the middle of absolutely nowhere, approximately 17 miles directly south of the desolate town to a place called Poston. It is a still, deserted area, too hot for settlement. This is where Japanese Americans were interned from May 8, 1942 to November 28, 1945. 17,867 persons of Japanese ancestry who lived in the Western part of the US were relocated here during World War II.

The fact that they survived the isolation and mustered spirit to build a monument that almost no one ever visits is the counter-balance of this story. It is a remote, ugly place to visit, and an even uglier part of history ever reminding us that war is ugly. We thought hard and deep. We were totally alone yet deeply moved. In our hearts, this will never be forgotten.

It was time to leave this part of history and country behind.

Lake Havasu City

If it was not for the **London Bridge**, one would wonder if Lake Havasu City would even be here. But its claim to fame, or even existence for that matter, seems to be the old London Bridge. In 1968, the McCulloch Corporation purchased the London Bridge for more than $7 million. Now, this historical landmark stretches across the Colorado River.

Lake Havasu City is more than a contradiction; it is both a question mark and exclamation point smack in the middle of a sleepy little river community dependent upon tourist trade for its very existence.

Moon Ride

As we drove through this part of the country, we could not help but feel it would look just like this ***if*** we were traveling on the surface of the moon. The topography seems so similar. The eeriness of the terrain keeps one interested and entertained.

Then suddenly, out of this vastness comes spectacular color and beauty. Mountains spring up from nowhere. In the distance, one can notice snow covered peaks, in direct contrast to this hot, dry, flat land.

The most unique sights spark one's interest. For example, we saw wild burros, horses, and even cows, in some parts, grazing on open range lands.

Bullhead City, Arizona

As we detoured through California to travel north because Lake Havasu had been invaded by swarms of grasshoppers, the words of the weathermen throughout western history echoed in my mind. "The hottest spot in the country today was Bullhead City, Arizona."

We were leaving 104 degrees at Parker and headed for Bullhead City, Arizona. We were going to ***fry!*** But as we parked the coach, it was the stench of black leather that permeated the air.

We went to the Bullhead Chamber of Commerce to gather information. It was here that we learned that the 16th Annual River Run was roaring into town the same time we were. They advised us if we were foolish enough to cross the river to Laughlin, we would most certainly want to dress in black leather--chains optional, but desirable!

40,000 Harleys Converge on Laughlin, and WE WERE THERE!

Across the River, but directly adjacent to Bullhead City is Laughlin, Nevada, a "rough and tumble" bad boy town reminiscent of Las Vegas in its early days except, as they said, "more casual." It was here that 40,000 bikers roared into town--and we were with them!

I have written about Ol' Tex's experiences when meeting up with a Biker named T-Bone back in Reno. Friday night, the spirit of T-Bone lived on when outside our bedroom window, a dozen bikers drank beer and swapped profanities. The one with one leg captured our hearts as well as our attention. We wondered if he had "parked his hiney" in front of some other motor coach and dared the driver to run over him.

Undaunted by the leather and chrome, we decided to brave the crowds and go for the one pound prime rib dinner (each). As many of you know, gambling places are well-known for there food as well as their casinos. We were standing in line waiting to be seated when a conversation from behind caused us to casually see *WHO* was there.

WHAT would have been a better choice of words. There stood a male human (we think) with every body part that was visible pierced and filled with metal (and probably, even parts not visible). He was talking to his 8 year old son (also fully pierced). We were distracted from their conversation not only by the heavy metal, but also by the head to toe tattooing—on both father and son, of course. It was difficult, but somehow, we managed to appropriately ease our fixed gazes to other interesting sights.

The memory of T-Bone's tenacity lives on!

Burros and Bikers

To avoid the congestion and whatever else a town full of motor cyclists might produce, we headed out into the desert on the famous and historic old Route 66, the first transcontinental highway west from Chicago to the Pacific Ocean.

We eased into the authentic western ghost town and gold mining camp of Oatman and could not discern which seemed more out of place--the burros freely wandering the crowded streets or the thousands of shinning chrome motorcycles lining the main drag.

Miraculously, we found a place to park and began meandering the streets and mingling uncomfortably with the bikers. (Okay, so we didn't exactly mingle.) We did, however, stand our ground while petting and feeding the donkeys. It was fun to browse through the shops and notice that the usual array of tourist memorabilia had been carefully replaced with Harley T-shirts and black leather apparel.

It was difficult to leave "hog heaven," but by late Sunday afternoon, most of the bikers had left town and those who remained were being escorted out of town by a motorcade of police cars--front, back, and beside them. When I glanced over at my partner, Ol' Tex was smiling to himself as he thought about "sweet justice."

With spirits high, we were going into Laughlin for one last buffet before heading to Death Valley the following morning.

Joshua Tree Road

We were rolling west with the sunrise shining on our tailpipes. Once we had gotten several hours out in the middle of nowhere, we turned onto Joshua Tree Road, a lovely name for a street in the middle of the desert, we thought. Within moments, we started noticing strange, but interesting tree-like plants of the Yucca family with sword-shaped leaves and greenish-white flowers grouped in panicles...Joshua Trees.

Needless to say, the desert has many miles of sand, but many unique sights and experiences as well.

Chapter 9

This Is MY Country – Land That I Love . . .

The Other Side of the Moon

Our travels have taken us through places that looked as if we were either on the surface of the moon or in an ever changing sculpture. Mountains with tufts of vegetation and mountains with no vegetation at all eased up and surrounded us as we found our way around and through landscape dotted with rocks, sand, and a multiplicity of dry vegetation. It looked as if some giant travelers ahead of us had taken gargantuan paint brushes and painted stage scenery for us to focus upon.

Climbing the mountains out here in the desert was so subtle that the only way one was cognizant of the elevation variations was by pressure in the inner ear.

This was a thrill of a lifetime for Ol' Tex whose head was bobbing from side to side. "Look at the flowers," he croaked in an effort to justify our being in this God forsaken country. We thought a lot about and discussed the Sahara as well as Egypt as we traveled along on this part of our journey.

Suddenly, we came upon a hotel and casino, but it was the five (5) saddled-up CAMELS parked out front that caught our attention!

Now that was a Kodak moment if ever there was one. We pulled to the side of the road and took photos. There really was no worry about having to pull to the side of the road since we were the only folks out there—except the camels, of course. One could not help but wonder how they managed to get saddles on them. Or better yet, why were they parked there?

I kept finding myself wanting to say, "Can we go home now?" But Ol' Tex was happy. And besides, I keep forgetting, "We are home."

Nevada

In the vast wastelands of Nevada, there are three items of particular note: exceptionally good highways, casinos, and brothels. ***BROTHELS???*** That's right! Out in the middle of acres of sagebrush or even less, you will notice simple, small buildings of eye-catching color--shocking pink or even a mustard yellow seemed popular. The names were equally attractive: Angel's Ladies and Shady Lady to name a couple.

Gradually, as the sage became more sparse and we moved deeper and deeper into desolation, we noticed there were no birds, then no snakes, no lizards. Nothing. Aside from the occasional empty beer bottle thrown on the side of the road, there was no evidence of civilization except for the road itself. Without immediate awareness, we were again climbing mountains.

As we began our decent, flowers popped up. We were being swallowed-up by rocks and mountains on a narrow, curving road. Dreamcatcher plummeted down deep into a canyon...***a valley of death.***

Death Valley Days (Destination: Minus Sea Level)

Ol' Tex has *always* wanted to see Death Valley. The Beautiful Bev, on the other hand, a person who has always had a keen fondness for words and their meaning thought there was probably a good reason it's called "*Death Valley*" and *never* wanted to go anywhere near it. We hit a compromise that satisfied both by meandering through desert country and spending two days and nights right in Death Valley.

During our stay, we visited Scotty's Castle, Ubehebe Crater, Grapevine, Sand Dunes, Salk Creek, Furnace Creek, Badwater, Shoshone, Death Valley Junction, Amargosa Valley, the place where

Borax is mined, and the 20 mule teams that took 10 days to haul their train from Death Valley to the Mohave Desert 165 miles away.

To this day, the Beautiful Bev remains grateful that Ol' Tex won the "compromise!"

Scotty's Castle

Truly a legend in its development and history but a reality for those who have stayed there in the past as well as those who visit it today. It is a mansion that no one would ever expect in the middle of no man's land. It is as unique as Death Valley itself. Was the owner-financier duped or did he know exactly where his money was going? He didn't seem to mind. A friendship that honors the best and the worst of trust built this castle.

Desert Flowers

They blame and credit the abundance and kaleidoscope of color on El Nino. It was a virtual transition in texture ever reminding us that Mother Nature is in charge.

In the end, Ol' Tex was on target. It is something one must experience; it is impossible to describe. Death Valley needs to be a must see on everyone's list of "What to do and see before I die."

The Best of Times...The Worst of Times

Las Vegas, a 24 hour amusement city filled with bright lights, theme casinos, shows, and shopping, was a welcomed treat after the absence of any decadence in Death Valley. But the temptations had to be tempered when Ol Tex took ill. (Too much Borax, maybe.)

We managed to take in a fabulous show at the Stratosphere, dine at the famous Luxor where one gets a sense he may have been kidnapped to its sister city in Egypt, and enjoyed buffets at several other hotels.

Theme hotels: Treasure Island, MGM, New York-New York, Mirage, and on and on, were sights to simply see in and of themselves. Usually we called it a day by mid-afternoon so Tex could rest and recuperate. We needed to get up early to enjoy the 49 cent, 7 pound waffle specials!

Southern Utah

Having once lived in Utah for a couple of years, we were aware of the natural beauty the land had to offer. But as we left Nevada, climbed the mountains and looked into vast canyons in Arizona, we were unprepared for the *take-your-breath-away* beauty we began to see in southern Utah. Our eyes could not begin to drink in the spectacular array of colors and textures as the panorama totally encompassed the Dreamcatcher.

We had driven right into a movie. The mountains were perfectly excavated while streams snaked through them—colors kissed in place to perfection, courtesy of Mother Nature.

As the song lyrics state, "Only God can make a tree," but His wind and water disciples must have worked tirelessly on the landscape that began unfolding before our very eyes. Sister spring took a paintbrush and dabbed bouquets of flowers into the mountainside. All this time you thought only Steven Spielberg could achieve such a level of greatness!

Zion

OOOH! Just look at that...!!!

There simply were no words that could begin to capture the majesty of the gallery of sculptured rock, waterfalls, and other wonders of nature before our eyes. The absolute beauty of it all was humbling. The stone was cut and polished by elements and time, dramatic drop-offs just appeared without warning, and green gardens with wild flowers sprang forth from nowhere.

This is Zion National Park. This is Utopia! Natural carvings, Navajo sandstone, and layers of rock bend and twist skyward. The higher we climbed, the more magnificent the ever-changing scene. Tunnels had been cut through the vermilion landscape; and, throughout the longest unlighted tunnel, a 1.1 mile spans, windows had been cut affording us an occasional peek into awesome beauty--***heaven!***

During our climb, precipitation that began as rain produced newborn waterfalls which cascaded over jagged, hanging cliffs polishing the surfaces and giving them sheen. Streams below gathered speed as they swelled and rushed down the lava swirls of the volcanic terrain.

As the storm intensified and hail pounded against the Jeep, waterfalls intensified. We could barely contain ourselves as we tried to drink it all in.

Pueblo Indians inhabited these lands over a thousand years ago. We looked with wonder at the "weeping rock" and were awestruck when we arrived at the *Temple of Sinawava.* It was there that we were joined by three wild deer and a Peregrine Falcon.

By nightfall, we could barely quiet our senses which were filled with freshness, color, and magnificence. We wondered if sleep would ever come. Memories made our hearts beat faster like the rush of the mountain streams pounding against the rocks then continuing to flow and fill the soul and the sea respectively.

Bryce Canyon

It was a **SPECTACLE** *beyond our wildest dream!* The amazing sights at Bryce Canyon were otherworldly.

Pinnacles and spires called Hoodoos cast their spell on astounded visitors from around the world. These pillars of rock were left by nature's erosion. Their phenomenal forms afford both excitement and serenity.

Elevation at the National Park ranges from 6,500 to 9,100 feet. The quality of air is worthy of bottling. The water is cold enough to freeze at night yet melts and adds vigor and freshness to streams as sunlight caresses the Canyon.

Fairyland Canyon

"The fanciful shapes at Fairyland Point offer a natural amphitheater of castle-like formations." From this view point, one can see Navajo Mountain and other magical sights that revel the imagination. It is difficult to pull one's self away and on to the next sight.

Rainbow

The clouds thickened and darkened as we climbed to the vista. Pellets of ice bounced off the windshield and danced across the hood of the Jeep. Lightening shot out across the sky as we looked out over Rainbow Point.

We just had to get out of the car. We took one quick peek and scurried back as thunder crashed around us. At 9,115, feet we feared being struck by the violent yet beautiful force of nature. It made us appreciate the true meaning of the word "awesome."

Reluctantly, we began our decent while the precipitation intensified. Before our very eyes, black, asphalt roads turn white and slippery with ice and snow. The frozen accumulation deepened and we carefully maneuvered our way back through the Canyon reminiscing that only days before we had concluded that we would like a homebase where four seasons are apparent.

You can consider this our "winter" for the year 1998.

Hoodoos Cast Their Spell

Soon the sunshine magically danced across the Hoodoos and cast a spell on us again. A Hoodoo is a pillar of rock, unique and spectacular in shape, left by erosion. These magical shapes are as exciting as Cinderella's Castle. Move over Disney, Bryce Canyon has you beat by 10 million years!

Paradise Lost

That evening, we settled in early not only to keep warm but to do some planning as well as reflection. It had been 20 years since we called Utah home.

Grand Staircase - Escalante

We tooted out of Ruby's Inn at Bryce Canyon and headed for Torrey. With the bright sunshine upon us, the scenery was nothing less than spectacular. As we drove, hoodoos changed to cowboy country. The new green of spring proudly served as backdrop for flowering trees and bushes.

The road narrowed as we climbed and looked with wonderment. Why are movies now being shot in dirty inner cities when young and old need more exposure to the beauty and grandeur of nature.

We passed through the Petrified Forest and began a series of hairpin turns with no shoulders and 10% grades. At 6,500 feet, I was looking directly over what would easily be that much of a direct drop.

We were still climbing. Our altimeter went out of range at 9,000 feet. ***We were still climbing!***

As we descended into the welcoming pastoral valley at Torrey junction outside of Capital Reef National Park, I relaxed my white-knuckled grip from the arm rests of the co-pilot seat and smiled as I glanced over at my proud partner, *Don Quixote.* He had conquered the mechanical dragons of the motor coach and now he was successfully *chasing the windmills of the road.*

Windmills of the Gods

We retraced some ancient footsteps of our past as we continued our search for our future. We drove in and out of each area becoming closer and closer to our next adventure, God, and each other. We are never quite certain where the road will take us even though it is clearly marked on the map. ***This is a Dreamcatcher's Journey***.

Butch Cassidy Country – Capitol Reef National Park

The legend lives! We could feel the excitement, sense the same danger as we climbed the same hills, walked the same paths, and ducked in and out of the same canyons, buttes, and domes that Butch Cassidy and the Sundance Kid once did. The colors were dazzling, the structure and texture of our surroundings took our breath away. Our hearts beat with both excitement and joy.

We were in *Capitol Reef National Park* (Utah), the "Land of the Sleeping Rainbow," as the Paiute Indians called it. Folks here now remember it more for the Wild Bunch who used the area to hide out rather than for the rugged landscape and brightly colored cliffs and terraces that seem to fill one's being with joy. Nearly impassable ridges were called "reefs" and dome-shaped rocks reminded the early pioneers of the nation's Capitol. Hence the unusual name for the area.

Elephant Skin

Traveling north and east from Capitol Reef to Price are some of the most unique land formations on earth. Rock mountains look like sand dunes; others look as if they have been covered with elephant skin. Another area of the moon surface complete with craters and "green cheese" loomed before us. Majestic and uniform stone fences adorned the tops of some of the highest land forms. In this mysterious land where vegetation is extremely sparse, we noted fences. Surely, no cattle could survive here. We wondered if they were perhaps for a few errant dinosaurs who once roamed freely over much of this land.

'Dem Bones!

Jurassic Park! For real, honest! Utah's Dinosaurland is home to the world's largest Jurassic dinosaur quarry. Can you believe this is yet another one of our National Parks?

We went first to the quarry where archaeologists are working. Since we had been there nearly 20 years earlier, we were eager to see how much more had been uncovered within the 200 foot long glass enclosed wall. It is also exciting to watch the geologists on the other side of the quarry chip away at our history.

We toured the rest of this large park by Jeep. The Green River runs through it and the water was moving swiftly.

Petroglyphs & Pictographs

Two of the most exciting things we saw on the last leg of our scenic journey through Utah were the petroglyphs and pictographs on several rock walls at various places throughout the park. Our first encounter with them had been at Capital Reef, but the final collection was even more distinct. One cannot help experience a sense of awe to realize you are standing where ancient civilizations roamed.

We stopped at the primitive cabin of Josie Morris. A college educated woman and "friend" of Butch Cassidy, Josie had spent the first 40 years and several husbands just north of the present monument area. She spent the next 50 here at Cub Creek where she lived alone except for friends and family who visited on occasion. A quiet, peaceful, romantic place, this is where Josie farmed and raised cattle. There were no modern conveniences. From where we sat to contemplate this, there was no need for them.

Flaming Gorge

Back again in the Dreamcatcher, we *CLIMBED* from the foothills through major geologic formations until we reached the one billion year old core and I cried, "Uncle"! Geological identification en route affords travelers the opportunity to note specific variations by name: Jurassic, Triassic, etc.

Highway switch-backs gave this passenger the distinct feeling that she was about to drop off the end of the earth. Roads began to go up at a 45 degree angle. Herds of white tail deer at the edge of the road were undaunted by our presence. I wondered if it would be easier to pray since we were getting closer and closer to Heaven—both figuratively and literally.

Road Warrior

If he had been outside of the coach instead of behind the wheel, Ol' Tex's tongue would have been covered with snow as it hung from his mouth and he looked down upon the waters he wished he could fish. It was sad really. I watched Ol' Tex while he focused on the view.

Then it happened. We missed the turn! 10,251 feet high on a narrow, winding mountain pass and ***we miss the turn!!!*** Aside from dropping off the edge, nothing could be worse! The edge of the road was completely unprotected. Undaunted, Ol' Tex said, "We'll just find a place and turn it around."

I wondered if he had been watching the same things I had...narrow roads, passes, steep drop-offs. Without warning, we came upon a large turnout with an entrance and an exit. As we pulled-out the other side headed in the opposite direction, I looked over at the bus driver.

"No sweat," he grins. I was in awe. Driving School personnel would have been very proud.

Although it was snowing more heavily by now, the rest of the trip down the mountain and on into Rock Springs was a piece of cake!

Chapter 10

BeeBeep . . . BeeBeep!

Rock Springs, Wyoming

Rock Springs is a ***very old*** and ***very rugged*** western town. If one was to put the politically correct spin on it, "rustic," would be a mildly appropriate term.

After completing our overview tour and picking up some supplies at the General Store, we were eager to leave in the morning. It was very cold and we watched while the sun melted the frost from the Jeep. We waited for the slowly rising temperature to sufficiently warm the diesel engine so we could start it. (It would not be until our next stop at Jackson Hole that Jim would hardwire a switch for the engine heater and put it next to his bed.)

Jackson Hole, Wyoming

Rustic in the better sense of the word, Jackson Hole is a hub of food, shopping, cowboys and cowboy wanna-be(s). The day we arrived, the town was holding its annual elk antler auction. Buck elk shed their antlers early in the spring each year and only the local Boy Scouts are allowed into the Grand Teton National Park to collect them. One weekend in May every year they sell their prize collection in the town's square. If anyone else is caught taking antlers from the park, they are arrested and fined.

National Elk Refuge

Fortunately, I had dug my snowsuit out from the basement storage the morning we headed out into the Grand Tetons. There was a significant amount of snow in the mountains and enough at ground level to make it cold, very cold.

We looked and looked for elk, moose, wolves, and other wild game that are plentiful in the park. Old Tex was a mite disappointed as our eyes searched out into the snow covered roadside and flats and all we saw was coyote pee!!

Grand Tetons

The snow-covered beauty of the majestic mountains contrasted magnificently with the rushing waters of the Snake River which wove its way in and out of our tour through the National Park. We climbed Signal Mountain and looked out over the flats where herds of elk and buffalo come to feed. But not today.

As we headed back to camp, a strange sight caught my eye. It was a very large, dark brown furry creature. Ol' Tex slammed on the brakes and we dipped into a convenient turnout. Before our very eyes (and cameras), were a half a dozen buffalo. It took us a few minutes to realize that at a distance from them, there was a small herd. We snapped pictures and watched as the immediate group began to head back to the herd--all but one, that is.

The Lonely Bull

The lone buffalo stood and watched what we were doing. He actually posed for the camera before moving. I held back, near the Jeep, while Ol' Tex moved in closer with the camera to get that perfect shot. (He is the professional, after all.)

Suddenly, the big, burly beast charged the fence! I was certain that Ol' Tex would be wearing a buffalo robe by evening. Tex started running for the car.

Fortunately, the buffalo had his sights set on greener pastures. Once free of the fence, he ran for the other side of the road. It would not be until the following day that we would be handed a **WARNING** from the National Park Service which read:

MANY VISITORS HAVE BEEN GORED BY BUFFALO!
DO NOT APPROACH BUFFALO.

Now you tell us!!!

Bald Headed Eagle - Up Close and Personal

Putting on an air show for our personal viewing pleasure, a rare bald headed eagle performed by flying solo around us as we stood beside the Snake River soaking in the serenity. We had been looking into the clear, rushing water for trout. Perhaps he was too.

We just stood still and watched the spectacle for a long time. In the quiet and the beauty of the moment, we heard voices in our heads tell us how remarkably blessed we were to be here at this moment in time. There may not always be eagles to watch, but we must stop and note what is and become just as observant of the beauty that is in that exact moment.

In Search of Bull Winkle

Undaunted by the earlier antics of our buffalo buddy, we saw several large herds of animals at a distance. We turned onto Antelope Flats Road for a closer look. I was eager to see a moose and my partner was willing to take a closer look too. As we moved in nearer to this large herd, we could see the animals were buffalo---and more buffalo.

Ho-hum. Buffalo. We had grown indifferent. After you have been chased by a buffalo, watching a herd watch you is a bit of a bore!

Yellowstone

The sights and sounds of the Grand Tetons were but a preview for what we would encounter in Yellowstone National Park. There were large herds of animals. Female buffalo with young calves romped nearby while herds of all male buffalo were separate and at a distance at this time of year.

And, there were elk, plenty of elk. As a matter of fact, it was necessary to walk with care when we got out of the car to take closer looks at geyser basins and hot springs. We were reminded of what fellow explorer, Buck Staghorn, used to say:

"And remember, watch where you step!"

Bubble, Bubble, Toil & Trouble

Caldrons of boiling, bubbling, splashing liquid with varying degrees of thickness, steam, and coloration enchanted the area at intervals throughout the Park. These basins often appeared as paint pots, taking on a cartoon-like presence before our very eyes. It was not uncommon, but surprising, to see occasional buffalo taking "a day at the spa" in several choice locations.

Old Faithful at Yellowstone

Forty-five minutes before the scheduled eruption, people began to gather around Old Faithful. As the time grew closer, one could sense the excitement building. Then, as it had for hundreds of thousands of years before, it started to tease us with pre-eruption burps followed by quiet times.

"There she blows!"

I tried to contain myself at this reverent moment. Other than my outburst, there was a unified "aaaahhhhh," from the large crowd that had gathered around the magnificent geyser. The burst of 204 degree liquid straight toward the sky lasted less than 2 minutes but was worth every second of focus.

The experience can only be measured in faith--faith that it will continue to happen for hundreds of thousands of years to come.

Yellowstone touched our souls and made us ***more aware of a higher power***. From the volcanic activity so abundant and spectacular to the birthing of buffalo calves less than 25 feet away, we knew instinctively there is more to life than war, corruption, government, greed, drugs, violence, shootings, struggle and despair.

With hearts filled with joy and life renewed, we tried to capture everything on film and video tape. We had equipped ourselves with two cameras each and tried desperately to hang on to each moment.

But alas, we realized all too soon—in the end, some things can be captured in spirit only. We need to capture the joy of each moment everyday. The spirit of Yellowstone lives on in our minds and hearts.

(News from Springfield, Oregon)

That same evening when we got home and turned on the evening news, we learned of a tragic shooting at Thurston High School in our beloved Oregon.

Exactly a year before this incident, we had arrived in Oregon and I wrote extensively about how Oregon had restored my faith in humanity. Major news stories were about rose festivals in the parks in comparison to the top three shootings on the streets of Baltimore and D.C. People cared—they really cared.

We have been to Springfield, Oregon on several occasions. The Dreamcatcher was born just a mile or so north of there. I experienced a deep personal loss with this particular violence.

It is my feeling that if this kind of violence has reached Oregon, society as we once knew it--is no more. Civilization no longer exists in this country. We feel a heart-wrenching sadness for all of mankind as well as an enormous sadness for our country and our culture. *(Author's note: This event took place in 1998.)*

Dreamcatcher Covered...with SNOW???

Our trip north through the Gallatin National Forest was cold, but spectacular. Snow was weighing down the evergreens and it was snowing lightly as we climbed the mountains. It had been snowing in this part of the country all night and the ground was covered with several inches of new snow.

Mountain streams ran along the roadside, cold and rapid. Lone buffalo foraged for food near streams. We were delighted to see two female elk teaching their newly born babies to follow them on an open hillside. Life anew. There was great joy in the new day, but will we ever be able to forget the news of the "dark night?"

A Day At The Spa in Montana

Barely 32 degrees outside, this was spring in Montana. We parked the rig and packed our swimsuits and towels into our tote bags and headed across the lawn of our campground to Bozeman Hot Springs. These particular springs are highly acclaimed for their healing properties. Ol' Tex and I were eager to drag our aching bones to the mineral water spa and check them out.

There were seven pools inside one very large room. Each pool varied by several degrees in temperature and all were readily available to climb in and out. So we did. There was also one large pool outdoors.

We warmed and we soaked until we were shriveled like prunes. I could not get into the hottest of the pools, but Old Tex, toughened with age and experience, soaked until he look like a cooked lobster! We both felt younger (and warmer) when we returned home.

Rite of Spring

Defying all odds, flowering trees and shrubs were expressing their determination to bring spring to the cold northwest by the time we got to Bozeman, Butte, and Missoula. I was convinced they were losing the battle. Consequently, we went out and purchased an additional space heater remembering we did not experience summer until we got back to Kansas last fall! This particular year, the plan was to head even further north.

Butte, Montana

During the days when the mines were still active, Butte had to be *one heck of a town.* But today, it is sad--everything stopped about 30 years ago. Downtown Butte had the potential for magnificent revitalization, but obviously, it did not have the energy. Houses which continued to see hard winters for 8 or 9 months a year had not seen a paint brush for 30 or 40 years. We did a "preview" trip the day we arrived in the area to determine how to best ration our time to see all of the sights the following day which was Memorial Day. After the preview, we decided it would be more prudent to stay at home and catch up on chores. The preview was sad enough. We prepared to move on after the holiday.

On To Missoula

In total contrast to Butte, Missoula was "home" to me. Maybe it was because it is a college town. The University of Montana is here. Maybe it was because I was in love by the time we got there. The countryside of Montana is magnificent and lush, filled with trees, rugged rocks, streams and rivers, and patches of livestock: horses, cows, sheep, mules, lamas, *all with babies!* I nearly fell right off the co-pilot seat gawking at the cuddly creatures. Montana is much like the Adirondacks where I grew up--only with fewer trees, bigger sky!

Another plus for Missoula was both the campground and our hosts. The owner raised thoroughbred horses and I spent most of the first 18 years of my life on a farm just outside of Saratoga Springs, New York which is home to the most elite racetrack in the world and the Horse Racing Hall of Fame. For the entire month of August, the area from Albany to Lake George, New York caters to horse racing fans and owners alike. Oh, did I mention that Saratoga is also a college town and has famous geysers and mineral baths? That's where the "springs" comes from in Saratoga! Perhaps we do long for our "roots" eventually.

Yup, I'm home! What's that you say? No Dillard's? No Nordstrom's?

"On the road again, can't wait to get on the road again...making music with my friends, I can't wait to get on the road again!"

Kamiah, Idaho

Route 12 from Missoula to Kamiah, Idaho is like driving down a postcard. The beauty is awesome and continues for nearly 150 miles along a clear, fast-moving river. At Kamiah, it is called Clearwater River. It is picturesque no matter what you call it.

We came to Lewis-Clark Resort at Kamiah to make it our home park in order to be able to join Coast to Coast Resorts and Resort Parks International, two networks of private campgrounds throughout the United States, Canada, and Mexico which allow only members to stay at them.

Lewis-Clark is a quaint, charming place filled with warm, friendly people. We stayed nearly a week, enjoying every moment of the great outdoors in the Idaho panhandle. The air has a "clean-clothes fresh" smell. Even the sweet scent of blooming flowers is an intrusion.

North to Deary

From Kamiah, we wound our way north to Deary, Idaho, home to the famous Gaylord Maxwell! Dear friends for many years, Gaylord and his wife, Margie, supported us during the agonizing years of preparation for this great adventure. Gaylord, renown in the RV industry is a writer, a teacher and developer/director of the Life On Wheels School at the

University of Idaho which we attended at Moscow and the Association to which we are charter members.

The Maxwell House

That's what it says on the ranch-styled arch over their driveway. Clever, huh? And, so are the talented folks who live there and call The Maxwell House "home." We spent a week with them at their ranch and enjoyed every minute.

Shortly before this book went into final edit, long-time mentor and friend Gaylord Maxwell passed away. He will be sorely missed. His contribution to the RV world and those who enjoy it is unparalleled.

Coeur d' Alene - Life Doesn't Get Any Better Than This!

Friends made arrangements for us to park beside them in the Foretravel lot, where they were parked for service. We toured downtown Coeur d' Alene and drove over to Spokane. The entire area is filled with gorgeous scenery. We did some walking, some talking, and rode out to Hayden Lake. Sometimes time passes too quickly. This was one of those times.

When we said, "Good-bye" to our Foretravel hosts, I said, "This is one of the best places we've ever stayed." I meant it. But it was time for us to move out to the other side of the lake where we had committed to KOA. They had a boat launch. Foretravel assured us we could stay on, but old Tex was itching to do some fishing and the spacious asphalt lot where we were camped was dry as a bone.

Testing the Waters

After spending most of the day running back to town to pick up parts to do yet more repair work, I convinced the Captain it was time to test the waters--inflate the yacht.

We loaded the vessel onto the top of the Jeep, put the motor, gas tank, life jackets and miscellaneous equipment inside, and headed down to the dock where we unloaded the boat, the motor, the gas tank, the life jackets, and miscellaneous equipment. After considerable *ado*, we got into the boat and sped off. Well, "sputtered" would be a better term. You see, in his effort to economize on fuel (since the motor requires so little), the Captain, in his infinite wisdom, got barely enough to keep the motor running while sucking air.

It was during this tour of duty I suggested we might return to port and purchase a fishing license and see about staying on at Camp KOA for a few days. (It seemed so necessary now that we had all this paraphernalia together in one spot--and ready to float.)

I manned the deck while the Captain booked us in for the extended weekend and bought his licenses. When he returned with the fishing gear, I hot-footed it back to the little necessary room then gathered food and drink for the voyage.

Soon we were off on our first ever together fishing expedition. Talk about togetherness!!! Some of you have heard me joke about surviving in the confined space in the Dreamcatcher, our motor home. Well, think about the joy of togetherness in our 3' by 4' floating vessel with both necessary and unnecessary gear, food, drink, motor, and gas storage *tank*-- in the largest sense of 6 gallons!!!

But, my trophy fisherman was happy, and that was really all that mattered when we pulled into the dock at dusk. It was nearly eleven p.m. by the time we finished dinner. But, no matter, he was happy. He had caught his ten inch bass and he was happy. That was all that mattered. All that ever matters—really!

A Fishing We Will Go

Day and night, four days and four nights, the Captain launched "Pop Fizz," the Zodiac inflatable yacht, and headed out to sea. Not unlike Savannah's Waving Girl, I waited--and raved, rather than waved. 'Space at last! Space at last. Thank God Almighty, I've [my own] space at last!'

But alas, the days passed and each day when I asked Moby Dick, "Where's the fish?" He'd mumble, "Too small to keep." Finally I couldn't resist but shouldn't have said, "Could we get a bowl and keep them as pets?"

So the great fish out turned into burned beef and beans. But he was happy, and that's all that matters--all that ever matters.

Lake Coeur d' Alene, Idaho

Ol' Tex was psyched about this fishing business. He bought himself another gas tank, more lures, more line, a seat cushion, a new boat anchor (he lost the first one), more rope (lost that too), but he was happy. "Got to get another new fishin' pole," he concluded. "This one's too light!" (The other one was too heavy.) "Too short, too," he added as if to justify the decision. I didn't respond. I had learned better. (And some folks say we are too old to learn.) I have my space, remember, and I know a good thing.

Moses Lake, Washington

Complete with a community of ants big enough to saddle and ride, we moseyed out of Coeur d' Alene and headed west. Old Tex was giddy from this fishing business, so we headed straight for Moses Lake, Washington--smack dab in the middle of ***nowhere***. We rolled into the Sunrise Coast-To-Coast Resort and told the "General" we had reservations. "How long ya gonnna be here?" she barked. "Oh, probably 3, 4 nights. How's the fishin'?" Tex smiled.

Disinterested in our concerns, she continued. "How long? We're filling up here," a misinformation if ever there was one. "Gotta know right now how long you're gonna stay."

"Do you have a phone line to the sight?" I foolishly asked.

The General gasped, "NO! Of course we don't, but you're going to have cable."

"I don't want cable. Do you have a phone jack I can use?"

"I can't let you use ***this*** phone. ***THIS*** is a business. You're gonna have to take cable. Two dollars extra a night."

"I don't want cable. We have a digital satellite system. Paid good money for it and we don't need cable."

"Well, you're gonna have to take cable. Didn't *she* tell ya? ("She" had to reference the phone-in reservation's clerk.) You are gonna have to take cable. Two dollars extra a night. Cash!" She bristled.

We moved to sight A-3. It had cable. $2 extra per night. I bristled.

Center City

Under the guise of "let's check out what there is to see and do around here," we headed off to town. What little enthusiasm I had left diminished as I got my first look. But, heck, there was still the possibility of a phone plug somewhere and the World Wide Web if I could find access.

Within minutes, we located the Chamber of Commerce and went into the little hovel on the main drag. "Is there any place in town where I can plug in and download E-mail? NONE?? "

"Does the library have internet access? NO??"

"Does any place have connections to..." I hesitated before I said what was on my mind and decided to try a new ploy and explain about E-mail and the art and necessity of communication in general before I alienated the director completely. I had noted she had several phone lines coming into the place that weren't busy.

"Well, I could let you use the fax line after nine. We use it for getting our computer information between eight and nine. The other lines are always busy." (Yeah, right. Not one jingle from the time we had entered the building.)

"Terrific. We'll be back."

"No, you can't use it now. After nine."

I had a plug. Of course, old Tex would be bobbin' somewhere off shore "after nine," but I had found a link to the outside world. I was happy. At least, I would leave the town a little more computer friendly for the next world wide traveler.

And, old Tex was happy. We were headed for Walmart where he could finger the bait and talk fish-talk with fellow bait-fingerers.

"Cheap" Entertainment

"Cheap entertainment," he called it. Disinterestedly, I looked over the latest slew of fishing gear Ol' Tex had purchased. Delighted, he popped one item under my nose with glee. It was tiny fish packed in anise. I was powerful hungry, but they had their little eyes popped wide open—looking at me from the bag. Poor little fishys. I suppose if I was packed in anise, my eyes would be wide open too!

De Planes, De Planes

It was very windy when we arrived in Moses Lake area and we noted large passenger planes low in the sky which appeared to be suspended in mid air--balanced and supported by the wind. There was a significant and unusual number particularly when you consider we were out in the middle of nowhere. We eventually learned that Japanese pilots were learning to fly these planes. Oh, oh...I covered my head and ducked. It was easier to accept my original thought.

Nowhere to Somewhere---More or Less

Tex hoisted the muddy anchor while I secured the land yacht and we headed due west again to Easton, Washington—a lesser area than Moses Lake. The post office looked like a mini doll house version of a real one. There were a few other sorry, "no longer in use" establishments like "Mel's Diner," for instance. But other than that, nothing. So we moseyed on up to Roslyn via Jeep. As Brigham Young once said to his persecuted Morman followers, "This is the place!" Well, Roslyn used to be, anyway.

Roslyn, Washington served as the setting for the once popular CBS-TV series *Northern Exposure.* The false-front buildings on Pennsylvania Avenue "used to be" Cicely, Alaska. The local hangout, Brick, with moose antlers still on its front, appears to be popular with Roslyn townsfolk now. Whereas Cicely had a population of approximately 380 people, Roslyn has a whopping 990! After a quick tour of the little burg, we decided to take a serious look north of town which was truly Washington spectacular with clear, see-to-the-bottom streams, crisp, sweet air, and lush evergreen forests.

The Bluest Skies You'll Ever See . . .

The greenest green you'll ever see--and, one of the most cosmopolitan cities in the continental USA. *Seattle. Man, I love it here!!!*

We started our tour uptown with the 72 acre Seattle Center at the *SPACE NEEDLE.* This is the city's symbol, left over from the 1962 World's Fair. There is a monorail which links this area to downtown, but we opted to take the Jeep and headed for *PIKE PLACE PUBLIC MARKET*, the oldest continuously operating farmers market in the US of A.

Pike Place is in the middle of the city. This indoor/outdoor European style marketplace consists of three floors, 300 stalls, and sits on seven acres of prime real estate adjacent to Elliot Bay at Pier 59 on Puget Sound.

While we were there, we took advantage of the opportunity to meander up and down side streets beyond the market. We visited well established, in-town shops also. We were not disappointed.

Hills went straight up and offered enchanting views. Electric street cars effectuated the metropolitan atmosphere. Shades of blue in every hue, clouds in various shapes, whiter than white, and green in every shade, created dimension unlike any other major city. Houses, high-rises, and skyscrapers punctuated the breathtaking scene.

No matter where you look, everything shouts, "This is Seattle!" You can't help wondering as you walk on if you are in a movie or if this is real. Seattle! ***Man, I love it here.***

Pioneer Square

With thoughts of going "down under," we headed for Pioneer Square, Seattle's oldest neighborhood. Seattle "under ground" tour takes visitors through the early days where original shops and business establishments thrived during the Alaskan Gold Rush Days.

There is something for everyone in Pioneer Square, an eclectic neighborhood with antique shops, bistros, parks, and the Elliott Bay Book Co., my personal favorite. Writers from around the world give free readings of their work in the book-lined basement while audiences sip espresso or microbrew beer. It is a very old building, multi-floored, and packed full of every kind of book anyone would ever need or want.

The Klondike Gold Rush is evidenced in lore and spirit throughout this area. It was home to the original "Skid Road," a term born when timber was slid down Yesler Way to a steam-powered mill on the waterfront, not all that far from less industrious sections today identified as "Skid Row."

On The Waterfront

Today, much of the waterfront consists of seafood eateries, shops and terminals for government ferries. The north end of town is home to the Fishermen's Terminal, the West Coast's premier commercial fishing homeport. It provides moorage to over 700 commercial fishing vessels, 30 to 300 feet long.

As I reflect on this place I have to admit it rains a lot here! I had to "wring out" my computer a couple of times, and Ol' Tex had to scrape off the moss growing on the sides of the motor coach. . . but, golly, *I love this place!*

Chapter 11

Simply Stunning!

Snoqualmie Falls

We stayed due east of Seattle between Snoqualmie and Fall City where the Snoqualmie River cascades 270 feet through a natural rock gorge and is100 feet higher than Niagara Falls. It is truly a breathtaking sight. The power of the flowing water is harnessed by Puget Sound Energy which maintains the two acre park.

Richer for the experience and very much at peace, we left the falls and drove into the small town of Snoqualmie where we took the train through the upper Valley to North Bend and back. The antique cars provided a melancholy experience along with an idyllic opportunity to preserve history. Being part of that history, we were convinced preservation is important.

North By Northwest Passage

It rained most of the time we were in Seattle, but the sun was in our mirrors the day we left. I wanted to believe there was a message in that fact as we continued our north by northwest passage. We had enjoyed the eclectic of downtown and the tranquility of our home base. The forests of the northwest are a virtual cathedral complete with their own version of "stained glass" windows. The "pews," if you will, were filled with God's creatures--great and small. We enjoyed their company, especially the many deer who were not in the least threatened by our presence. Unlike traditional worship places, if a person feels compelled to burst out in prayer or song, he or she may do so at any time.

Practice, Practice, Practice

Experience tells us to anticipate problems and so we did a practice run of crossing the border into British Columbia. After all, as the bus driver likes to say, "We are 59 feet long, 102 inches wide, nearly 12 feet tall"... *and nervous!*

We pulled off and parked the Jeep approximately 150 feet from the crossing and got out to see what we could see since there had been controversy over using the truck crossing. As it turned out, both types of vehicles cross at Canada's Route 15. Comforted by this knowledge and fully equipped with all kinds of documentation papers, we popped back into the Jeep and headed north!

The processing was curious: on my far right, I could see uniformed officials boarding motor coaches and other RVs parked along the side of the archway. Ol' Tex kept his eyes fixed on the straight-away challenge of entry. Then, in what seemed all too soon, it was our turn. The border guard began to fire-off tricky questions: "Where are you going?"

"Campground. Surrey. Visit."

"How long will you be in Canada?"

"Just today, sir."

That did it! WRONG ANSWER. The crossing guard was a woman. Now what will we do? Then, a stroke of sheer genius. Mr. "No-Sweat" caught his error, "Errr, ah, mam," he coughed.

Phew! Now the big one, "Where are you from?"

At that point, I didn't have a clue, but Old Tex was back in control. "Oregon. Tillamook, Oregon."

Bingo! I would have said, "Texas," but thank goodness he remembered Oregon. (We were from both places at this point.) But, Oregon matched the information on our plates, insurance papers, and drivers' licenses. ***"Way to go, Tex!"***

Preview Tour

Bolstered by our success, we easily navigated the next 0.5 kilometers to the visitor information station where we got great maps and great information for finding the two destination stops on the Dreamcatcher's schedule.

First, we high-tailed it to Peace Arch RV Park in Surrey where we would spend the first night. Then, feeling somewhat jubilant, we headed for Vancouver. Now, this was a challenge. We were ever so grateful we had left the bus behind when we tried to locate the Capilano Park under the Lions Gate Bridge.

*ee*Ykes! We landed smack in the middle of a shopping mall which encompassed both sides of the highway with shopping to die for!!!

Well, what can I say? ***"Stop! I wanna get off the bus!!"***

Ol' Tex's tongue may hang out for fish, but put me in the center of a premier shopping district and . . . What's that you are saying, Tex?

NO??? Now this is down right selfish!

We did find Capilano eventually, but everything after the shopping mall seemed anticlimactic.

Crossing the Border

We didn't sleep well that night before and so we were up and ready to roll early in the morning. This Customs' business, we had heard, could "take all day."

At the border, we got into the truck/busses line and were slowly routed out and around to an official looking outpost where two uniformed guards were checking the big boys through. Soon it was our turn.

"Good morning!"

We guessed it was and nodded affirmatively.

Now for the drill.

"Where are you going?"

We had practice, remember; got that one right.

"Do you have any goods to sell or fire arms on board?"

"No."

"Have a good stay."

With that, the gate opened, and we moved ahead--free to go..."*Oh, no Tex....*"

In an effort to look relaxed and in full control, Big Jim (did I mention he didn't wear his signature cowboy hat for the crossing in order not to aggravate the customs officials) pulls ahead through the raised gate. Then, of all things, he hangs a right hand turn to (we're still not sure where) and eventually we swing around to a *serious* barrier evidently for the 'bad boys'. (We know we are in trouble now.)

"Well, I see you've had the full tour today," says the uniformed official. He looked tougher than most.

We sat at attention. "Lucky for you, I have a gate card...."

Off we go! The irony in the end was that from Ferndale, Washington to Peace Arch, Surrey, (including the side trip to nowhere),we were parked and all hooked up in less than 50 minutes, ready for a full day of exploring!

Canadian Countryside

We were impressed with the well-maintained properties in our general area. White Rock and Surrey were heavily populated communities, but homes and yards were well cared for and attractively landscaped. It was a pleasure to drive along the shore and see Semiahmoo and MudBays.

We ventured inland to Cloverdale and on toward Langley. As we drove all around the area of Peace Arch, we were impressed by the fields of fresh fruit and vegetables on dark, rich soil. It was all we could do not to stop and buy blueberries, raspberries, and other delectable items, but I was committed to using up the rest of what we thought we would have to hand over at the border.

Happy Birthday, Canada

On the next leg of our journey which was by motor coach, we were accompanied to West Vancouver by Canadian friends. It was in picturesque West Vancouver we celebrated Canada's birthday, a national holiday. We enjoyed a picnic in the community park at water's edge with these friends and their family as did most of West Vancouver. We were entertained by a changing scene of musicians and entertainers during the festivities. For those who had the stamina to keep going, fireworks originating from Canada Place could be seen throughout the entire area.

Touring Vancouver

Although the English Bay is posh and elegant, crossing the Lions Gate Bridge into downtown Vancouver offers tourists yet another banquet of treats. Since we had watched cruise ships departing the Burrard Inlet, we decided to begin at Canada Place, the cruise ship terminal. We also wanted to see where the sea bus from Lonsdale Quey on the north shore would come into town since we would be using it during the week. Seeing the Alaskan cruise ships brought back fond memories.

Gastown

Vancouver's first community, Gastown, provides visitors a flavor for yesteryear with its Victorian street lamps and cobblestone streets. Boutiques, restaurants, and galleries are located in restored warehouses and alleyways. The main attraction, however, is the one-of-a-kind steam powered clock which emits thick clouds of steam and tones every 15 minutes.

Gastown is the terminus of both the sea bus and sky train. Therefore, it is selectively located to be the hub of night-life and visitor attractions.

Chinatown

Second only to San Francisco, Vancouver's Chinatown is a busy and crowded area of the city. We came upon the bustling scene by accident entering from Hastings. Hastings is Vancouver's "skid row" and borders Chinatown on the south. Shops extended out into the streets where crowds clamored to make selections.

Granville Island

Formerly the heart of Vancouver's industrial center, Granville Island is now home to more than 250 artistic, educational, and commercial ventures. It has its own public market along the waterfront like most communities throughout Vancouver. This is European marketing at its finest.

Stanley Park

No tour of Vancouver is complete without visiting Stanley Park, home to Vancouver's aquarium. Stanley Park is located at the tip of Vancouver where it connects West and North Vancouver to the mainland via the Lions Gate Bridge. The park offers visitors and residents a place to swim, to walk, and to enjoy nature.

Vancouver's Northern Countryside:

Park Royal: within 2 minutes, we walked to a gorgeous mall complete with all one's shopping pleasures and needs.

Ambleside: an affluent community filled with posh shops. We were invited to spend the day where we watched the local grain expert make porridge and whole wheat bread--from scratch.

Capilano Suspension Bridge: located 230 feet above the Capilano River is 450 feet of swinging, swaying cedar planks. It is a foot bridge only. It is an entertaining challenge to cross but provides the only access to the wilderness on the other side.

Grouse Mountain: the peak of Vancouver and one of three mountain ski areas within minutes of downtown.

Whistler: world class ski resort with delightful Alpine Village filled with first-class accommodations and shopping.

Market at Lonsdale Quey: an international treat, the market offers a wide variety of seafood, fruits and other edible delectables.

Sailing The High Sea

We waited for *good* weather to make a voyage out onto the Pacific with Captain Lloyd, our personal host, on this 42' sailing vessel. The trip was worth the wait.

The country, from seaside, is magnificent, and the ship was delightful: two bedroom cabins, a living area, and a full galley inside. Although the weather was very cool, we spent much time topside to get a better view of the fjords, coves, and islands. Yet, with the living quarters so pleasant, we opted to dine in rather than disembark at one of many choice coves.

Sailing along the coast is breath-taking and picturesque. So, too, is Vancouver, British Columbia.

Going Home

As hot and dry as it was in the USA, it was as cold and wet in Vancouver, B.C. The day of reckoning came. The big question--to muddy the motorcoach or not to muddy the motorcoach? But that was not the only question.

We were low on supplies. Supplies cost big bickies in Canada. Everything was unjustifiably expensive in this foreign land. And the weather, at best, was dicey. Ol' Tex was eager to return to the land of the *all night Wally World*, and I was ready to do time in Oregon's *no tax Nordstrom's*. And, a killer volcano, which we knew all too well from personal experience some twenty years earlier, was on our way to both commercial attractions. It was time to see Mt. St. Helens up close and personal.

Mt. St. Helens

Loowit was an old Indian woman, keeper of the sacred fire. Klickitat legend has it that after many years of loyal service, the Great Spirit rewarded her with one wish. That wish was "to be eternally young and beautiful" and so she was transformed into a beautiful, "white-clad maiden," ***Mt. St. Helens***.

Although it was at rest during our visit, it was far from dormant. This blown away mountain percolates, hisses, and emits steam and gases day and night. Yet, there was far less activity on the day of our visit than there was at 8:32 a.m. on May 18, 1980. This was when a 5.1 quake on the Richter scale lasting 20 seconds would have been "just another day at the mountain" had it not jarred loose its north flank and created a landslide which tumbled down the mountain at 150 mph, the largest landslide in recorded history!

Along with this, superheated ground water and molten rock exploded like nuclear bombs creating a titanic black explosion which melted billions of tons of glacial snow and ice. Within minutes, a towering column of ash and pulverized rock rose 12 miles into the sky.

This event turned high noon into midnight as sixty mph winds carried the ash north and east. It became a superheated hurricane with 670 mph winds and gases which toppled, crushed or scorched everything in its path. Trees were ripped from the ground or severed from thick, eight feet in diameter bases. 230 square miles of lush forest became ashen wasteland while ash encircled the planet.

Where there were no lakes, there became lakes; where there was a large lake, part of the mountain top dropped in, splashed the water 800 feet high then filled it with debris before the water returned.

Fifty-seven people died. Among the dead, old man Harry Truman, "man of the mountain" who many remember because he was interviewed so frequently for television news *before* Mt. St. Helens erupted. The noise from the explosion was heard in Canada. But the area surrounding the mountain went totally silent following geologist David Johnson's final transmission: ***Vancouver! Vancouver! This is it!!!*** David Johnson was absorbed into the silence.

At the time of the eruption of Mt. St. Helens, we were living in Salt Lake City, Utah. We had been transferred there a year and a half earlier. We saw the darkness, we saw the ash, and eventually, we experienced resplendent sunsets two per night for months.

This site was poignant to us; it will be extraordinary and moving for you as well.

Back Home In Oregon

Oregon is truly a magnificent place in every respect. It has breath-taking beauty in ocean frontage, awe inspiring mountains, step-back-in-time lakes and parks, and, as I said when we moved here, it is "civilized." Folks here are interested and interesting. There is both serenity and excitement. We enjoyed all it had to offer. At this point in time, we opted for the excitement.

Dreamcatcher's motor had not cooled down before the Jeep's wheels were in gear and we were headed for Camping World (Tex's favorite place) next to Walmart and Radio Shack. He was one "happy camper." New chrome pipe for his generator exhaust, hmmmmm, he was a'hummin' as we headed south to Wally World. I was upbeat because I knew "my day" was not far away (even though he pretended not to remember).

Nordstrom's

My heart quickened when I saw the name over the top of the door at the mammoth Washington Square Mall. As I crossed the parking lot, I watched folks carrying specially decorated shopping bags. "No! Could it be? Had I really..........I HAD!! Yup, just in time for Nordstrom's Anniversary Sale, *the big one.*"

I was filled with glee as I pinched the fabric, smelled the potpourri, and listened to the familiar piano music. I drank it all in and became intoxicated by it. I was home. This is how life should be, filled with beautiful stores, beautiful merchandise, and beautiful days. Like I said before, *civilized.*

All too soon my 15 minutes of joy ended with the reality that I live on a motorcoach and my limited closets were bulging already. I abolished the foolish dream that I might store some things in the basement. No--folks were indeed right when they warned me, "Men claim territorial rights to the bays (basements)and women *share* the remaining, limited space upstairs." Whatever I put down in the basement comes back to haunt me usually in less than a week with that irritating question, "*Do we really need this?*"

LESSON: Joy is such a fleeting thing. It is important to live in the present, find *joy* in the moment, and live each moment to its fullest.

Monaco Factory: Coburg, Oregon

Some stories are best left untold but, here goes anyway.

We arrived at the Monaco factory in time for our appointment right on schedule. They did not have room for us. That was quite a disappointment since we had made our appointment months in advance so as to guarantee we would not run into exactly this situation.

The service department had not ordered one of the parts which, at best, was a week and a half wait. The recall part was still being negotiated, so that was also unavailable. Consequently, we settled on doing what they could do now and thanked God that Tex had done all of the rest of the repair work himself. "Be back here tomorrow by 8:00 a.m."

We did. We parked it in the lot and no one came near the coach until 1:00 p.m. when they took the Dreamcatcher behind the fence.

By 5:15 that afternoon, all the coaches (except ours) had been returned and parked in overnight spots with water and power. The overnight spots were completely filled. We were getting very upset and our service writer who was supposed to keep us informed had not been seen since the early morning report-in call.

"They're going to lock our bed behind the fence," I sniveled to Tex. "Think maybe we ought to track *someone* down.....***pronto!!***"

We did, but it was not our service writer. He had gone home without a word to us. We did get our coach out, nothing had been done, the parking spot he had promised us had been taken by someone else, the parking lot was full, it was very hot, and we had nowhere, at this time of night to go!

Need I say, "We were *NOT* happy campers?"

Like I said, "some stories are best left untold." *This is one of them.* This story will give you a flavor for some of the realities of living on the road. They are different in facts but similar in emotional response to living day to day wherever you are. Movin' on . . . .

Oregon Coast

We had come full circle when we arrived on the coast at Florence, Oregon. Friends had come down from Desert High Country to be with us through the factory ordeal; and, we all needed a "vacation" on the coast. (The four of us had lived on Netarts Bay a year earlier waiting for new coaches to be delivered.) We parked the houses-on-wheels side-by-side at Heceta Beach. It had been quite a year for all of us, and we appreciated this special time together.

The air temperature was at least thirty degrees less than inland and when they say, "There's always a breeze off the Pacific," you'd better believe it. By evening when I took my walk, there were "gale force winds" which made it impossible for me to go in one direction. It was necessary for me to walk among the imposing evergreens that had been nestled along the coast for many years.

Florence is filled with tiny shops and fine eateries. We shopped and ate for three days and nights. We laughed a lot, too. We had all been through a year of significant and traumatic experiences and these days together were a catharsis, a time to unwind and enjoy not only our magnificent setting, but each other. Life doesn't get any better!

Camp Nazi

Peace and quiet, yes! But, at what price?

Randy, Der Fuhrer of Camp Heceta Beach RV Park, advised the four of us, "There are rules and regulations strictly enforced to insure solitude." He didn't have to mention signage. It took several very slow trips through the campground to read all of them! We drew straws each time information was needed and a visit to the Gestapo headquarters was necessary. Without doubt, the Camp Nazi was a source for many good laughs, but we also acknowledged, this Fuhrer had a good heart. (It said so---on a sign!) *Just kidding.*

Sea Lion Caves

A few miles north of Heceta Beach are the famous Sea Lion Caves, a place where one can watch these warm-blooded mammals who give birth, nurse young, and breathe air. Oh yes, and make a lot of noise, especially the males. (So this is news?) In the spring and summer the females give birth and then nurture their young on rocks along the coast.

The vast cavern which began forming about 25 million years ago is over 12 stories high and longer than a football field. This natural rock structure alone is a remarkable sight. It is a natural amphitheater for watching these fun-loving creatures.

Wonderful entertainment; gorgeous setting; fabulous days along the Pacific Coast.

Chapter 12

On the Road Again . . .

Heading Inland

It was difficult to say so-long to our adopted Oregon home. It could be several moons before we returned to this area and we were "homesick" already.

Leaving the 50 to 60 degree weather in Florence did not seem like such a bad deal until we rolled inland. As we tooted north to Portland, then east along the Columbia River Gorge, even this writer, who rarely is warm, began panting when we ticked off 109 degrees, cruised into The Dalles, and parked the Dreamcatcher under the camp's namesake, Lone Pine. Just as we were hooking into shore power, the camp host pulled in to say "Howdy!" and "Heck no," he continued, "This ain't so bad. Wait till it gets to 117-118 like yesterday."

As if that wasn't bad enough, when our insufficient 30 amp power failed within the first two minutes, we unhooked, hopped back into the coach, and rolled right back out of there. Surely it would be cooler in high desert country, our next stop. Actually, it was--if you can believe that! ***And,*** we enjoyed 50 amp service along with the indoor pool and spa. Life is good!!

To Tell or Not To Tell....

This writer had heard enough mean-spirited comments and constant whining from her companion to pick up the phone herself and call the RPI (Resorts Park International) reservation desk and book us into Willow Bay Resort, a hit on Ol' Tex's priority list. That was mistake number one.

Mistake number two was when I believed the description in the Resort Parks International book as being fact instead of complete and utter fiction! And, perhaps mistake number three is deciding to write an account of this miserable place at all rather than deciding once again, "Some stories are best left untold."

It began when we pulled up to the check-in desk/security gate some 30 to 40 miles out in the middle of "Tin buck ...." west of Spokane. At the time, it seemed like a million miles, but who was counting? The uniformed attendant ignored us. "Excuse me!" Nothing. We got out of the bus. (Talk about mistakes--are you still counting?)

"Got reservations?" he barked. Ol' Tex responded dutifully and politely eyeing the big lake in front of us. The guard shook his head side to side in negative fashion. Knowing it was too late to get back out of this hole and find another place, I chimed in. "They told me that 'Sue' was the person to ask for." Again, he shook his head "no."

"RPI also told me the manager said to 'Come right in,'" which was true even though I wondered why at the time. Another shake of the head along with a "You got to be kidding," look from under the frowning eyebrows.

He shuffled a bunch of papers and continued to ignore us for what seemed an eternity. "Who needs this?" I thought. "Let's get out of here," I said under my breath. Tex remained planted with a semi-smile on his lips.

"Number 10," he finally growled after ignoring us for several minutes and acting as if he wished we would simply disappear. (Yeah, right! 59 feet of equipment pointed straight ahead with no place else to go and he points to an undefined maze of green adjacent to the lake!!)

"I told them we required 50 amp service," I asserted.

"Any good fishin'?" Ol' Tex cooed.

Again with the eyes, plus that look that says, "Ya gotta be kidding."

The gate went up. He pointed out into the heavily treed field. Tex hopped back into the bus as I peered out into this jungle of grass and low, gnarled trees. "I think we need to find the spot before we start driving," I said through clenched teeth.

Tex eyed the guard who impatiently waited with his finger on the switch which held the gate open. "Na...we'll find it. Get in!"

"I want to find it first."

With that, I heard the air being released from the brake. I quickly moved out of the way and the bus rolled in through the gate. In desperation, I started searching for a sign of any kind of hook-ups and could not find one. Old Tex begins to see the problem himself and stops the bus. Eventually, Mr. "You-gotta-be-kidding" leaves his post, takes off for the middle of the field and points at a place. Tex follows the finger with the bus. I feel faint as I see the Dreamcatcher bobbing up and down over the rough terrain missing several of the trees by only inches.

Not to labor the point, the "hook-up" was an inadequate 30 amps, there was no sewer, and the so called drinking water was probably fresh out of the lake! But Tex was happy and that's all that matters!

We maneuver for half an hour or so to work the bus into a reasonably level, half-way acceptable position. In time, we got to the hooking up of the electric. Faulty wiring--unacceptable power source! Therefore, we had to go back to Mister "You gotta be kidding" and beg for another 30 amp spot providing, of course, there was one. We also had to work the Dreamcatcher in and out of hundreds of low-branched, gnarled and threatening trees. I headed for the driver's seat. Ain't no way I was going to assume responsibility for directing us in and out of this mess.

Finally, we were parked and nearly hooked to shore power when I remember we had cruised in with full tanks which Tex had been "cleaning" enroute.

Again, back out of the gnarled forested jungle, back to the guard station, and a 25 minute maneuver into the dump station. "Guess I should have told you to dump before parking," the guard said with noticeable "gotcha glee."

"No problem," Ol' Tex smiles. He was happy. He was eying the lake and he was happy. It was about one hundred and two degrees, we were no closer to calling it a day than we were when we rolled in the gate about an hour and a half earlier, probably less. I'm "ticked," but Ol' Tex was happy, and that's all that mattered. All that ever matters!!!

Dem Bones!

"Want to know the difference between a small mouth bass and a large mouth bass?" Tex smiles.

"No."

"Here! Look!"

"I don't care."

Grinning from ear to ear, Old Tex stands back and admires his catch. "Here, you can see..."

"Just clean them. I'll eat them."

About 45 minutes later, the remains of two decent sized fish had been reduced to a small pile of flesh, blood....and bones! "Better rinse this off," he intoned proudly, as he handed me the pitiful mess.

Lunch that day consisted of more than our daily supply of calcium. Unfortunately, Tex didn't know the difference between a bass and a squaw fish--the later, the "catch-of-the-day" and what we tried unsuccessfully to eat.

Camp Grenada

"Hello mudda. Hello fadda. Here we are in...Camp Grenada!"

By Thursday night, the campground started filling with tents--and people, every size, shape and degree of loudness! *It was a zoo*. Trailers, campers, tents, and dogs--three per person, I swear, bounded on into the jungle of weeping trees and soggy grass which had been kept over-watered by the "Ya gotta be kidding" security patrol. Babies screamed at the top of their lungs, bugs became disturbed and nasty, weekend warriors popped beer cans and set up camp. Ol' Tex? He was happy. Took his fold-up chair right out and sat in the middle of the fray. Lord, he was one happy camper.

I stayed inside and contemplated. Did I mention we couldn't get a television signal? Either the jungle was too thick or the place was too remote. From my personal vantage point, I decided it was both.

Back To Big Sky Country

No matter where you look, your eyes are drawn to the sky. This is "big sky country" in the bluest sense of the word.

Missoula was a comfortable stop to gather supplies before heading north to Glacier National Park. Although it was not far in distance, it was a long drive up through Polson and around the enormous Flat Head Lake...***Montana!***

Glacier National Park

Glacier is unremarkable *only* because it is typical of the inclusive beauty of the entire northwest: crystal clear lakes, cool mountain streams, cascading falls, and pristine rivers. Okay, it's awesome!

We conquered ***Going To The Sun Highway*** which offered visitors breath-taking overlooks and "hold-on-to-the-car" drop-offs. Wildflowers grew abundantly and colored the mountainsides. The higher we climbed, the greater the offering.

We watched carefully for noted wildlife. Grizzly bears, mountain goats, rams, etc, but evidently they decided to leave the area during the peak tourist season. That is exactly what it was—peak and *crowded!*

After several hours of dodging tourists, Tex felt obligated to head the jeep out toward a remote area called Polbridge, a backwoods settlement some 25 miles out in the middle of primitive land reachable mostly by horseback or hiking boots. We, of course, had a 4-wheel drive vehicle equipped for on and off road driving.

The rugged drive made me feel as if my brain had been put in a paint can mixer on super shake. As I held onto the top of my head and watched out the windows, I could see signs of Montana Freeman on summer maneuvers! I wanted to go home but Ol' Tex was determined to persevere on to the Polbridge Merchantile. (He's the shopper in the family.) Dust billowed and stones flew. We saw occasional hikers and bikers as our heads bounced off the roof of our 4-wheeler. Tex enjoyed calling the hikers "grizzly bait," and the bikers, "drive thru grizzly bait."

Polbridge Merchantile was both a destination and a reward—a truly remarkable step back in time—well worth the potential headache.

Best Laid Plans...

We had planned to spend a few days at the Montana Ghost Towns but when we arrived at the Anaconda Coast to Coast Campground, the host relegated us to a hot, dry field which he determined was the only thing available to Coast to Coast members. Perhaps if it had not been well over 100 degrees and we had not been hot and irritated, we would have blown our coupons on these "accommodations." But, we were both—hot and irritated because there were plenty of spaces available. Consequently, we opted not to put up with such nonsense. We pulled through the campground and kept right on truckin'.

The next problem we experienced was there were no more desirable campgrounds available until we reached Bozeman. "On the road again...."

Billings, Montana

I had been reviewing articles which I had judiciously cut from earlier issues of *MotorHome* and faithfully filed for future reference. From our research, we were led to believe that whereas other Montana towns were western in flavor, Billings was larger, more culturally remarkable, and filled with mansions! Yeah! Right!! Just goes to prove the adage: "Don't believe everything you read!" (*Whoops!)* With no other choice, we pulled into the Billings KOA, the first KOA--*ever*!

The first thing I noted as I directed Tex into the parking spot was the lack of sewer in our "full-hookup" site. I won't belabor the point, but that sort of put a "damper" on my spirits! That was the beginning of what should have been only a minor irritation!

It could have been overflow from Yellowstone; it could have been pre-Montana State Fair hoopla; it could have been that there was a motorcycle rally nearby; or it could have been the only campground in the entire area and every misguided R-V decided to stop and stay at the same KOA as we did.

Whatever! It was worse than a Class B movie--and louder. They barbequed, brought all their kids, grand kids, and every dog this side of the Mississippi. And, it was hot, really hot for that area. 90 - 100 degrees hot! All the power in the park failed. Smoke from the BBQs summoned fire department attention, dogs barked, kids went ballistic, and black leather on Harleys rode the range. We're talkin' "he-haw!"

I clenched my teeth and longed for the good ol' days of grizzlies and gators!

But, there was fishin'. Ol' Tex was having fun, and that's all that matters. (Can you hear the words whistle through my clenched teeth?) It was *his* birthday, but I was the one who got older!!!

Cody, Wyoming - Yahoo!!

When we found out that the Montana State Fair is only for wusses, we headed for real cowboy country, Cody, Wyoming: Yippi-kai-oh-kai-A! This was the land of Buffalo Bill Cody and his Wild West Show.

It took two days to go through the Buffalo Bill Historical Center, world class and headquarters for four individual museums: the Whitney Gallery of Western Art, Cody Firearms Museum, Buffalo Bill Museum, and Plains Indian Museum. It is remarkable in both its content and its completeness.

Rodeo Capital of the World

No visit to Cody would be complete without attending ***the* Cody Nite Rodeo**. Held every night of the week from June through August, this is highfalutin, rootin' tootin' entertainment. In its 60th year when we visited well over ten years ago, it is the longest running rodeo in the country.

We were not disappointed when we sat in the Buzzard's Roost above the chutes and watched cowboys from around the world compete. We learned a lot too.

"Buckin' horses buck because they like to buck," the announcer said. "No one hurts them to make 'em buck--those bucking horses!"

But what really caught my attention was when the Buzzard's Roost started bucking. I clutched my bucking seat in bucking fear. Brahma bulls were being herded to the chutes in front of us. They didn't want to go! I didn't want to stay**! *I was buckin' scared!!!***

Gettin' Outta Dodge

Before we could "get out of Dodge," e..rr Cody, Wyoming, there was a shoot-out at the Irma Hotel. With so much black leather in town, we "held up" at the Ponderosa where we were staying rather than dodge the Harley Hogs in town. Bikers from around the world had filled the northwest to participate in the annual International Motorcycle Rally held in Sturgis, S.D. As you may recall from River Run at Laughlin, Nevada, our timing for motorcycle events is impeccable.

Evenings were comfortable for walking, so I took off on foot enjoying the exercise and exploration of the canyons. Imagine my shock when one of the bearded bad boys on a bike cruised to my side and asked, "You wanna ride?"

You bet!

Awesome!!!

Thermopolis

Greek for "hot city," Thermopolis is literally Wyoming's "hot spot" where hot springs abound. Here, the Wind River flows through the beautiful Wind River Canyon and the bison roam freely. A unique display of terraced land forms are left behind from the overflow of Big Spring. Waters from the springs have legendary healing qualities.

Through treaty with Native Americans years ago, these are free-to-the-public baths for soaking. We languished in the medicinal waters and for one remarkable afternoon, experienced the unique healing provided by Mother Nature.

North and East

After a peaceful night at the Fountain of Youth Resort, we continued our journey north and east. We passed through Worland, a bustling Western town, then on through magnificent Ten Sleep, spectacular in both land formations and color where ranchettes line the fertile valley and streams rush through awesome canyons. As we continued, lush trees replaced the oil pumpers and, once again, we were reminded how fortunate we are to have this great opportunity to become immersed in the beauty of nature.

Suddenly, we started climbing and climbing until I felt we couldn't go up any higher. "Geronimo," I cried, and still we climbed. The road became so narrow and steep that I began to think we might begin to go backward. We down-shifted again. When we crossed Ten Sleep Creek, I peered out my window looking for snow pack.

Still we climbed, higher and higher. The clouds became bigger--and closer. Then blue, bright sky blue...and rich forest green. Had we passed over? Were we on the "other side?"

We downshifted and climbed some more. Dear Lord, if my ears hadn't popped earlier, I would have listened for the choir of angel voices.

We passed through Big Horn, Sitting Bull, and climbed higher. The air got thinner, the water became purer, the sun--brighter. Still we climbed. There were no people. There was no pollution. There was no barrier between us and God.

We climbed higher. The road narrowed. The blue faded into grey. We were in the clouds and heaven bound. We had left the heat of Hades. 9,600 feet and crossing through Powder River Pass.

"What, Saint Peter? Where's the pearly gate?"

Had we missed the turn?

Geronimo! On to Buffalo! Wyoming, that is! Lunch at Buffalo and on to Gillette. *Chugga-chugga. BeeBeep!*

Fireworks Convention

Did you ever think you'd get to go to a Fireworks Convention? Neither did we! But, when we arrived in Gillette, Wyoming and found that the campground where we had *planned* to stay was involved in an RV rip-off, we just saddled up and moseyed over to High Plains.

Low and behold, we found out that very same night that we were parked in the midst of a fireworks convention. People came from miles around to see this spectacle. Here we were, comfortably parked, right at the edge of the most fantastic show we had ever seen.

For years, I've not had the stamina to fight crowds on the 4th of July or New Year's Eve in order to watch the fireworks--even though I really enjoy them. But, on August 12, 1998, right from our living room window, we were privy to the world's best display! The convention and nightly displays went on for several days.

Ka-BOOM!!!

On August 17, 1998, when we were safely parked in Rapid City, S.D. and listening to the news, we learned that Gillette, the little berg that hosted this big event had been blown away in a strong storm which devastated the area.

Ironic, but true. *Go figure!!!*

Deadwood, South Dakota

This boomtown of yesteryear has turned itself into a national treasure of restoration through entrepreneurial money-making skills--primarily legalized casino gambling. Risk-takers that we are, we took all of our gambling money, two quarters each, and parked our stakes on the Deadwood Trolley to tour the town. Hot afternoon turned to cool evening as the trolley tooted up and down the streets of the Black Hills to every nook and cranny of the historic gold rush town of 1876.

Our laid back visit to Deadwood got livelier real quick when we stopped by Saloon #10 for a drink. #10 had been someone's gold stake that didn't pay out as such and in its place, a saloon (#10) became infamous. We soon learned why.

In a stunning enactment, we saw Jack McCall shoot Wild Bill Hickock in the back--right before our startled eyes. Later, town folks chased old Jack down and ran him in for trial. In this same place, we saw a portrait of Calamity Jane who claimed fame as lover to Wild Bill. She's gone now. I'm not clear exactly what wiped her out at age 53; but, I doubt it was either the chewing tobacco or the quart of whiskey per day she consumed.

A few doors down the street we stopped at Kevin Kosner's place, Midnight Star. We were nostalgia stricken when we saw his memorabilia from *"Dances With Wolves."*

We ended our visit to the Black Hills with a visit to Mt. Moriah Cemetery; and, let me make it clear right now, "There ain't no 'dead wood' in Deadwood." They have found a way to make a buck on everything in this town--including the Boot Hill Cemetery!

It's a pleasant climb as you trek from grave to grave and wonder what life was like back then. I expect not all that emotionally different than in our lifetime. The promise of success and riches in earlier years which matures to philosophic wisdom if one makes it to later years. Opportunities exist to enrich our own lives as well as others should we choose to accept the challenges and risks. As one gets older, wisdom comes in the knowing we should have taken many more risks when we were younger.

Rapid City, South Dakota

It was both comforting and disconcerting to note the many severe weather shelters in Rapid City. We stopped by the Mt. Rushmore Mall and before I could think to count, I saw several well marked shelter signs within the mall itself.

My cause for alarm was grounded when during the middle of the night Tex woke me to tell me he was going out to anchor the ground satellite system to keep it from crashing into the coach during the storm. Wind howled, thunder crashed and lightening danced across the sky. This was the beginning of a series of midnight storms and the end of Gillette, Wyoming as we knew it.

August 17, 1998

I title this piece by date rather than subject since the date and other noteworthy events seemed far more significant than the stone wall of presidents at Mt. Rushmore on this day. This was the day that the *office of president* of the United States was denigrated by the man who addressed the nation this night and could not even apologize for lying.

Yes, we saw Mt. Rushmore. It was a wall of stone faces but it was insignificant to the face that stonewalled a nation of trusting Americans once again. Both events left me feeling quite empty.

Bad Lands of South Dakota

Traveling I-90 across South Dakota was about as exciting as watching paint dry. Let me mention some of the sights: Wall Drug, Grasslands National Park and Visitor Center, Bad Lands. I'll let you be the judge.

For those of you who are eager and excited about visiting the moon before Nordstroms, Walmart, or civilization gets there, Bad Lands is the place for you. Get off at Cactus Flats as we did, pass by the prairie house of the homesteader who didn't make it, and you'll be "nowhere" or "now here" depending on how you see it.

We stopped at the BP Amoco "last chance" gas station to fuel-up but, 9 miles down the road, there was yet another chance!

The silence was eerie, the scenery, other worldly. The heat was thermal. The land formations, created by thousands of years of water and wind erosion, were spectacle.

Spirals turned to pinnacles. Winds of geology, sands of time, and a sea that drained 65 million years ago. We were at the bottom of the sea where spectacle turned to spectacular when yellow turned to red fossil soil, pinks and purples mingled to make mauve, and all but the prairie grasses which cupped bunches of Black-eyed Susans here and there were the only traces of earth as we knew it.

Then prairie, mixed grass prairie--too tough for most animals to chew to eat and survive--opened into planes where five hundred bison *with good teeth* live. So do snakes with rattles. Here the "water is too thin to plow and too thick to drink," said the last pioneer as he loaded his wagon and left.

We ended our tour in Wall, home to Wall Drug and yet another town of T-shirt shopping. Although I usually don't fall prey to tourist trendy T-shirts, I desperately wanted to find one that said, "I did my time in the Bad Lands: Let the fun begin!"

And so it did. Wall Drug is souvenir shop and tourist trap extraordinaire! In the land of "put a quarter in" and hear, see, taste, smell, pull and/or ride, I found Tex looking over a stuffed buffalo.

"You want ride him?" I asked.

"No," old Tex replied. "I'm looking for where ya put the quarter in. I want to see him sh..!"

***TEX!!!* God love him; you can't take him anywhere!**

Chapter 13

Moseying Around!

Thoughts from the Roads of South Dakota.

I was getting our publication ready for a mailing as we bumped across South Dakota where I found myself wondering what I would write for our next issue that would interest our readers. With fall semester rapidly approaching, my mind and heart longed to be back in the classroom teaching. Lord knows, it would have been an easy semester with current events practically writing lecture plans in Law, Communication Process, and Public Speaking--say nothing of Ethics! What's ironic is that the same holds true today, over ten years later in time!

We passed a huge field of sunflowers all in full-bloom and facing east. Would readers think that was noteworthy? I thought it was cool!

Right along the open highway we passed a beautifully erected ghost town complete with train stopped dead in its tracks a long time ago. It had been deserted, nobody there. I wondered what happened.

I wondered what happened inside the D.C. Beltway today. I wondered also why no one was seeing the problem concerning the President. I wondered, too, with so many, many national polls being touted why no one had asked me what I thought. (Again, the irony ten years later!)

We passed round bails of hay in open fields, piled high on top of each other. Long, cold winter, I expect.

Will there be a melt down in Russia? Will someone launch a biological attack? What about Asama Bin Laden, the wealthy terrorism financier? Is anyone looking after national security? Does anyone know about these things? *DOES ANYONE CARE???*

(…and, ten years later!)

Why do these silly signs say "Dakota Territories?" Doesn't anyone outside the Beltway know the Dakotas became part of the Union? Does the *Outside* know what the *Inside* is doing?

I wondered what was going on inside the Beltway *right now this minute.*

Maybe that's the problem. Perhaps we are in some kind of time warp where *what really matters* like morals, honesty, respect, decency *has been lost in time and space?*

Maybe I should write about *INTEGRITY.* (10 years later—does anything change other than the players?)

Whoa . . . the bus is slowing—what's this???

Corn Palace

Now "ears" something to write about! And we are off the bus!!!

Celebrating 100 or more years, (not ears), the Corn Palace in Mitchell, S.D. is popping with excitement. (Excuse the pun.) You won't miss it. For a 150 miles or so coming in from the west, there are signs everywhere imploring you to see it. It is, after all, the "world's only corn palace. Thousands of bushels of corn, grain and grasses are used to redecorate the Corn Palace each year." Says so on the hundreds of thousands of post cards they have for sale.

From Corn Palace to corn fields, the parade marched by our windows: stalk by stalk, row by row, field by field, farm by farm. We left Sioux Falls and entered the Corn Belt. The land was flat and sprawled for miles, green, tousled out silk in amber and brown. Silos and shinny barn roofs broke the monotony of sameness.

I wondered if we were safe here in the middle of cornfields. By now, we had heard news of American attacks on Sudan and Afghanistan. We were waiting for retaliation. Early morning, I had made the comment

I was relieved we didn't have to fly. As we drove through this farmland, I thought about the Oklahoma City bombing, ever reminding each of us that nowhere is really safe.

(Now today, Ft. Hood, Texas terrorist attack and New York City where we are to bring the mastermind of the 9/11 attacks back to ground zero.)

I saw dark clouds and looked for funnels on the ends of them. More corn, everywhere corn. I thought, "For now, we are safe in these well established farmlands; but why are my thoughts weak with fear?"

Perhaps it was the weight from the emotions I felt that weakened me.

Camp! So many interpretations…

Without warning, we were back in the world of poor accommodations, "an us versus them world" where campground hosts act as if they are doing you a big favor by over-charging and letting you park in over-crowded, under-equipped facilities. There was not enough power to run my computer let alone the air conditioners. Yup, this is the land of screaming kids, barking dogs, and far more permanent campers than transients. Rain. Bugs. High humidity. Low tolerance.

The last straw was when the host came around the bus, walked into our living space, put wrist bands on me and my mate, and treated us like we were prisoners of war. "You must wear these arm bands the entire time you are here."

Beaver Trails Campground, "*the great outdoor experience*," so their brochure says, this side of nowhere in southern Minnesota. "Yeah, right! Expect me back soon." For those of you who might have missed it, scratch this one off your list of "*things to see and do.*"

Wisconsin Dells

Instinct told me we shouldn't go back to "The Dells" as they are so fondly called and fondly remembered in our minds. When we lived in Chicago in the 1980s, we used to make a trek each summer to this tourist trap where beach deprived Midwesterners flock and overwhelm the small village. Here, vacationers use man-made water parks, buy T-shirts, souvenirs, and eat all day. At the time, we always looked forward to this annual experience. Mostly, we watched the people, and of course, we *had to eat!*

This time there were many more waterslides, many more T-shirts, and last but not least, many, many, many more *people*! So, after a short stay, we headed for Indiana, childhood home of *Jimmy Paul Lorenz aka Ol' Tex.*

Our Indiana Home

Because there are practically no RV parks in Indiana but mostly because he is (contrary to popular belief) a really good guy, our brother-in-law installed a 50 amp outlet on the concrete double drive behind his home providing us the opportunity to park at one of the nicest "resorts" in the country. We enjoyed a front row view of their completely lighted, beautifully landscaped, and well-stocked private lake. Now, if this sounds good to you, you haven't heard the half of it.

Meals and entertainment were provided by the host and hostess. We enjoyed an old fashioned family picnic and bar-b-que on the grounds on Sunday where relatives gathered to enjoy good food, good times, and each other.

Louisville, Kentucky

It had been forty years since I had seen Uncle Chuck Lane, but I would have known him anywhere. His coal-black hair had turned snow white, but he looked and sounded the same as when I was a child!

After a delightful visit and tour of the area, we had dinner at the Feed Store which had been converted into a first-rate BBQ restaurant. Noting the highway complexities after crossing the Ohio River, we felt it prudent to move to the southeast side of Louisville on Sunday morning. We parked the Dreamcatcher on a 40 acre lot and enjoyed Sunday breakfast together. With promises of a return visit, we said a reluctant farewell and were on our way.

(*Author's note: We remain grateful for the opportunity for what became my last visit with this dear gentleman. He passed away a short time later.)*

Labor Day Weekend in the Midwest

Although it was Labor Day weekend, signs of fall were upon us. Fields of tobacco were turning from rich green to brilliant yellow. Occasional dry leaves on trees were beginning to turn color and drop prematurely. Autumn was in the air even though it was a summery 95 degrees.

It was quiet on the highways as we headed East passing through beautiful Lexington, Kentucky and the surrounding horse country. We noted a slightly different terrain as we continued on south to Renfro Valley, home to Kentucky Country music. We decided to stop for a few days and cool our wheels in this scenic area. By the end of the holiday weekend, we were eager to "head 'em up and move 'em out!"

Asheville, NC

We stayed in a coast-to-coast park about twenty miles west of Asheville in the heart of the Smokey Mountains' Maggie Valley. The terrain is rolling and vast, but one has a sense that he needs to keep wiping the fog from his glasses in order to better see the beauty of the land. But then, of course, this is the nature of the mountains...*SMOKEY.*

We toured Waynesville, Hendersonville, and even the Cherokee Indian Reservation. We were looking for a homebase, a place to put down some roots, and this is country we needed to consider. We had heard many good things about this area. We decided Asheville did not feel like "home," but of course, the Biltmore Estate could be the exception.

Biltmore Estate - (America's Largest Home)

With tickets costing at least as much as any amusement theme park including Disney World, you know you are in for a special treat, or at least you hope so! This 8,000 acre palatial estate with its 250 rooms filled with treasures from around the world overlooks vast gardens, a conservatory, and an award-winning winery. It is the legacy of George Vanderbilt III, a bachelor when he built it. He completed the project on Christmas Eve 1895.

65 fireplaces, 43 bathrooms, 32 guest rooms, hot and cold running water, an indoor swimming pool, billiard room, all of the most modern appliances of the day and every amenity known to man at that time. Vanderbilt also enjoyed and housed the finest art and furnishings. Indeed, the Biltmore Estate is both a treasure and a "must-see."

The Search for Home Continues

With paradise still illusive and campgrounds even more so, we didn't get an opportunity to enjoy Winston/Salem to the extent we would have liked. It became apparent that if we planned to park the coach, we needed to scout out spots first.

Reluctantly, we surveyed the *only* campground that was located between where we were at Tanglewood and where we wanted to end up which was Chapel Hill, NC. This sorry sight was a now defunct KOA, dusty, dirty, and adjacent to the busiest highway in the country with the exception of I-95. (Let me assure you, it was not easy access as one might have thought it would be. We really had to scout it out. We felt like we were playing hide-and-seek just to get into the place.)

Since we had wasted over half the day, and were halfway to the Triangle area of Raleigh, Durham, Chapel Hill, we opted to drive on and see if we could find where and how we would arrange an extended visit in that area since we had the Triangle high on our list of potentials for establishing a homebase.

Spring Hill Park at Chapel Hill

Unbelievable! The *only* park in the *entire* area was a mobile home park. Okay, there were two State Parks on reservoir lakes that locked the gates at dark for your protection. (Sure! Now what happens if you get in some traffic and are just a tad late for curfew? Convince me that someone wanting to do harm couldn't find a way into the area! Trust me, it is possible.) At any rate, it serves to keep legitimate campers away and this turned out to be a very good thing for us.

We ended up being able to spend our entire two week stay at Spring Hill Park, right in the heart of Chapel Hill. Spring Hill was hidden in a dense but beautiful forest, with the nicest people you would ever want to meet. The original arrangement had been for three nights. This is really not a campground and the two to five places that they have available are for long-term rental. As it turned out, (and I thank you again, God), when we rolled in, the RV we would replace was rolling out!

Chapel Hill

Of the three, Raleigh, Durham, Chapel Hill, hands down, Chapel Hill was our pick for a potential permanent residence. Although the entire area is rich with possibilities, a college town has always been my choice. Chapel Hill is the personification of this. The area is growing so much and so rapidly, we ended up thinking it could be too much of a good thing. Traffic is fast and heavy, roads are complex, and parking is unavailable. There are no communities with lakes for Jim to fish and those with golf, tennis, and other amenities, required a commitment to a more material life, one which we had decided to leave behind.

Although we would not completely rule the area out at the time, we were ready to roll toward Charlotte when our two weeks were complete.

Carowinds

The only place to park in the entire Charlotte area was the campground adjoining Paramount's premier water and theme park. The clerk behind the counter the day we checked in was part of the show troop and gave us passes to visit the theme park over the weekend.

Having experienced the fright of my life by accidentally going on Disney's Magic Mountain (roller coaster) many years back, I stood in awe looking at people eagerly awaiting their turns on these tracks of terror. I remember seeing the "Vortex" on television a couple of years earlier as being one of the country's (how do I say) "worst" in a positive way?

We skipped the rides except for the space needle and showboat and took in the shows. My personal favorite was *All Shook Up*, a 1950s revue featuring pop vocals and rock-around-the-clock choreography. And yes, for those of us who believe, *Elvis lives!*

(Again, an aside: Seven years later, I would personally meet Elvis back in the Charlotte area when I interviewed him for a special story I was writing for the newspaper. By this time, Ol' Tex had evolved into my professional photographer so we have some great photos of the King. We also got to see two of his shows, a year apart and enjoyed every minute.)

Southern Accents

Tex was having a hard time hearing and understanding "southern." When the cashier behind the counter said "f--eye--ve dollars and feeevtie-ate ce-ents," I had to whisper the interpretation in his ear and assure him that was what she wanted. (Several years later, we would become totally immersed in a complete study of both the language and people!)

Charlotte, NC

Charlotte is a lovely, southern city. Equipped with real estate books and maps, we set out to see what the area had to offer. We checked out Lake Norman at the most northerly end and Lake Wylee at the most southerly end. So much for Charlotte—or so we thought at the time!

Hendersonville, NC

Just south of Asheville is a busy little town called Hendersonville where we decided we needed to stop and spend the night. We had done a very quick tour of the town when we visited Asheville, but since it continues to be mentioned as a retirement "hot spot," we decided it was worth another look. So far, we are not convinced.

(*Author's note: Life has taught us direct lessons on the adage—never say never. It is evident throughout this book.)*

On To Knoxville and Tellico Lake

The best part of any place, as I'm sure most of you are aware, is the people We spent considerable time at Tellico Village which has not only a lake and lovely homes, but golf courses, club houses, marinas, restaurants, tennis courts and pools. This was a community rich with possibilities--and it was lovely!

At the time of our visit, a development by the name of Rarity Bay was just coming on stream. We were favorably impressed with it all. In time, the developer, Rarity, would develop 9 similar communities throughout this area.

It was time to move on.

Nashville, TN

Our first visit to Nashville was short and sweet due to the complexities of where we were staying. Our return was quite another story! Surrounded by gun toting National Security Agents in the Grand Ol' Opry, we experienced one of the most exciting adventures in our lives.

But alas! That's another story!!!

P.S. Nashville

We returned a few years later and managed to break into a highly confidential meeting of the **National Security Administration**. It had seemed so innocent, really.

Ol' Tex wanted to show me where he had stayed during a conference with his big oil buddies back in the days of his life with Amoco Oil. There was lots of security around and at the time, we had no idea why. So I whispered to Tex, "Just act as if you know where you are going and we'll get there."

So we did. Before we knew it, *we were surrounded with gun toting special agents* who wanted to get to know us better. ***And, they did.***

We've had some pretty ***memorable*** "experiences" in our life; this was only one of them. *And,* this was one *experience* my writing muse tucked away for future use.

(Don't ever try to tell me there wasn't more to the Salahee Whitehouse break-in than meets the eye. The Secret Service is plenty capable! There is something more to that story.)

Goin' To Memphis

You may have heard this writer say on occasion, "They ought to 'nuke' this place and start over." With the greatest sense of sadness, I must tell you that I feel similar thoughts about Memphis. We drove all around the downtown area hoping for signs of life.

We parked the Jeep and went into the old Peabody Hotel where we saw the famous mallard ducks in the fountain and the impressive **Duck Walk**. If you've not seen it, it's a real treat.

From there, we went to the famous Beale Street and felt even more sadness for what must have been as it originated—blues and jazz in the day.

The city of Memphis was sad for us. It had enjoyed a past of strength from being on the Mississippi River as well as home to the King of Rock and Roll. This sadness seemed to overwhelm us when we visited Graceland. It was our personal good-bye to *the King* who we appreciate even more today.

Elvis Presley's Graceland

From the moment you turned off the city street and drove up to the first guard who collected a parking fee, you began to sense it was a money-making machine. Worse, you knew, you really knew Elvis is dead. As certain as I am that he once lived and changed a whole generation, this whole money-grubbing "machine" was proof certain that he is dead.

Tears filled my eyes the entire two hours we were on the compound. The home and grounds were not nearly as big as our last home in Forest Hill, Maryland. The mansion personified life in the late fifties and early sixties. There was dark wood paneling in the "jungle room" which was his family room and a glitzy 50s bar in the basement. I would prefer you think of it as simply "retro," but at one time I had a home with similar decor—right down to the lavender bathroom!

He was too young to die. He was the King of Rock and Roll. He personified my youth. Elvis was only forty-two when he left and I never felt as if I had an opportunity to really say good-bye. Perhaps the tears were not only for another time, another life, but most of all, for all those years that can be no more.

Elvis keeps the soul of Memphis alive, but when one visits Graceland, you know for certain in your heart of hearts, Elvis is dead.

PS

Since that time, my newspaper writing career gave me an opportunity to meet and interview a real Elvis impersonator. Chad Champion works in and around the Charlotte, NC area; and, I can tell you for a fact, the spirit of Elvis lives on. *Long live the King!!!*

Little Rock/Hot Springs, Arkansas

Our search for "paradise" continued as we dropped anchor just outside of Little Rock and headed for Hot Springs Village. We had read about the Cooper development here and wanted to see with our very own eyes what paradise looked like.

Hot Springs Village is a very large area in the middle of forests, lakes, and golf courses. It did not prove to be the paradise we had hopped to find. All the homes were well hidden in a thick blanket of trees and the numerous lakes were visible only from specific viewing points.

We had been courted by a real estate woman for part of the tour. Once she realized that we weren't "buying it," the real estate woman is the one who finally convinced us both that there was little else here. She said that she HAD to work for her own sanity and survival. (She had "retired" here from another part of the country.)

We had no trouble deciding to head for Texarkana in the morning.

Texarkana

Bordering Arkansas, Louisiana, and Texas, Texarkana combined the warmth and friendliness of all three states. We parked the Dreamcatcher at the Four States Fairground, an interesting concept in RV parking, and went out to mingle with the nice folks. I experienced the greatest camaraderie with the lovely women in Dillard's while Tex saddled up to the clerk behind the fish counter in Wally World.

Is this pitiful, or what???

Nacogdoches, Texas

A recently acquired magazine, *Where To Retire,* featured and praised the retirement advantages of Nacogdoches. Since we were in Texas and still looking for a place to put down roots, we headed to this highly acclaimed town.

Nacogdoches is quaint. Quaint is one of those writer words one uses like "interesting" that really says nothing but allows the reader to draw his or her own conclusions without negative (or positive for that matter) connotation.

Personally, we left the area with little doubt about the old cliché: Don't believe everything you read!

Headin' Home

I want to tell you, "It's good to be back!" Yet again, when you are consumed by a sense of longing for a home, rolling into a mail forwarding address seemed well…a tad less than perfect. But, our research had not afforded us any positive feelings toward a permanent place to hang our hat, so we headed on into Livingston, Texas to park the Dreamcatcher and re-assess where we were in our life and handle "home base" type of business.

We reached Rainbow's End but there would be many more miles before we would find the "pot of gold."

Chapter 14

I'm Going To Houston . . .

Rainbow's End

That's what it's called. REALLY! The "pot of gold" is found within the people who are there. Although I was personally discouraged and facing daunting tasks, it was difficult to keep an "unhappy" face.

Rainbow's End located in Livingston, Texas is the headquarters for a major RV organization called Escapees. Among the many things this club offers is a professional mail forwarding service. At Rainbow's End, there are permanent structures such as the headquarters building and the huge hall which offers day care services to those who have to come off the road because of illness. There are other buildings and services as well.

Additionally, there are permanent homes and a nice campground for members who are just passing through. There are several Escapee RV Parks throughout the country, but Livingston is the headquarters.

We did the welcome tour and went to "happy hour" the very first afternoon. Happy hour at any Escapees park is the 4 o'clock gathering of all the folks in the campground where any and all types of announcements are made, people arriving are introduced, and people leaving tell where they are going. It is an information exchange extraordinaire! It is that magical time when you *welcome* friends and find out "what's happening."

Walmart at Livingston, Texas

With little else to do on Sunday afternoon, we headed down the road to the local Wally World. So did everyone else in Polk County, Texas. It was a fun-filled, educational experience. The store was a living museum in ethnic diversity. The crowd seemed to be enjoying the day and the experience.

During our extended visit to Livingston, this "community hall" proved to be the gathering place and entertainment center for the entire area. When they started calling us by our first names, we knew it was time to roll but not without one last Texas friendly: "Y'all come back now, ya hear!"

Licensing

During our extended stay in Livingston, we decided it might be a good plan to switch motor coach and tow vehicle plates and registration from Oregon to Texas. We were perfectly legal in Oregon, our first official home-away-from-home on the road, but neighboring states had begun to force Oregon officials to keep tabs on possible phoney residents. Since we also use Escapees' mail-forwarding service out of Texas in addition to our original Oregon one, it seemed a good idea to transfer all official documents to Texas in the event we should be summoned to account while on our future sojourn to the northeast coast and Nova Scotia in 1999. Therefore, we set out to accomplish this task.

We easily and successfully got both vehicles inspected, registered, and plated. The Inspection Station was most accommodating and the Texas Tax Department (where we paid for our registration) was eager to take our money. Buoyed by these successes, we headed for the Department of Public Safety's Driver Licensing Bureau, a tiny room in a small building adjacent to the local lock-up (jail).

Ol' Tex was determined to have the proper credentials. Therefore, when the Driving Examiner said, "Fill out this application and come back. I'll give you your licenses for $24 each," Ol Tex would not settle.

"Don't I need to take a road test?" he persevered.

"No, just an eye test," she replied with finality. "Next!"

"But," he persisted. "I thought I needed to have a road test."

"No."

"I'm over 26,000 pounds! I'm driving a bus! I need a special license!!"

With that, her officialness reaches down, whips out a paperback book, hastily writes something on the cover and shoves it at Tex. "Read chapters 1, 2, and 15. Come back after you have read them. **NEXT!!**"

I had tried my best to kick him in the shins early on when she was willing to let it go with an eye test, but the room was so small I was unable to bring my foot back for the wind-up.

So, book and papers in hand, we went home to the campground, filled out applications, and Ol' Tex studied for the exam. He determined that she should have told him to study Chapter 8 as well after carefully perusing the entire book over the weekend. I suggested it might be ill advised if he told her so before he had his new license in hand. He agreed.

Completed applications in hand, we returned to the licensing office. Our turn came and we took eye tests, answered questions, and "solemnly swore that the facts we rendered were true...." Ol' Tex knew the material backward and forward so taking the test took only a few minutes longer. But whoops, "You missed one," the examiner told him.

"Which one?"

"The one about the taxi cab," she pointed to the examination.

"Wait a minute," he growls, "That information is NOT in the book but it would have to...."

"Wrong..."

Well, you get the picture. By now, I am hiding at the edge of the outer office ready to make a beeline for the door with my coveted new license. Finally, the conversation stops and Tex bristles out the door of the examiners office. But just before he is completely out, the driving examiner snaps, "You have to make an appointment for the driving test."

I nodded for him to return to the little room. She studied her calendar." I'm off Friday. [Pause.] Monday at 9:30 ---- if it's not raining. We only test on Mondays and Wednesdays," she snapped the calendar closed. "We don't test if it is raining. NEXT!"

So with my hand clenching his arm, Tex and I headed out the door to wait out the next three days in a muddy campground with heavy, persistent rain pelting the 26,000 pound motor coach.

Will Monday Morning Ever Come?

The rain did stop as Monday morning dawned. We unhooked the rig, piled into the pilot and co-pilot seats, and rolled down the road to the driver's licensing office. It was 9:28 a.m. exactly when we parked the rig on the edge of the highway in front of the chain-link, barbed wire encompassed prison adjacent to the licensing examiner's office. 9:30 a.m. on the nose, we walked through the door to meet the "make or breaker."

The tiny outer office was crowded. Tex moseyed up to the door of the examiner's office, a courageous move considering the number of folks waiting ahead of him. I was not inclined to follow. After all, it was ***his*** appointment. Besides, I'm very little!

I saw his demeanor immediately begin to change as I watched from afar. He had announced himself, that was for certain, but I had no idea what had precipitated such a change in both his posture and his facial expression. But then, I was standing quite a distance away from him, trying to look nonchalant, yet brave. Tex had, after all, cut to the front of the line. Others who were waiting knew nothing about road test appointments, rain, or 26,000 pounds!

Eventually, I worked my way near enough to see that a different person was sitting at the examiner's desk. Handling six other things at once, I heard this stranger say as she turned her head toward Tex, "She called in sick."

"But, I have an appointment to take a road test."

"Sorry."

(No, not really!)

"Isn't there anyone else who can give me the test?" he pleaded.

"No!"

The stranger continued her business. Tex looked at me. His eyes were wide, angry.

I tried to show my support and shrugged my shoulders. I didn't say, "You just had to have the special license. See, I could have told you. Fine mess you've gotten us into--now what are we going to do? You don't have a license to drive the rig and neither do I!!! Stuck! We are stuck here forever...."

Well, perhaps I *wanted* to say all those things, but I didn't. I just shrugged my shoulders and quietly bit my tongue.

The rest of the story is even uglier. I'll spare you the grief and jump to the end of our stay at homebase Livingston, Texas.

Leaving Rainbow's End

With a "pot of gold" in terms of accomplishment, Dreamcatcher and company were ready to travel on November 22, 1998.We would leave Livingston, Texas and head for Houston on Sunday morning.

Medical business including complete physicals, lab work, colonoscopy, mammogram, Pap smear, and prostrate screening had been accomplished through local doctors and the CARE Health Fair. The nurse in charge of the CARE facility at Escapees headquarters would remain forever in our minds and hearts for the comfort she brought.

There is a special camping area adjacent to the CARE facility for members who are living on the road yet have special needs to be addressed. Fellow RVers are available to help either at the facility or drive people in need of medical services as far as Houston where world class care is available.

Recommendations and assurances throughout the whole ordeal kept us going. We were most grateful to have this piece of "what if something happens" information as we continued our journey.

Hope, Happiness & Good Health

The month of accomplishing the necessities of life was made easier because we were among RV friends in Livingston, Texas. Now it was time to get those wheels a- rolling. We both were licensed, plated, and registered to vote in the "great state of Texas."

We were happy to have the physicals and legalities behind us. We looked forward to our tour of southern Texas and the Rio Grande

Valley. When we counted our blessings that holiday season, there were more than ever.

Dateline: Houston, Texas – (November 22, 1998 – Sugarland, Texas)

It was a virtual banquette for the senses! Store after store, shopping area after shopping area. Things to do, places to go, sights to see. MECCA!

Our first shot out after arriving at the USA RV Park was nearby Colony Mall, a beauty if ever there was one. Two anchor stores, Folley's and Dillard's, made the adventure enticing! But, Old Tex had a cold, so we hustled back home before I could pinch the poly-fibers!

Galveston

Galveston is another sad example of better days. The reason these towns and cities are particularly sad is that their potential remains.

Author's Note: That was my "take" on Galveston before the 2008 Hurricane came and took it away. The world economy tanked immediately thereafter. I have a strong feeling that it will be rebuilt one day, perhaps not in my lifetime. Surviving during this period will have to come first. It is a gorgeous piece of real estate, too luxurious to go to waste.

Surrounded by water, Galveston is primarily a large island. At the time we visited, off shore oil rigs in moth balls lined the harbor area and fresh seafood markets were mixed in with restaurants along the harbor shores. The University of Texas Medical Branch seemed more alive and functional than most of the rest of the island. I'm almost afraid to think about what might have happened to some of the proud "pillars" that held Galveston Island together.

NASA Space Center Houston

In the far outer reaches of Houston near Galveston, is the Johnson Space Center. It offers a hands-on display of space related exhibits as well as IMAX Theater presentations. We were invited to touch a piece of moon rock over three billion years old.

A tram took us to the actual working facility that occupies 1,600 acres and employs more than 14,000 people. It is here that astronauts are trained and the Space Shuttle program is managed.

Mission Control

From seconds after launch until actual landing, Space Shuttles are run from here—Mission Control. It was overwhelmingly powerful to me to be right there. Tears of joy welled up in my eyes when I saw the interior of the facility with its computer monitors and TV screens. I know deep in my soul how fortunate I am to have been able to personally see these most remarkable places which are significant in our history. I remain forever grateful.

It was interesting to note that all of the major news organizations had trailer facilities parked adjacent to and just outside mission control: MSNBC, CBS, ABC, Associated Press. They were all there. Because of my background and field, I was personally delighted by this particular observation.

Thanksgiving

Counting blessings on Thanksgiving Day is a tradition in my life. There were really more blessings than we could count that year. In an ever evolving life, it takes perhaps more planning and adjustment; and yet, we enthusiastically welcomed this opportunity for reflection.

Corpus Christi

We parked the rig in a little burg called Sinton just west and north of Corpus Christi. When we went out exploring with the Jeep, we noted that the traffic was considerably heavier as we got closer to the city. We investigated RV parks closer to the Gulf of Mexico, but found none that suited us. We were comfortable with our decision to stay in Sinton.

We took the causeway across to Padre Island. Once there, we enjoyed taking the Jeep on the beach where we rode along the shoreline and watched the surf break and wash toward us. It gave us a new appreciation for all-terrain vehicles.

We drove further north on the open highway and continued to look for potentially desirable places to park the coach and explore for a few days. By day's end, we decided it was not meant to be this time. Where we were was, after all, the best choice for us.

Before we returned to the Dreamcatcher that day, we bought the equivalent of both our weights in shrimp right off the boat at Aransas Pass. We took the ferry back to the mainland and headed back to Sinton for the night. In the morning, we continued on to South Texas.

Chapter 15

"and miles to go before we sleep . . ."

Harlingen, South Texas

We arrived in the southern most part of Texas and sat in a delightful resort for a week and a day debating whether to head east or west. I had become overwhelmed with the desire to have a home and felt we would be remiss to not head back east and keep focused. Tex had put up some powerfully good arguments that helped me re-think my position. In the end, you will readily see, we did indeed head west but with the stout and positive assurance from the bus driver that if we weren't having fun, we would turn the bus around and head for the east coast (and I mean on a dime!)

There is much to share about South Texas, a far different place under the sun, so I will break it down by place and/or subject. I would hate to have you miss a moment of the diversity.

Four Seasons Resort

We had the 90 degree heated pool and a fabulous Jacuzzi whirlpool to ourselves. I'd like to believe it was because we were more spry and exercise conscious than the other guests but, in fact, it was because all the other folks were dancing through night!

I thought I was "in shape," when early one morning one of the elderly ladies caught me on my morning walk and invited me into their exercise group. Halfway through the low impact aerobic workout, (and gasping for air), I vowed not another day would go by without both morning and evening mile jogs along with a pumped-up version of my pathetic excuse for cardiovascular fitness.

Rather than to move several times, we ventured out and explored South Texas, “the Valley” as it is called, from where we were parked in Harlingen which is located on the eastern side of a chain of small snowbird towns that spread west to McAllen. There is a strong Mexican presence and influence in life here in southern Texas. Brownsville, a Texas town which is farthest south and adjacent to the Mexican border, is entirely Hispanic from all appearances.

There Goes the Neighborhood!

When this story was originally told to me, I shared great empathy with the man who was telling it. I could not help, however, enjoy the significant irony in the situation.

We had driven around the hustle and bustle of downtown Brownsville looking for a place to park on the street. It wasn’t easy but we did get occasional opportunity to do so. Shops were crowded and busy but merchandise seemed somewhat different. We opted to forget the crowding and confusion of the in town area and made a stop at the mall which was just outside the downtown area.

Only Spanish is spoken in the area, so when one of the merchants began visiting with me in English, I stopped and spent some time with him. He spoke with a very heavy Mexican accent, but I had no difficultly understanding his complaints about downtown Brownsville. "No good, anymore," he complained. "Chinese have taken over. Nothing is the same."

I continue to try to rectify in my mind and find words to help me write my reactions to the struggle throughout America for ethnic groups to hang on to their cultural heritage, their roots. Why doesn't anyone seem to realize that American was meant to be a "melting pot," a blending together of people from around the world in order for them to live in harmony? Now no one wants to tolerate “others” while each group struggles, and yes, fights, to remain separate and different. Is this what America is meant to be? Divided? Separate? Un-united? Culturally diverse!

These were my thoughts and reactions in the late 1990s. Today, over ten years later, there is an even greater division in this country. Our founding principals are being challenged more than ever before. Our freedom of speech is being both threatened and compromised and what little commerce and industry is left is being taken over and regulated by government.

I am not so certain I really want to know what is going to happen.

Progreso, Mexico

We parked the Jeep on the American side in Mercedes and walked across the border at the International Bridge. Beggar children had tied large containers to the ends of long sticks to reach up to the top of the bridge where Americans crossed. Streets were also peppered with begging children and people.

The streets were lined with shop after shop. Smells from restaurants and pharmacios were overwhelming. Music wafted the air and merchants strongly encouraged you to purchase their wares. It was a far cry from the self-service/no-service stores we had become accustomed to in the States.

Unfettered by the clamor and attention, Ol' Tex set out to purchase his Christmas presents in the event Santa might not locate him this year. He gleefully tried on hats and belts, and checked the prices of "spirits" in all the shops. He bought himself a "drop dead" ranger buckle and dropped quarters and nickels in cup after cup extended by handicapped people sitting on dirty streets. He also put nickels in tiny hands which extended from everywhere, jeering, begging, then running off to another potential candidate.

We didn't eat or drink even though we were assured the food was good in several restaurants. That was what finally brought us back across the border, through Customs, and home. We were hungry, tired, and exhausted by the over-stimulation of our senses. If Progreso, Mexico was one of the "quieter cities," we were not confident we would be able to handle a crossing at Matamoros, one of the larger cities.

South Padre Island

We came close to moving to one of the resorts at water's edge on South Padre Island but I was not inclined to want to give up our private swimming pool and spa. We enjoyed watching the shell seekers and fisherman during a day trip however.

The debate over whether to turn the bus east or west raged on. We decided to stay put and enjoy the amenities of where we were located. (We also enjoyed making several trips to "Wally World" just to finger the fishing lures.)

Zapata, Texas

The decision was made to head west and "play" for the winter. Being a person who has always been dedicated to task, it was a heavy, thought-filled decision for me. Being ever so considerate, Ol' Tex decided we would follow the Rio Grande and head on over to Zapata and, as he said, "Just kick back for a few days." Ever so casually he mentioned the huge *fishing lake* which was on the map. "Maybe I'll do a little fishing."

So early on a Sunday morning, we headed west along the Rio Grande. The further we traveled, the less there was to see. Towns became less frequent and those occasional spots on the map became less inhabited. Finally, we arrived at Zapata, which felt eerie with quiet and inactivity. We turned left off the main highway and headed toward the Four Seasons Resort on the lake. It was a far piece as well as a far cry from the Four Seasons Resort at Harlingen.

A very pleasant couple met us in their golf cart at the secured gate and led us back to the area where we were to park. The first spot we were directed to left part of the Dreamcatcher's 40 feet blocking the road. But, with the second choice, and in the opinion of the "bus driver," we were only sticking out into the road about five feet. "Not much traffic back here anymore anyway," said Gus. "You'll *probably* be alright." Edna nods in agreement.

Feeling pretty good about life along the Rio Grande, Ol' Tex begins the "golly gee" talk specifically aimed toward fishing. "How's the fishin'?"

Gus stumbles through a few choruses before he reveals the near obvious, "But, I don't do no fishin'"

"Got a good place where I can put my boat in?" asks Tex.

By that point, I was more consumed by the fact that we are parked in the road and how we are going to divert traffic before being plowed into as vehicles come down the road at night----*after dark.*

It was not until after lunch that we piled into the jeep and headed for the boat ramp. Tex took a quick left turn and headed down a cement roadway (or former ramp) of sorts when I immediately noted a tall iron stake protruding upward at the foot of the incline in the middle of this pavement. "Where are you going?" I shrieked.

"The guy said the lake was over here." he barked back.

"Where???"

"He pointed over here."

In front of us were acres upon acres of tall scrub brush that had been in place so long that they looked like established trees. There was a tall metal stake at the low end of the cement road which led to nowhere except the scrub brush. I hated to be the one to tell Ol' Tex what I thought and fortunately, an old man with a very long beard and hunched- over shoulders showed up. After an exchange of pleasantries, (and me feeling pretty foolish sitting on this road to nowhere) Tex inquires about the lake.

"Dropped about 55 feet or so 'bout five years ago. Used to be right out here." He pointed to the ugly scrub brush in front of us.

"But how do I get to it now?" the desperate cowboy fisherman persisted.

"Well, if you go down to the next road...."

By the end of the conversation, it was still not clear to poor Ol' Tex that we were sitting on what used to be the boat ramp to the lake that once was but was no more.

We headed out of our "lake resort" to the next road that Ol' Tex deliriously believed would offer access to a body of water that had dried up five years ago. It was pitiful. So pitiful.

The next "resort" was Lakeview. Then there was another, "Lake Haven." Wherever we went, it was evident, there was no lake.

Beleaguered with disappointment and seething with frustration, Tex took us on a tour of the area and determined there was 'no joy in Zapata, the mighty fisherman had struck out.'

As soon as the office opened in the morning and we could pay for our overnight disappointment, we were *dust!*

Del Rio

We had been traveling adjacent to Mexico and Del Rio was right on course. Mexican influence was everywhere throughout south Texas and in many ways, the area is far more Mexican than American. Del Rio was no exception.

We enjoyed seeing the history of the area in a unique in-town museum called the Whitehead Memorial. A piece of property was set aside and housed several representative buildings which were historical exhibits in and of themselves. Tex was rather taken with the history of Judge Roy Beam and Lilly Langtree, but no matter what took one's fancy, the history of South Texas is rich and imaginative.

Amistad is the name of the national recreation area and a name which means *"friendship."* It is the international park on the United States-Mexico border. It is adjacent to where we parked the Dreamcatcher for our stay in the area. There was not much in the way of recreation going on in the area with the water all but gone.

In severe contrast, it was overwhelming to us to see the evidence of the fall floods in downtown Del Rio which had destroyed many homes and ruined several areas. It is hard to describe such contradictions: draught on the one hand and dried-up flood waters on the other. The "Queen City" of the Rio Grande was a rather sorry place in the fall of 1998; it was nothing like it was in its glory days when it was called San Felipe Del Rio, a fertile farming community which produced crops for nearby U.S. forts and camps.

Ciudad Acuna, Mexico

I must admit, I was a bit insecure as we boarded the Mexican bus at the Border in Del Rio and crossed the bridge into Acuna. We were surrounded with Mexican people carrying bags of supplies which filled seats and floors making it difficult to find our way to the back of the bus, the only spot left to accommodate two foreign American visitors. We did not understand a word of the constant chatter that filled the bus during the short trip. I felt as if we were in a movie.

My nervousness and ignited sense of humor nearly got me into serious trouble when the bus stopped and an armed guard boarded the bus. The chatter stopped abruptly and everyone came immediately to attention. There sat two lonely Americans, one with a Cheshire grin from ear to ear. I lost the grin. Instantly, I looked guilty.

The armed, uniformed guard walked very *slowly* toward the back of the bus where we were sitting. He looked into the seats and over the collection of bags strewn helter-skelter throughout the bus. I held my breath as he approached. Satisfied, he turned and very slowly retraced his steps. I knew I was going to burst before he ever got to the front. Then, without a word, he descended the steps and disappeared.

The bus driver closed the door, chatter resumed, and we were on our way. Who says uniforms *and guns* don't speak???

Never - Never Land

A couple of days in Del Rio and we were more than ready to head 'em up and move 'em out. We didn't bother spending more time within Amistad because we could really see it all from the bus--dry desert and a place where the water had been.

We tooted on through several dried-up Texas towns and finally arrived at Ft. Stockton at High Noon.

The nice manager at the Ft. Stockton Walmart was willing to let us park the rig at the side of the store and head out in the Jeep to pick up our mail. Hallelujah! The priority box was in and we were on our way. The concern was whether we should head on to the higher elevations in New Mexico or continue west to El Paso. We decided to go north to Pecos, Texas and make a decision in the morning after watching weather conditions.

It is presently interesting to note that so vast is the State of Texas, that over the years, we frequently stopped and stayed in Ft. Stockton to break-up a long trip.

Pecos, Texas

Never, ever head out to Pecos this late in the season. Aside from the fact there's nothing there, it gets mighty cold as it did the night we stayed at the Escapees RV Park there. Folks were welcoming and very friendly. However, the weather turned bitter and we headed back Southwest.

Rain began and it was so cold it was near sleet as the wind began to move us off the map.

We made it through El Paso, but on the west side of town, we pulled into a Flying-J Truck Stop and stayed with the Big Boys to wait out the sand storm. We thought we would have to spend the night with the truckers. Fortunately, when Jim called Doc's RV Park in Las Cruces, NM, the gal said conditions were good there. We watched the local weather as wind gusts pitched us back and forth. By mid afternoon, the wind had eased enough to head on into New Mexico for the night.

It was fun to be back in Las Cruces. We revisited and enjoyed many of the sights.

Tucson, Arizona

By the time we got to Cactus Country RV Resort in Tucson, we began to feel a little like we were "living on the edge." Booking places to stay seemed more of a challenge than we had hoped. We were, after all, into December.

"Got a place for us to stay for the night?" we inquired at the desk.

At first, the Hostess, (and I use that word liberally), curls one side of her upper lip with a smirk and says something like, "We are booked solid for February!"

We waited quietly not wanting to pursue this attitude further. Finally, with the bus running outside the door she pulls out some paperwork, deliberates for a time, sighs, then says, "When'd ya say ya want that for?"

"Tonight, mam. Just tonight. Maybe add on a day or two if it's possible later on."

The real irony came when we drove to our relegated spot on the east side of nowhere and passed by skaty-eight empty spots along the way. Someone like me just can't help wondering, "Am I missing something here???" Perhaps it was a subtle form of punishment for not booking last year.

The moral of the story? If you've got your heart set on one fine piece of desert sand, I suggest you book now for February!

Deb Webb's Sunflower - Tucson

Retirement community developer extraordinaire who made a Mecca out of Sun City in the Phoenix area has begun to spread the charm and development of these age 50+ communities around to other areas. A very nice one was underway in Tucson. Although we enjoyed seeing the models, it left little doubt in our minds that we were not full-time "desert people." As soon as we are able to make it through the threatening winter weather conditions between west coast and east, we were heading back to Georgia, South Carolina, and Florida for a serious look for a place to put down roots. No desert for us! At least not at that time. This subject will be revisited one day. (Perhaps more than once!) I have now learned, *"Never say never."*

Yuma

Quartzsite with hookups! RV Heaven!!!

For those readers who have not shared the challenges and joys of RVing, you are probably not familiar with either Quartzsite or Yuma, so let me begin by telling you about the former. Quartzsite is pretty much open desert land in Arizona. Most of the land belongs "to the people." In other words, it is Bureau of Land Management (BLM) land which means it is "ours" and available for us to use. True, it is probably more available and desirable to those who have self-contained motor homes.

The largest gem show and swap meet in the world is held annually at Quartzsite. At the end of January, first part of February, people come and stay in the desert, have parties, reunions, and shop. At least fifty thousand RVs or more were coming annually to this great show and party when we were on the road.

Yuma is totally different and is located at the extreme southwest corner of Arizona. It is adjacent to Mexico and California. Although we had never been to Yuma before, we had heard of it through many RV snowbirds. We decided we had to go there ourselves to have a look. We could not believe our eyes! RV Resort after RV Resort...and if that wasn't enough, private RV lot after RV lot with beautiful brick corrals around each and every one of them. There were hundreds of thousands of RVs. It was a sight to behold!!

Friends had offered us a place to stay in one of the little corrals in the Foothills of the unique Chocolate Mountains that surround the area. These mountains are most unusual and give one a sense that you are camping on the moon.

Yuma was or is a territorial prison. It was December 20th when we arrived in Yuma. The next morning when I got up and looked at the calendar longing for an old fashioned, traditional Christmas, all I could think of was the prison. I wanted to go "home." As the familiar song says, "There is no place like home for the holidays...no matter how far away you roam."

Yuma is unique country. It is different from anywhere we have ever been.

So You Thought You'd Heard It All

On my morning walks through the neighborhood of lot corrals toward the mountains, I began to note plastic bottles of water set in front of the mail boxes or gates to many of the properties. In general, they were simply old two liter soda or juice containers refilled with water. The more I thought about these jugs, the more puzzled I became. "Why?"

Water is at a premium in the desert, and for those readers who have not spent much time in Arizona in particular, *"Don't drink the water,"* is not the name of a Hollywood production, it is a fact of life. You must buy drinking water. There are "filling stations" everywhere. In Yuma, there are drive-in filling stations; that's how bad the water is.

Therefore, to have bottles of water setting along a street would be a puzzlement anywhere, but in Yuma, Arizona desert, *one HAS to wonder.* I met a couple of men on my route and stopped them.

"Say, can you tell me why there are bottles of water all along the street?"

"That's to keep the dogs away."

"Say what?"

"Dogs. To keep the dogs from doing their ahh, well, you know..."

I squinted my eyes and cocked my head not understanding what on earth they were him-hawing about.

Finally, seeing I wasn't beginning to comprehend where his friend was trying to go with his story, the other gentlemen chimed in, "To keep dogs from doing their duty on the property."

I did understand what the man had said, but I was not even close in my comprehension. "You gotta be kidding!"

"No, that's what they say."

I stood there with a silly-looking grin on my face for several minutes. Finally, the first gentlemen added, "And, if you get thirsty, you can always use it to drink!"

Right neighborly, don't you think???

Unfortunately, there was no one else to ask!

Algadones, Mexico

The Mexican town that borders Yuma is Algadones which showcases the most aggressive city of merchants we have seen in our travels. Since English is so well understood by the local Mexicans, it was easy and fun to converse with them. Most vendors had a fairly good sense of humor and were prepared to joke if you let them know that you were not ready to believe their every word.

Each merchant was determined that he would sell you a piece of his wares no matter what. If you were at all interested in purchasing anything, you would be a fool not to dicker over the price. Unfortunately, this writer and Ol' Tex are not especially good at this barter business. But seeing the necessity of dealing this way early on, I became far better at "haggling" than I ever deemed possible. It was challenging and great fun, but exhausting. I'm not certain whether it was because it was Christmas or if it is easier in general, but returning across the border into the United States was a simple: "Are you a US citizen?" "Yes." No question about what we were bringing into the country. Actually, we were asked more questions about goods as we crossed the Stateline from Arizona into California.

Author's note: I have a lot more to say about this today, but that's another story.

Chapter 16

Cal..i..forn..ia... here we come . . .

Christmas Day 1998

We were eager to leave Yuma but the earliest we could book a spot in southern California was Christmas Day. It was cold and brisk in the desert and we were ready for "balmy" San Diego.

We turned the engine heater on in the middle of the night so that we would be ready to roll at day break. BUT, the old "Dreamcatcher" refused to go! A problem with the fuel filter rendered us immobile---for three hours!

Tex was relentless in efforts to start the engine. When it finally turned over, we were like a pit crew at the Daytona 500. In a matter of seconds, we were headed for Lakeside, California, just a few miles outside of San Diego.

As we moved further west, the terrain was different than anything we had seen so far in our journey. From austere desert flat land which went on for miles and miles, we eventually began to see huge, irrigated fields for growing crops. Migrant workers were bussed in from either Mexico or the only city along the way, El Centro.

The stark, brown mountains that had always been at a distance began to get closer and, before we knew it, we were climbing from sea level to over 4,000 feet. Up close, the brown mountains began to change to huge bolder covered inclines. We had never seen so many rocks all in one place. "I'd sure hate to be here during an earthquake," I remarked as I clutched my seat in disbelief.

This desolate area began to fade into scrub brush and scattered housing. Within a few minutes after our descent from the heights of the Chocolate Mountains, we eased into beautiful Southern California. Maybe it was worth it all!

No Room In the Inn

Losing an hour somewhere in the mountains, we arrived at Rancho Los Coches somewhere around high noon. The manager had told us that she would leave information for us on the office door. *WRONG!!!*

Okay, so we knew the site number that we would be calling "home" during our stay here. We unhooked the Jeep and headed out to find it.

"But somebody's been sleeping in my bed..." and he was still there!!!

We found the manager on premises (whew!) and set out in her golf cart for the next hour or so in an attempt to rectify the problem. As it turned out, the "bear" that was in our "bed" had decided to stay on, "but would move if he had to."

The manager looked at us sitting in the golf cart. Would it be a thumbs up or a thumbs down on the fate of this poor old soul on Christmas day?

"Let him stay; we'll try to squeeze into that *itty, bitty* spot next to the dump station with minimal electricity. ***Merry Christmas!***"

And, so we did. But, we were in California, and folks are darn right friendly here! We warmed up right quick!

It took some doing, but "big bird," the Christmas turkey, got cooked with a promise that "same time next year," the bird would get cooked in a traditional oven with a traditional HOUSE around it! "Amen."

San Diego & Southern California

The "oouu--ahhhhh" of this gorgeous area was short lived when Ol' Tex remembered that he couldn't drive in California and that everyone *else* on the highways was a *maniac!!!* I suggested that I drive but even I had to admit the offer was weak when I realized that without warning, the freeway could bank my driving-phobic body skyward on an approach ramp that would make the height of the Empire State building pale in comparison. We're talking about concrete ramps that swirl skyward and are worthy of sculpture classification. They are monumental to be sure.

We tried to work out a feasible plan to maximize our stay with minimal stress--a monumental task. We went nowhere for two days adjusting to the ridiculousness of the situation we were in. Finally, we spent the serious bucks and bought yet another map.

My Kind Of People

Let me interject here that the *people* of California are the friendliest and most helpful in the nation. (At least they were at that time.) If they think you need help, you don't even have to approach them; they find their way to you! They are good-humored, always smiling, and exude warmth. (I hoped it would rub off on us. We were in need of a better attitude.)

Let the Good Times...Roll!

Map and magnifying glass in hand, we hopped into the Jeep and *rolled* out toward the California *Freeways.* There was no way around it, we had to learn the ropes (or asphalt, I should say). If nothing more, we had to get the Dreamcatcher from Los Ranchos to Desert Hot Springs on January 4th. And, like any other major league sport, practice plays a big part. Moving from San Diego, through Los Angles to Desert Hot Springs on New Year's weekend is the equivalent to the Superbowl on the Highways. *Let the game begin!*

Superbowl I-8

The first hurdle would be Interstate 8. Yet, even as we whirled out onto the Super Highway, I remembered that there is a certain aura of happiness or joy about California. I don't know if it is because everything is so beautiful, the weather so perfect, or if it is a left-over from the Gold Rush Days, but one simply immerses into the ambience that this indeed is the land of opportunity.

We tooted along at 80 miles an hour, slower than most of the traffic, until we identified the approach to Interstate I-5 where we needed to head north. Here, Ol' Tex had to grip the wheel and "gun-it" onto the off/on ramp. He clutched the steering wheel, I shut my eyes, and we were off. Vehicles passed us from everywhere as we merged onto the next scene which immediately had two exit lanes that expanded into many more.

The trick was, we did not want to exit; we wanted to remain on I-15. "Gun-it again, Sam!" And off to the left we went hoping for a space in the on-coming. I shut my eyes while Ol' Tex put the peddle to the meddle and we headed north. Now it was time to breathe.

"Where to now?" my chauffer asks with amazing calm.

"Where to? Heck, I just want to try out my breathing apparatus again."

I lowered my head toward the map on my lap, pried the handle of the magnifying glass out of the palm of my left hand, and began to study the possibilities of getting turned around and headed back home.

It was daunting. This definitely needed more practice but time and courage would weigh in heavily. Lord have mercy! We were getting closer and closer to the Parade of Roses and Super Bowl; more and more people (and vehicles) were arriving in Southern California each day.

Seaport Village

We toured more local areas for a day before heading back to Freeway practice. Ol' Tex was eager to get "back on the horse" and I knew it was necessary if we were to get on with this western tour.

Like a pro, he got out and challenged the surfers. We ended up at the San Diego Zoo. Whoa! Proud and smiling.

Discouraged by the countless amount of cars parked everywhere near and around the Zoo, we decided nothing was worth that crowd and headed off to tour downtown. It was a pleasant, beautiful experience and eventually we parked the car for a carefully allotted one hour and forty minutes to tour Seaport Village, a charming area along San Diego Bay. Like everywhere else in Southern California at holiday season, it was crowded with tour buses and band buses and football players.

And, like everywhere else in Southern California, it was comfortable and friendly-----a day well spent. On our way home, we stopped off to buy a new electric blanket and ran smack into two furniture items I had been searching for since we moved into the motor coach...a very good day, indeed.

San Diego Zoo

No visit to San Diego would be complete without a trip to the world renowned San Diego Zoo.

Our day began with an overview ride and guided tour around the entire park on a bus. The zoo is very large with seven zones, and this tour took us up close to the animals as well as through every zone. We would return to spend time with some of the most interesting creatures once we disembarked from the tour bus.

After watching and listening to the noisy yet beautiful pink flamingos, we were happy to snuggle-up to the Koala bears that napped and played peek-a-boo from their heat-lamp-warmed bedrooms. The camels were as interested in us as we were in them, and, the elephants entertained us while they played with their toys.

Giant Panda viewing meant we had to get into a line, three deep, to enter the area where Shi Shi and Bain Yun were being studied by behaviorists. Bain Yun was busy eating his favorite food, bamboo, while Shi Shi hid from the crowds. These Chinese natives choose to live alone except for mothers when they are rearing their cubs.

As we meandered around, we saw many interesting birds: storks, vultures, falcon, etc. Rare species of the deer family and gazelles were tucked uniquely away in natural habitats. It was a pleasure just to walk the grounds where unusual plant species were identified and thriving.

The polar bear plunge was a fascinating exhibit and we were able to see them in a vigorous self-imposed swimming program before we returned to see them settle down for their afternoon nap.

The beautiful Bengal Tiger was snoozing when we went in for a closer look. It was a good thing that there was glass between him and us because the temptation was to pet the well-marked, carefully defined fur coat.

Soak Zone

Signs appropriately parked near fun animals such as the rhino and giraffes stated "Soak Zone --- 20 Feet!" So it was not surprising then that when these "bad boys" back their butts in our direction, Ol' Tex ran for the hills.

One of the most fascinating sights was the Hippopotamus exhibit. Two humongous hippos entertained us as we watched these thin-skinned animals soak in water. A glass shield afforded us an opportunity to get a good look at their entire bodies. At the surface, we looked eyeball to eyeball. I love those guys!

Kissed by a Llama

His name is Poncho and, well, golly gee, he was smitten with me. First stolen kiss I have had since marriage. I still remember his really big, beautiful eyes, those soft lips, the warmth of his breath on my face. I think I'm in love!

Skyfari

The Skyfari Aerial Tram provided transportation from one side of the vast zoo to the other. The view was awe inspiring and I did not want to disembark. San Diego is a gorgeous city, and the sky view was yet another way to appreciate not only the beauty of the zoo, but the city's skyline from a whole different angle. San Diego will always be one of my most beautiful memories.

Beautiful Places, Beautiful People

All aboard for: Palm Springs, Desert Hot Springs, Palm Desert, Indio, Cathedral City, Rancho Mirage........you get the picture.

In the vast desert between San Bernardino and Phoenix exists the land of "good and plenty"......plenty to see, plenty to do, plenty *GOOD FOOD & SHOPPING!*

I had found Mecca; and, Ol' Tex? "We need to defrost the refrigerator," he decided again in his infinite wisdom. Actually, there wasn't much else left to do since we had done our fall and spring cleaning during the long New Year's weekend. (You know how we love to celebrate special holidays!)

Resorts A-Plenty

We stayed at a Hot Springs Resort looking off into the little San Bernardino Mountain Range. Resorts were plentiful--and lush.

Posh Retirement Communities

Now that we have decided we do not want to live in the desert on a permanent basis, it was interesting to see that some of the best of the best retirement communities, with all the necessary amenities, are located in this most spectacular desert valley. Where there was sand, they have brought in grass. Where there was total dryness, they have brought in ponds, fountains, and water falls. Entertainment abounds, and world class shopping is available. For nine months of the year, the weather is perfect; and, when we inquired about the summers, they scoffed and said, "We have air conditioning."

We toured Del Webb's Community and were not disappointed. It is class and, if there had been a fishing lake, I believe Ol' Tex would have plunked down the money right then and there.

Palm Springs

We evaluated "The Valley" as one of our top ten picks of places in the country. It may move into the top five, but we have more to see and enjoy before we make that decision.

Chapter 17

"Under the Desert Sky"

Quartzsite

A contrast in conditions: the serenity, tranquility, and aura of the desert along side the chaotic collection of vendors hawking their wares. It is, in fact, the largest swap meet in the world. 50 million RVers and countless merchants. We were there for the preview and truly enjoyed every moment of both worlds.

The Great Light Show in the Sky

Sunrise on the desert is spectacle and sunset is spectacular!

Sunset. For at least an hour each night, we watched the Master Painter add and change color with strokes of rich, warm, ever evolving color. From this vantage point in the middle of the desert, sun setting is unlike anything you could ever imagine.

Serenity. It was palpable.

We left the desert with a longing for more. And yet, we have learned the message well: "Know when to go...know when to stay...."

We embraced the au natural existence in the vast desert and delighted at the emersion into the world's largest flee market. It was time to go---and we knew it! Thousands more were on their way to this paradise. We knew we had experienced it at its best.

Trains, Planes & Automobiles

If memory serves me correctly, there is a movie called, "Trains, Planes and Automobiles." Our first stop in the Phoenix area put all that together when we arrived at Leon's in the Sun City area. Across the street from the park was an automobile dealership with a loudspeaker which called, "Al, Al, Al," or "Mike" or "Joe" or whomever she wanted.

Then, "De planes, De planes" from the air force training school, droning overhead, canceling one's every word--or thought. Finally, just after I said, "Well, at least we don't have the 'lonesome whistle,'" a train headed down the track some 500 feet away sent out that lonesome "wooooo...wooo." We had 'em all, but our stay was to be short and busy. We would soon be moving to the east side of Phoenix.

Mesa, Arizona

Snowbird communities are plentiful throughout Arizona. Mesa is a perfect area for many of these active adult winter homes. We stayed at Silveridge where there are park models as well as RV parking spaces. Activities and amenities abound. It is a fun place to winter.

After nearly a week in this spot, we reluctantly took a deep breath and said, "Good-bye." Instinctively, we knew that we would not be back next year for our annual southwest sojourn. As we pulled up anchor (the sewer and water hook-ups) on January 23rd, we officially began our trek back east to put down some roots. We were excited; we had a good itinerary, and we were looking forward to the trip.

Lulu's Back In Town

Throughout the past year, it had become a necessary habit to check the news at every opportunity. (War had broken out frequently!) True to habit, we checked the Saturday morning news on January 23rd before leaving Phoenix. Ho, hum, a winding down of President Bill Clinton's Impeachment Trial which had kept me personally entertained for months. Anti-climatic, but inevitable.

Less than three hours later, we pulled into the campground at Benson, put the satellite dish up, a quick check of the news before lunch to be sure we were not at war or under terrorists' attack, and... what's this? "What did he say?" I shushed Ol' Tex who was eager to level the coach. "Hold everything!" I shrieked. "What's the matter?"

My mouth had dropped open several inches. "I don't believe it," I gasped with glee. (Monica Lewinski was winging her way to Washington.) "Lulu's back in town!"

And I thought the story was over. A story teller myself, I couldn't have written a more intriguing novel. What's that Mark Twain said about "truth being stranger than fiction?"

Note on the Past

Over a decade later, it is interesting to note the irony of our concerns at that particular time in our country's history. It was not until September 11, 2001 that we would experience the attack on the World Trade Center in New York City and the Pentagon in Washington, DC. Yet we, personally, were vigilant even then. Evidently things did not look good to us. Too bad that those in charge were less vigilant.

Benson, Sierra Vista, Bisbee, etc.

No surprise, Benson is a wide spot in the road, a staging area for more prestigious areas such as Tucson, Phoenix, Palm Springs, and so on. We stayed with our Hawaiian friends and set out in the morning for a day of touring southern Arizona.

Sierra Vista is really just an outgrowth of Fort Huachuca, nothing more. We stopped to stretch our legs, and were glad we had not decided to drag the coach along.

When we came to the Y in the road, we decided on the spur of the moment to head into Bisbee for a quick look-see. Holly Toledo! Old? Let me tell you, this copper/gold mining town looks to be older than the hills on which it sets. It is spectacular not only in age but in the way buildings and homes are "perched" on the rugged terrain. The huge open-pit copper mine as well as the underground mine have been closed for years. The city runs tours of the mines and uses the tourist revenue to keep the town going.

Queen Mine Tour

We donned our mining uniforms: rubber jackets, hard hats, battery packs, and hopped on a miner transport which would take us into the interior of the mine. The driver of the train, a man who was also our official tour guide, was a former mine worker with 40 some odd years of experience and a good sense of humor. He had lived in Bisbee all of his life except for his years in the army in the early forties.

We stopped after we had made the first bend into the cold, dark, interior of the mountain. Jake offered to let anyone off the train who had claustrophobia and monies paid would be returned in full.

I thought long and hard about this offer. We rattled forward. Ol' Tex was thrilled.

We stopped occasionally and climbed up to interior excavated rooms which, when mining, they call "home" for the day. We saw where they lunched with "pet" rats; we saw where they...well, neither you nor I really needed to know about that, but you will be relieved to know, it was trolleyed out!

The thing which seemed to interest *ME* most came late in the tour when I finally noted a light other than the ones which hung from our necks. Forward in the distance, I could see just a trace of light. It grew bigger as I watched intently and hopefully. Indeed, it was a light. A great sense of relief washed over me. It got bigger and bigger.

My burden of fear began to ease as I realized for certain it was ***the light at the end of the tunnel.***

There Is A Light at the End...

Both metaphorically and literally, the tour of the Queen Copper and Gold Mine at Bisbee spoke volumes for our Nomadic experience of two years. We had seen and done more than most folks ever get to do. Yet, we still have a whole lifetime of new and completely different opportunities to look forward to. We were leaving Arizona behind physically, but the rich memories of our experiences in this unique desert country would always remain a light in our hearts.

UN-BE-Lievable!!!

We pulled into the Escapee Dream Catcher RV Park in Deming, NM and eagerly set out to see the sites. We stopped in town to buy a newspaper, walk the streets, and twenty minutes later, had hunkered into our motor coach for the night. Deming is challenged in its size and scope.

None-the-less, we ran into friends here by virtue of belonging to Escapees. This synchronicity is always a delight when you are on the road and we were thrilled. It was a great way to spend time, catch up with each other's adventures, and make future plans.

For those readers who are just beginning this life on the road, you will enjoy the serendipity of these occasions as well. One neat circumstance of RV life is that you are able to make friends quickly without going through the formalities and superfluousness that "real life" often demands. You have much in common with other RVers and appreciate the ins and outs of life on the road.

El-Paso

From Deming, it was on to Texas. For us, it was always a joy to experience El Paso--without wind. This visit was "wind free." It was no-jacket weather, comfortable seventies and sunny.

El Paso is a true western city, a cowboy's place to shop. Tex was ready to shop, and shop he did. We bought hats, pants, shorts, and looked at boots and belts. He was one happy cowboy.

El Paso is also a lady's place to shop with three, count 'em THREE Dillard's all in the same town!!! I could hardly contain myself. Fortunately, Ol' Tex was doing the driving. He contained me, but I did manage to find some pretty spiffy duds for myself.

Again, it was difficult to pull up anchor when we were having such a good time, but like the old cowboy song says, "Know when to go...."

Melancholia Sets In

It is amazing how familiar we had become with Texas. Two years ago, we knew nothing about Texas. Now this vast expanse of land has become, out of necessity, our home state.

West Texas is, as Ol' Tex likes to say, "Miles and miles of nothing but miles and miles." West Texas is immensely vast in space with little if anything of significance to report on. On our long haul from El Paso to Odessa, Ol' Tex got melancholy. "This may be our last trip across Texas. We may never see this particular stretch again."

Overly sentimental by nature, I felt a certain sadness, a "neuvo" nostalgia, if you will. Suddenly, it occurred to me. "Get a grip! Do you ever want to come back to West Texas???"

Pecos, Odessa, Midland, Abilene, reward us best as memories of another time.

Oil Patch

The immense stretch of vastness began to fill with oil pumpers as we moved closer to Odessa. Fields filled with oil rigs, where other fields in Texas had been filled with cattle.

There was a certain romance about the area in a rough and tumble sort of way. The excitement was enhanced with a sense of foreboding as dark, heavy clouds began to rapidly move in. We had to take shelter; a storm threatened and we knew we could not out-run it. One does not want to "mess with Texas" storms.

Odessa & Midland

We enjoyed Odessa-Midland and had a good time. We liked the people of the area, and again, we were saddened by the evidence that Midland and Odessa had both seen better days. When we were there, oil prices were at an all time low which meant that Texans were not pumping as much oil and what little they did pump was not bringing a good price.

As is true with many parts of our country, there was a nostalgia, a sadness, a longing for "the good old days," the better days of yesteryear.

Abilene, Abilene...

"Prettiest town I've ever seen." Ol' Tex was singing his cowboy heart out as we rolled in to Abilene, Texas. We parked the bus in a campground the likes of which I expected for Abilene and took a "one night only." *I insisted.*

After a bite of lunch, we headed out for the grand tour. It didn't take long and soon we were heading back to camp. "Abilene, Abilene...'worst town I've ever seen.'"

Now, he was singing my song!

Georgetown, Texas - Retirement Community by the original Del Webb

We have a great appreciation for the lifestyle communities created by the original Del Webb. The first, of course, was Sun City just west of Phoenix. We especially liked what the developer was doing in Georgetown just north of Austin. The homes as well as the grounds are picturesque. The facilities are first rate.

We did the tour and marveled at the gorgeous indoor pool, fitness center, computer lab with many computers, sewing labs with machines that did everything but make you lunch, craft rooms for art, stain glass, pottery--to die for, ballroom with stage, lighting, curtains--the works, and numerous other rooms of entertainment including a lovely library. The social hall and auditorium were all first class as we expected. The Wood Shop was a separate entity away from this group of buildings but not far from The Worship Place, a church-type building, non-denominational, for all to worship. Indeed, this one was a class act in a gorgeous setting.

There is within the community, a Village Market with shops, a filling station, a place to eat and a golf cart dealer complete with repair shop. Also within is a Fire House complete with ambulance and an EMS squad. Of course, there are several Golf Courses, pro shops, restaurants, etc.

We visited most of the thirty some model homes and while in the courtyard, we were delighted to run into people we knew from another life. Lee was the refinery manager at Salt Lake when Jim was the asphalt manager there. He and Georgina had retired to Hot Springs, Arkansas, one of the lovely Cooper Communities which we had visited in October. We had decided against that particular one and it was interesting to note that they were looking for a different area. (The Cooper Development in Hot Springs is really remote.)

We left Georgetown unconvinced that Texas was for us—mostly because we had never considered it. We did keep a folder of information along with two videos--just in case our dreams of finding similar communities in SC, GA, and FL did not pan out.

(Author's note: Georgetown, Texas ultimately provided us with a large, beautiful home and five years of wonderful memories! Texas was a good place to live.)

Livingston, Texas

Back "home" again at Rainbow's End, we had enough projects, appointments, and well earned R & R to keep us in Livingston for a week. Now for those readers who have been wondering about our association with Texas, let me try to explain.

In order to function in this modern day and age, everyone has to have an address. First and foremost, Livingston was our mail-forwarding address. Second, we had to be registered and licensed in a place, and Texas served as that place. It is a place for us to register and vote; and, it is a place for us to pay federal income taxes. So legally, it became necessary to become "residents" of Texas.

Our "residence" in Livingston was a hanging file in a very large room, or "neighborhood" with other hanging files. All of these hanging files belong to members of a "community" of RVers who belong to the very large organization of RVers known as Escapees. They use their power to achieve goals as a group that individuals could have difficulty doing. Although people who belong are called members, they soon become fast friends.

Escapees publish a monthly magazine keeping members current on happenings within the community. Now, of course, they are able to make good use of the internet with their own website. When we were traveling, magazines and rallies were the only mode of mass communication.

The organization owns and runs several campgrounds and co-op parks throughout the country. Members are eligible to stay in the parks at member rates which are nominal. One of the goals of the Escapee organization is to provide members with opportunities to purchase at more reasonable rates. Profit is not a goal. Friendship is.

Escapees have a CARE facility at National Headquarters in Livingston. The CARE Center supports members who are dealing with medical needs and concerns at nominal cost and maximum support. The truth is, they really do care.

Consequently, for the period of time that we were living on the road, Livingston, Texas was a "home" of necessity.

Hold Up Again in Livingston

Our planned time in Livingston became extended when packages did not arrive and appointments got put off. It gave us time to "smell the flowers" which were blooming everywhere; and, we enjoyed 80 degree temperatures. (This was the first week of February in Texas!)

It also gave us time to catch up on a few chores we had relegated to the background. One of the chores was bookkeeping which is so astutely performed by my financial advisor, 'Ol Tex. Now I admit this is far from exciting travel news, but I thought you might enjoy knowing more about incidental ins and outs of the road, in other words: "The road traveled, more or less."

In the official financial record there was a column identified as "clothing budget." It was better known as "Bev's Clothing Budget." At the close of posting, my financial advisor reported, "The clothing budget is way, way over this month." He looked at me with grave and piercing eyes that would force even an innocent person to feel guilty.

A well-learned defender of my vice, I was prepared to address this challenge. Old Tex had met his match and extemporaneously, I was prepared for "***W-A-R***!" It didn't hurt that I was looking at enough recently purchased cowboy hats to carry him through the new millennium----hats that he could not begin to stow away because of space challenges!

I put on one of the ten gallons and said, "What's that you say?" Need I say more?

Louisiana at Festival Time

Realizing we were heading in the right direction at the right time, we bailed out of Livingston without our packages and headed for Cajun Country in time for Madis Gras.

What a blast! Things always seem to happen in perfect timing; so why do I forget so easily?

Fat Tuesday - One Week Early

As they say in Acadian Country, *Laissez les bons temps rouler!* Translated: **Let the good times roll!** And so we did. Beginning seven days and seven nights before Fat Tuesday, we ditched the diet and ate our way through Cajun Country cooking.

We had received excellent advice concerning fine dining and ate at the finest of authentic Cajun restaurants. Crawfish pie, gumbo, catfish, and bisque of every flavor. Spicy? Some were scandalously HOT! But Ol' Tex just loved them all the more. As he dug deeper in, I occasionally had to set back and cool my tongue on hot, fresh-baked bread! Ahhhh, life is tough.

Tabasco - Avery Island Tour

No trip to Cajun Country would be complete without a side trip to Avery Island and a tour of the Tabasco factory.

In the post Civil War era, Edmund McIlhenny developed and produced the flavorful pepper sauce from capsicum pepper plants which he grew on Avery Island. Now, the family grows these pepper plants on the Island for seeds for the following year's crop to be cultivated in Mexico, Columbia, Honduras and Venezuela, The crops are picked at the peak of their ripeness for Tabasco. It remains a family owned and operated business. Today the product is sold around the world.

No tour is complete without a stop at the gift shop. Tex left the establishment armed with a bottle of the new, sizzling hot habanera sauce, lip smacking good.

Eating Our Way thru...FAT TUESDAY

We started going to award-winning Cajun restaurants: Prejeans, Chez Kitty, Cajun Cafe in Lafayette area to des Amis in Breaux Bridge, and so forth. We feasted on such delectables as dirty rice, jambalaya, shrimp, crabs, sausage, gumbo, boiled crawfish, and my personal favorite, varieties of crawfish pie. But, that was just the warm-up for the fun!

Corencro Country Parade

Not far from where we stayed was the rural town of Corencro. Since each town or city has its own celebration, Corencro was no exception. So on Valentine's Day, we found ourselves elbow to elbow with the revelers at the festival parade in Corencro. It was good that we got started early because one does need to practice!

Let the good times roll...and they did. Each float, *loaded* with participants, rolled by with its own version of rhythm. Beads, beads, and more beads were thrown at the crowds that lined the streets.

I began to collect the beads and other goodies which were tossed my way. I was actually beginning to learn to snag them mid-air when some fraternity boys invaded my turf. That set me back a bit. However, when I learned to let them have the loot tossed from the pretty, young girls, they gave me berth to gather my share--even helped me. All was going well until a couple big bruisers planted themselves between me and my boys. This was when things got tough! They could out shout me, out catch me, and out do me in every way. Not only did they tower over me and out weigh me by about four hundred pounds, they had about sixty years of practice at this sort of thing.

But my spirits were naturally high and theirs were even higher buoyed up from the liquid they chug-a-lugged from brown paper bags. Gradually, I began to be able to out maneuver them--and did!

Now I know where the expression, "eat, drink and be merry" originated!

Cathedral of St. John - Lafayette

After such an engagement, we did some down time by visiting the Cathedral of St. John. The parish itself was established in 1821 in what was then known as Vermilionville, now Lafayette. The cathedral was built in the early nineteen hundreds.

The Cathedral Oak, a mammoth oak tree to the right of the church, was one of the largest in the U. S. and estimated to be over 450 years old. The tree's diameter at the trunk is 8.5 feet with a circumference of 26.7 feet. It is 125 feet high and has a spread of 210 feet. Tree lovers would have a difficult time hugging this baby!

Although I have not had the opportunity to check it out again since Hurricane Katrina, I have a feeling the Cathedral Oak is still there.

The Cathedral Cemetery does date back to the beginning of the parish in the early eighteen hundreds. The above-ground vaults are a tradition from the French and Spanish influence in the area. I always thought it was because the swampy land, mostly below sea level, made burial below ground impossible.

Mardi Gras in Lafayette

We had been advised repeatedly to "get there early." So shortly after 8 a.m. the morning of the big day, ***Fat Tuesday***, we headed out to claim our spot on the parade route.

When we arrived in town, folks had obviously been there for hours. Barbeques were fired up, drinks were flowing, and folks were dancing to music which filled the air. Police had closed the streets on and near the parade route, so people freely walked back and forth, and up and down the streets.

Moment by moment, the crowds grew larger, louder, and more festive. This in itself was a sight to behold. We were glad we had staked out our spot early.

The noise and excitement grew with anticipation. As the parade got closer, there were "parade scouts" who revealed this information. Then, as the parade got close, many of the women in the King's Court Reviewing stand descended from their perch and lined up in front of us. Whoa!!! Not only were they blocking our view, but they were in line for *our* beads.

The meanest and nastiest of kids formed a threatening band behind us positioning themselves in primo territory under the box in order to catch the rebounds. It seems the bead throwers on the floats sling beads with all their might trying to reach the chosen few in the boxes. They don't always make it to the box. Therefore, these mean little guys with greed in their hearts had staked out the turf behind us.

The King came in on his float first and stopped at the reviewing stand where he pledged his love and his faith, and whatever else he could dream up to his lovely Queen who received a huge bouquet of roses and gifts from him.

Once he had laid on the troth, it all happened fast and furiously. Beads were flung as floats came and went. We couldn't catch a strand; we were grossly outnumbered and out-witted. These were seasoned beaders!

At the end of the parade which was not nearly as colorful, as long, or as good as the rural parade, my "guardian angel of the beads" came over and dropped about 5 pounds of beads around my neck. This was the same lady I had originally tried to block from my turf! Just goes to show, **one never knows an angel in disguise**!

Chapter 18

The Bus Is Eastbound . . .

Natchez

You really didn't need a tourist information packet to know that Natchez is run by the DAR. Well-dressed, yet fragile-looking in their suits and stockings, these southern belles are far from demure or helpless. They are solid stock, survivors!

The town of Natchez has several well-preserved antebellum mansions on its historic tour route, but perhaps the one held in highest esteem is Longwood. Time limitations did not afford us ample opportunity to tour this estate, so we elected to drive near the area and view the plantation from distance.

Or, maybe not! We were met by a no-nonsense "daughter" in the strongest sense of the American Revolution who flagged down Ol' Tex and advised him in no uncertain terms, "You have run the gate!!!"

"Not me!" he countered, "The sign said exit this way."

"You ran the gate!"

"The sign..."

"You ran the gate!"

"I'll turn around if you move out of my way...your royal high--neee."

Author's note: For those of you who don't know authority appreciating, rule abiding Ol' Tex, let me assure you, he, of all people, would never "run the gate." Further, the "royal high—neee" was spoken under his breath but you could read it in his eyes!

A Study In Contrasts

What is so remarkable about this area of the country, Natchez and Vicksburg, is the marked contrast between the antebellum mansion homes and the nearby cotton-picker shacks. It was disquieting as we soaked it all in.

On To Vicksburg—Another Jewel on the Mississippi

Vicksburg was saved, in most part, from critical Civil War burning by the Union army. We stayed at the Isle of Capri RV Park and by the time they gave us coupons and discount tickets, etc., we ended up money ahead! That was *only* because we didn't put a nickel of our own money in the slot machines available at the casinos up and down the mighty river.

Vicksburg had more than its share of antebellum homes, and we did an historic tour to see most of them. We stayed but one night and it was another one of those places where "knowing when to go" was critical. It left us feeling reasonably good about the place--mostly because the people were very friendly.

Meridian, Mississippi

We gasped as we drove into town; it was not a pretty picture. Meridian had seen better days.

Fortunately, we found a shopping mall on our way back to the motor coach and got a different flavor for the area. Ol' Tex saddled up to a buddy in the over-stuff chairs which were provided by the mall management as a gentlemen's gathering place. I enjoyed visiting with the ladies in Dillard's and McRae's.

The visit was not a waste. Tex discussed the various retirement topics with his crowd but left puzzled by a remark concerning one of our prime prospects, Georgia. "Iiiii like Mississip and Alaaaabaaaama, but Georgia, Iii wouldn't feed my dog their shortbread!"

"What did he mean by that?" I asked Ol' Tex who relayed that valuable piece of information to me.

"I don't know," he responded. "I guess he doesn't like Georgia shortbread."

"You don't think he has a problem with the place or the people?"

An interesting personal observation to note: In the end, a place is really about the people. Meridian clearly personified this.

Alabama

We visited friends in Birmingham and toured the general area while I contemplated suing the publishing company whose retirement guide book I was following. Better yet, a serious talk with the author was not out of the question.

Our opinion of suggested retirement prospects here in the Birmingham area might have been colored by the fact that the temperature plummeted to twenty degrees during our *short visit!*

Now I ask, do you think of Birmingham as cold? We decided to cross Alabama off our list of possibilities--at least until it thawed.

Heading South from Birmingham

We thought we wouldn't get far enough south fast enough. We started rolling just after 7 a.m. and didn't stop until we got to Valdosta, Georgia! There were blooms everywhere. Azaleas, tulip trees, fruit trees, and bulbs opened wide inviting spring.

Valdosta, GA

Valdosta is a lovely, little old town at the southern most part of central Georgia. The town square is well preserved and a credit to the community which has worked to preserve it. The downtown area also hosts an attractive University campus, well-maintained, and bustling with activity.

While we were there, I visited with a couple of students and a former professor which made me miss college life all the more! I noticed, also, a not so quiet desperation in Ol' Tex's voice as we toured the area looking for fishing lakes with retirement communities. "I've given-up on fishin'," he moaned, but I noted that we continued to look for water.

Further South to Orange Lake, Florida

Although it was pleasant and spring-like in Valdosta, we headed south to Florida. Our first stop was Orange Lake in north central Florida. We were in good position to investigate the Gainesville/Ocala area.

Back with the BAD BOYS

We had plans to head for Daytona Beach and meet up with friends. BUT....

Ol' Tex looked grim when he got off the phone. "What?" I inquired with much skepticism.

"You're not going to believe this," he lamented in obvious pain.

"No room in the inn?" I guessed.

"Not only that, but 50,000 bikers are about to converge on Daytona for a rally."

"You are kidding," I shrieked. "How do we manage to do it?"

This was the 3rd Harley Davidson Rally we had run into in less than a year. After Laughlin's River Run, and Sturgis, South Dakota, I was not up to another round of black leather!

Nor was he. You must remember Ol' Tex's exchange with T-BONE! *He ain't been the same since!*

Spruce Creek by Del Webb

After a very exhausting day of riding and looking for potential retirement communities, we meandered into Spruce Creek, the community we wanted to see based on information we had garnered in the west.

Spruce Creek is similar to the preferred "lifestyle" communities we had discovered in the west, but a strange "this is not the place" feeling must have enveloped both of us at the same time. Certainly, it was nice, but we did not achieve the same level of confidence with the development as we had with other Del Webb communities in the west.

We revisited Spruce Creek several years later after it was sold out. Our re-evaluation said it had to be a good choice based on the ratio of people to facilities. It is located adjacent to the largest of communities called The Villages.

The Villages

In a funky kind of way, *The Villages,* south of Belleview, had some appeal at that time. We were too tired to accept their offer for a real tour, but off-handedly decided if someone wanted a second home, this might be worth a second look.

Live entertainment was going on in the town square of Spanish Village while business establishments were quietly active. I sensed the place held promise. The only problem was, I didn't have stamina to really check it out and Ol' Tex was pooped! We decided we would return when we were older, perhaps looking for a last fling.

That was back in the 1990s. Now, one would have to consider the thousands of additional homes built in the area. *How do you spell gridlock?*

Gainesville, Florida

To satiate my need to be near university, we took an exploratory trip to Gainesville, main campus of Florida State University. It was fun to see palm trees lining the campus, but, so far as one could determine, Gainesville did not offer much in the way of adult retirement communities. I was, however, pleasantly surprised by the community.

Years later, I continue to believe that Gainesville has great potential for many reasons.

Lake Orange

We stayed at Grand Lake RV Resort to get a feel for the area. My biggest surprise was that Gainesville and Ocala are farther apart than I envisioned. Tex's biggest surprise was that Lake Orange was a fishing resort as well as a golf resort.

I had to take the big guy by the hand to the boat landing, but he got the message and promptly returned with pole, hook, line, and sinker! He had become so comfortable complaining about *not fishing,* he forgot *to fish* when he had the opportunity!

The things that always bothers me most near water in the southeast is the inevitable signs that say, "*Don't feed the gators!*" I'm okay with not feeding them; it is the implied message that always gets to me. The second is the airboats. Just as you begin to mellow-out and feel reasonably serene, a deafening blast from the final docking approach leaves one wondering if the captain might just have launched into space.

Back to "Tim-Buck..."

We left Ocala area and headed east to a remote area called Eustis, smack dab in the middle of Tim-buck...nowhere.

"Isn't this a really nice campground?" Ol' Tex cooed.

I looked out the window at 1200 plus units parked within three feet of each other on grass, sand, and fire ants and wondered what he was seeing that I was not.

"It's okay," I venture hesitantly wondering where this exchange is going.

"Nice place. Nice and quiet."

I turn my head slightly to see an emergency vehicle racing down the highway, siren blaring full blast.

As co-pilot, I had looked at the map just as well as anyone else noting the chain-o-lakes area in the middle of nowhere. We were parked right there, but, I decided two could play this silly game.

"You can get to just about anywhere from here," he persists.

"Specifically?"

"Anywhere."

I let that hang hoping to have an opportunity to lob one in at a later date.

"Good place to just sit back for a week and wait for the weather to warm farther north."

"Mmmmmm," I responded with painful restraint as I reckoned with the already paid-in-full 7 days that were ahead of us in the middle of Tim-buck.

After a few more pitifully self-serving, yet ever so innocent exchanges, Ol' Tex excitedly decided we should get in the Jeep and go out to check our surroundings.

Lake Eustis, Lake Yale, Lake...

Yadida, yadida, yadida.

"Oh! There's a lake!" says Tex with such innocence it could make one...

"Mmmmm, a lake."

"Maybe I'll do some fishin'," he says nonchalantly.

"Mmmmm, maybe."

"Got nothin' else to do..."

I let that one go with the grace of God.

(Nothin', you'd better believe it!)

"Well, guess we'll just hunker in and do a little fishin'. Heck, nothin' else to do."

(Nothin'!)

Hate the Message – Not the Messenger

This story was not anticipated when I wrote the preceding. Furthermore, I am humbled by it--at the very least. As you read, try to remember, I am strictly the messenger. A media guru once said, "Hate the message, not the messenger."

I fear I have created a readership that is pretty soft on "poor Ol' Tex." Before you do any judging, let me first tell you the story. But first, ponder this.

'Fate. . . or?????

Many, many years ago, my wise old philosophy professor asked, "Is there such a thing as ***Justice?***" I pondered the question for a full semester before he and I engaged in our discussion and my final thesis on that very subject.

My professor presented some powerful arguments against my position that ***there is*** justice. His opposition was valid; and, from that day forward, I have pondered the question, watched, and waited. It takes great patience and time.

I stand firm with my original position: There is justice.

Mercury Motor Succumbs

Many will remember when Ol' Tex bought his Zodiac (inflatable) boat in the desert of Las Cruces, New Mexico then spent a month in the desert of Phoenix, Arizona buying the 10 HP Mercury motor to go with it.

Well, "Pop-fizz," as I call the inflatable, lost its mate. The Mercury motor simply went ca-put!!!

Tex made a few calls, and we headed out with the sick motor to find a doctor. We drove for hours through heavy traffic to the "hospital." When the motor hospital advised Ol' Tex that they would have to ship it out because "We don't do boat motors here," Ol' Tex lost his cowboy cool and demanded his money be returned.

"We don't refund money here," stated the clerk behind the counter. (Right, as if we didn't see that one coming!)

"The motor isn't any good to me, I am leaving town, and I can't wait."

Finally, after Tex and the clerk had a go at this no-win conversation, I asked, "Who can?"

"Maybe a store..."

"Good, how do we find out?"

The merry chase took us into the heart of Orlando, a not so easy place to get to and one that Ol' Tex would never have come to had it not been for this situation. But, we were running out of warranty, and the problem needed to be addressed pronto!

Good News - Bad News

First the good: he got his money back--a considerable piece of change, I might add. The "bad" news? Ol' Tex is miserable. He doesn't have a motor for pop-fizz! And, there is *nothing* more miserable than a miserable Ol' Tex.

Nothin'!

And so, philosophically I ask you, *is there such a thing as justice???*

On the Road Again

Yup! That would be us, traveling north on I-95, the busiest highway on the East coast-- made busier yet by the departure of the 50,000 bikers who attended the Harley Rally at Daytona! Yup! Here we were, all together again! *"Making music with my friends, and I can't wait to be on the road again!"*

How did we manage to do this--our 3rd big motorcycle rally in a year? I mean we had absolutely no idea that they would be traveling north on I-95 the exact same day that we were.

Whoa! What's this up ahead? Five mile back-up! It's time to listen to the old CB.

As news travels down the wireless, we learned that a biker hurdling down the highway at high speed had hit the pavement head first.

Now you had to be in the middle of this three lane, five mile parking lot surrounded with Harley Hogs, revving-up their motors and sucking in their exhausts to appreciate the next communication over the wire.

"Can't somebody scrape that biker off the cement so we can get movin'?"

Honest. That's what the trucker said. Some things one just never forgets.

On the Banks of the Ogeechee (Georgia)

Fishing! The Ogeechee River offers the best of two worlds: "Freshwater fishing, Bream (Blue Gill), Red Breast, Bass and all the other species are yours for the taking. Downstream to Brackish-Saltwater area for the very best in Striped Bass fishing and all other species of Saltwater Fish."

This is what the advertisement told us about the Waterway RV Park just south of Savannah. I'm not sure we were convinced of the information, but it was a good location.

The camp owners were having a cook-out for their guests when we arrived and so we had lunch with the folks.

This was a nice experience. We had been on the road for six hours with all the motorcycles and we were tired and hungry.

Who says there's no such thing as a free lunch?

Sunday In Savannah

We didn't have much time left for entertainment that day by the time we got settled into Waterway RV Park. We needed a new set of wiper blades so the bus driver was willing to venture out to address that problem.

Ol' Tex generously stopped at the local market so that we could pick up some supplies. He also dropped a couple of wine bottles into the shopping buggy. *We were there anyway, right?*

The gal at the check-out carefully waved the bar code of each item over the magic eye of the scanning device as it came down the delivery shoot. When the wine reached the front of the line, she promptly announced, "It's Sunday!" and stopped short the conveyer operation.

Not to be foiled by this unimposing clerk, Ol' Tex immediately countered, "I'm from Texas! We drink every day of the week!"

Unimpressed, the stalwart Georgia peach did not even smile as she read Tex the total of his expenditures---minus, of course, his spirits.

Thumbs Up? Thumbs Down?

Was it a thumbs up? Or was it a thumbs down on calling Savannah home?

I loved it. It had plenty of water for Ol' Tex, universities for me, golf, shopping, libraries, cultural entertainment, and, it is lovely.

Although there were several developments with potential, Ol' Tex seemed disinterested in looking further. A one day tour and we were history.

Note: As it would turn out, many years later, we did get to live in the area. Full time in Savannah is a lot different from a transient tourist stop.

Score a big one for Ol' Tex!

Lake Marion

On a map, it looks to be ideal. In reality, it is actually smack dab in the middle of nowhere between Columbia and Charleston, SC.

Santee and Cooper Rivers are dammed to form one huge body of water called Lake Marion. The Corp of Engineers went off to fight the War before clearing the ground, leaving tree stumps, and other debris in the area which formed the lake, making it a perfect place for trophy fish to breed and thrive. Ol' Tex tried his best to justify the proximity of Charleston, Columbia, and Sumter but when it took nearly an hour to work our way from the lake to the meager offerings at Manning, I was unimpressed with Wyboo Plantation, the community where we would live. Even Tex had to admit that on a lake this size, it seemed a bit much to have to use electric lifts and card locked channels to get to the big water. This was not his or my version of "living on a lake."

Doomed

After chasing so many dreams just to have them dashed by not meeting even minimum requirements, Ol' Tex declared: "We're doomed to travel forever!"

At that moment, we are sitting in The Barnyard, *literally*, at Columbia, South Carolina where we had exhausted all possibilities at Lake Murray. Again, Lake Murray in South Carolina appears to offer great potential—on the map.

We were watching weird and honking geese, a mama goat with kids, and white ducks trying to drown black ducks in the barnyard pond. Horrified by what I was watching, I looked away and on the horizon I could see... "What's this?" The largest flee market I had ever seen! How bad can this nomadic lifestyle be?

Catch you later. Time to "shop 'til I drop."

Author's Note: Looking back now some ten years later from my present "brick and mortar" life, I am inclined to believe the "travel forever" is not such a bad fate after all!

Chapter 19

Nothing could be finer than to be in Carolina. . .

Columbia, SC

The city of Columbia, SC is impressive. It is clean and very non-threatening in appearance. The centerpiece is the large, yet quiet, University of South Carolina. I felt a sense of "warm fuzzies" when I envisioned myself surrounded by rows and rows of books that extended from floor to tall ceiling in large rooms with ornate architecture of yesteryear.

I enjoyed the warmth of gentle spring that kissed my face as I meandered from the mammoth library over to the nearby Museum of Art, a quick walk across the capitol lawn. Upon my return, perhaps I'd stop and look at the interior dome of the old capitol building as I headed back to my car which I had easily parked nearby.

Perhaps not! This was a dream sequence after all. We hadn't gotten out of the car since early morning once again, and this was a hopeful delusion to keep me going.

Aiken, SC and Augusta, Georgia

Aiken, quaint and reasonably rural, is horse country. It is picturesque. Its adjacent neighbor, Augusta, is a hub of activity with facilities and necessities both places enjoy. Augusta offered ornate, old mansions and gardens that one would hope to see in the "old south." The Savannah River separates the towns.

Savannah Lakes on Savannah River

We parked the Dreamcatcher right out on the "outer banks" of the Savannah River at Baker Creek State Park. We were surrounded by water affording Ol' Tex access to fishing. We planned to look at a small community on the Savannah. But allow me to digress.

I realize that this may sound simple enough to you, but with walkie-talkie in one hand and Jeep steering wheel in the other, I guided the bus driver through the narrow, winding roads of the thick forest to get to the perfect parking spot.

Several times I had to say, "You'll have to bend in the middle for this curve." Or, his favorite, "You'll have to go real slow here because you are going to hit on one side." You must understand, once we had gotten inside the park, there was no turning around or going back the same way we came in!

Indeed, this was a harrowing experience for not only the Dreamcatcher, but the two residents who live in it full time. This was where we really learned how to communicate extraordinarily well and have enjoyed this benefit ever since.

The Village at Savannah Lakes, McCormick, SC

We wanted to see the Savannah Lakes Cooper Community which we had heard much about during our travels throughout this area. We did the tour de force with a salesman who could not look us in the eye. With each point, the possibility of living there moved farther down my list, but I listened. I'd looked enough and decided to let Ol' Tex be the judge. (By this point, I was ready to accept *any* place that had a land line for phone access and internet!)

We walked the property and drove in and out of the woods. We climbed through the thicket to get to the golf course where we admired the views. It was beautiful; *it was remote.* Aside from the duffers and deer, we would have little else to keep us company. So, what's wrong with that? Did I not mention really remote?

Baker Creek State Park

Baker Creek State Park is peaceful and serene. This was where we parked to take in Savannah Lakes. This is what "camping" is all about.

Remote to be sure, yet in a State or National Park, one expects and enjoys this ambience. I walked the woods while Ol' Tex fished the banks of the Savannah River.

The delicate scent of the pine forest wafted through my nostrils and I felt intoxicated by nature. Ol' Tex, my hunter-gatherer, was doing battle with the beasts of the water, or so I thought.

After a long walk through the woods, I returned to enjoy sunset over Savannah Lake just in time to see the last of four, ten-man canoes filled with girls from the prestigious Skidmore College in my home area of Saratoga, New York glide by on the water right in front of him. There he stood, fish pole in hand, and a silly grin on his face.

"TEX! *I thought you were fishing.*"

"Crystal," he bubbled grinning from ear to ear. "There goes Crystal."

As the last canoe glided into the setting sun and out of sight, I could hear the coach with his megaphone in the accompanying power boat: "Crystal, you're going to have to...."

"Did you catch any fish?"

"Crystal. There goes *Crystal....*"

Keowee Key on Lake Keowee

Directly north and through Sumter National Forest, we headed to Lake Hartwell where we stayed at a private campground just north of Anderson so that we could investigate *Upcountry, South Carolina.* We were surprised and delighted to find the clear, blue waters of Lake Keowee not nearly as remote as we had anticipated.

We moseyed on to the town of Clemson.

Clemson University

My soul embraced Clemson. As we drove through the large yet concentrated campus, I marveled at both the landscape and the architecture. It exuded history; it had an obvious past and an exciting future.

Clemson is located adjacent to several hundred acres of the State Botanical Gardens with miles and miles of nature trails. The campus explodes with possibilities.

As we reluctantly drove away, we saw a first class, brand-spanking new *Purdue University* student transport bus. Ol' Tex saluted as tears welled-up in my eyes for that which once was, and our wonderful experiences on the Purdue Campus.

Lake Lanier, Georgia

Gainesville is a bustling little city in the heart of Hall County, located in the northeast Georgia mountains. It offers lakes for fishing, educational facilities, cultural opportunities, medical facilities, shopping which would be enhanced to an even greater degree when the huge southeast shopping center opened in a year or two. Things couldn't be much better than they were when the real estate person concluded, "Hall County is not made up of *all* 'red-necks' as some think." She continued, but we both tuned out unintentionally after that statement.

Ol' Tex told redneck jokes all the way back to the grocery store where we immersed ourselves into the interesting and distinctively colorful local citizenry.

"Know when to go . . . ."

Lakes Burton & Rabun

Our tour de force of Rabun, Lumpkin, Habersham, and Hall Counties was all inclusive and complete in one day. I was dizzy from twisting in and out on the roads which hugged the waters. We even took in the wild and scenic Chattooga River as we whipped through the towns of Homer, Hollingsworth, Cornelius, Demorest, Mt. Airy, Toccoa, Habersham, Cleveland, Clayton, Clarksville, Helen, Dahlonega and more. We crossed Tallulah Gorge, a 1200 foot chasm and enjoyed the stirring scenery of the Appalachian Trail which winds through the counties. Much of the area is in the Chattahoocee National Forest and is a paradise of natural and rustic beauty.

We returned from the higher elevations into the north and west areas of Lake Lanier. The dramatic scenery was tantalizing with the excitement of spring bursting from the woodlands and lakes.

Atlanta's Playground

We moved and parked the Dreamcatcher just south of Athens in Bishop while we explored Lakes Sinclair and Oconee.

The list of exclusive communities around Lake Oconee seemed endless: Harbor View, Reynolds Plantation, Greatwaters, Port Armor, Lakeview Terrace, and Cuscowilla, to name a few. We sampled two of them which took up one full day.

Harbor View was interesting with all of its amenities including Polo Club, professional Croquet courts, tennis, swimming pools, aerobics studio, golf courses, marinas, restaurants, etc. Mickey Mantle as well as several Atlanta Braves are part of this community.

Reynolds Plantation

A first class operation, this lovely community had three of everything that was available in the other communities. I won't elaborate on the luxury of the setting, the beauty of the homes and the facilities, but it was one classy place. It was also remote which made it desirable to those escaping from the hustle-bustle of the city. It lacked the convenience of shopping, libraries, universities, and medical facilities. Its desirability was somewhat enhanced by its proximity to Augusta and Savannah.

This area is clearly a great escape for those who live in these cities and want a second home. For those who want convenience and cultural enrichment, it is too far away from everything.

All Aboard...?

We are on the ***Chattanooga Choo Choo!!!***

It was time to 'kick back' and have some fun. We toured some of the city and checked-out some of the fine shopping opportunities in the area. Since we were uncomfortable in the heart of downtown in a city that was strange to us, we only took in Warehouse Row and a quick look at Riverfront Park from the car as we crossed the Tennessee River at Market Street. We slipped back onto the major arteries and headed west of town to the large and aesthetically pleasing Hamilton Place Mall...it was a beauty. Somehow, I lost Ol' Tex in the place. *Hmmmmm...how ever could that have happened?* But, all good things must come to an end, and soon he remembered he had me on his frequency and paged me on the *shopping* walkie-talkie.

What's that? Oh, didn't I tell you? He has me on a short wave length! For our anniversary, rather than diamonds or gold, Ol' Tex bought me a shopping walkie-talkie, one that fits comfortably in pocket or purse so that he can call me from anywhere, anytime.

Back then, it was especially embarrassing, I might add, to have it go off when I was in either the dressing room or ladies room! Someone once suggested "Life is one cruel joke." Now, of course, with cell phones, we are oblivious to this type of thing. Back then, a man's voice in the ladies dressing room would have been rather startling.

Carrying The Cross

On Good Friday in the Southeast, significance and meaning for one of the holiest of all Christian observances was brought to the people by way of symbolic cross-carriers and followers. Between noon and 3 p.m., at different places, we observed reenactments of Jesus carrying the cross to the hill while others followed. I have to say, however, that not every technological improvement appears to be as aesthetically advantageous as it might at first seem--the cross on wheels being a good example!

Knoxville and Vicinity

Our timing couldn't have been better then when we arrived in northeast Tennessee. The hills were alive with buds that were ready to burst--and they did. As if on cue, the Master Director forced life into the dormant flora and delicate white, pink, and lavender buds began bursting throughout the Tennessee Valley. The production was so magnificently choreographed that I could hardly contain myself in order to wait for a look at the next morning's act. Apple, peach and cherry trees demonstrated breathtaking spectacles; tulips, azaleas and miscellaneous other blooms joined the ensemble throughout Easter week.

We took our time in this area enjoying the birthing of spring at the magnificent lakes, mountains, valleys, towns and within the city of Knoxville itself. It was a great time and Ol' Tex even got to fish on Tellico Lake.

Master Painter

The hills and valleys were infused with a warm, *new green,* forming a lush back-drop to spectacular terrain. Sunday morning when we climbed gently out of the valley at Knoxville into the Smokey Mountains, we were surrounded by trees of rich lavender-pink lace with white and off-white dogwood sprinkled throughout the landscape. The color was so warm and rich you could practically feel its beauty.

The threatening weather preceded us as we experienced a colorful and changing skyline. By the time we parked the Dreamcatcher at the lake in North Carolina, the sun was shinning and more blooms were bursting from earth and trees. We opened the door and stepped out into fragrance so potent that it could have been bottled up and sold.

I walked through the woods and around the lake noting I was alone except for several mallard ducks and three Canadian geese that began following me. Ol' Tex had fed these feathered friends earlier but they looked at me in eager anticipation for perhaps another hand-out. The warm air combined with the delicate, sensual, fragrance intoxicated me with springtime.

Hickory, North Carolina

Picturesque and darn near perfect, Hickory exemplified Hometown, USA. We eagerly drove to Lake Hickory to check out Oliver's Landing. Again, picturesque and perfect as well!

We were positively impressed with the Piedmont section of North Carolina. Historically impressive towns such as Statesville, Salisbury, Mooresville and others were scattered throughout the area. We even visited the northern most end of Lake Norman and enjoyed our tour.

"We shall return to the area once again," we decided, but Ol' Tex wanted to take a quick look at Pinehurst and Southern Pines before we head out to visit family.

At the time of the 1990's visit to the area, we had no idea how prophetic those thoughts were. In 2006 we moved to the piedmont area which we call home.

Campgrounds in the East

In the Eastern United States, it was difficult, at best, to find campgrounds that would accommodate a 40 foot motor home. Hook-ups with sewer and water were limited and power connections were often inadequate. Florida was an exception.

Ratings were poor at the time we were traveling, and getting someone to answer the phone was a challenge. We never did get to stay in Pinehurst area because of this. Perhaps things have improved.

During this particular run through the southeast, the weather got very cold and windy. We visited Ft. Chiswell and the old town of Wytheville, VA but contending with the elements took most of our attention. We continued to head on to "west by God Virginie."

Huntington & Charleston, WVA

Charleston was the "jewel in the crown" of West Virginia. Both cities were adjacent to the river, and Huntington even had a flood wall and gate to protect it from the rising waters of the mighty Ohio River.

Charleston's State Capital building was adorned with a gold dome. Its brilliance exuded grandness while nearby trees were ready to burst into spring. It is an old city but in mint condition.

After an all too quick tour of downtown, Ol' Tex took an unexplained turn and we immediately left the gorgeous interstate which was guiding us graciously back and forth across the Kanawha River. Within moments, the "highway" became a one lane road weaving itself skyward through the ridges. Trailer homes and shacks clung to the edge of a narrow pavement barely wider than a footpath which went on for miles and miles. Similar footpath ridge roads sprung off from the one on which we were driving. There was no place to safely turn around, so we continued.

We became more and more tense. Ol' Tex was the first to address the situation. "I hope they don't think we are Revenuers!"

"Ridge-runners???"

"Yup!"

And no way out. I shut my eyes and prayed. The unkempt, overgrown campsite we would call "home" for that night was looking better when we returned--with but a *hint* of buckshot!

Lexington, Kentucky

Speaking of "jewels," both the city of Lexington, and the State-owned Horse Park where we stayed were "top of the line."

A very large facility, the campground is adjacent to the Technicolor acres of first-rate, championship quality horses, activities, and shows.

The grounds of both places were well-maintained and picturesque. New blooms were bursting everywhere as we looked over hundreds of acres of Kentucky Blue Grass surrounded by white, rail fences, a *class act*, to be sure.

The city of Lexington was quite probably the most *pristine* of all the cities we have seen so far. It appeared to be safe, free of trash and in its original state. Large, beautiful, mansions line the street as you leave the main section of the downtown area.

Magnificent!

Cincinnati, Ohio

It was unfortunate, but circumstances did not allow us enough time to explore and enjoy Cincinnati.

We pulled into Oak Creek Campground with holding tanks full. We had reservations but we immediately became cognizant of the fact that there were no sewer hook-ups; we were not so sure we would stay. *Then we remembered, **there were no other choices***---we were back in the east where any kind of campground is a premium!

While I went in to register, Ol' Tex took the bus off to the dump station where he proceeded to dump the tanks *on his PANTS!!!*

Surely you don't want me to finish this story.

Home Again In Indiana

We parked at the private first-class pad next to the lake behind Jim's sister's home. It is still in the country, but the "country" is filling with beautiful homes and golf courses. This private resort remains one of our favorite campgrounds in the USA.

The biggest treat of all in this part of the country is to reunite with Ol' Tex's family when we visit Ft. Wayne.

Spring Comes Late To New York

Forsythia were just beginning to bloom as we headed across northern Ohio, western Pennsylvania, and on into New York. Rather than the usual thruway route, we decided to take the southern tier route and enjoy the rural scenery along Route 17 as we headed east.

Whoa! We *bumped* all the way to Corning! This road had to be at least as bad as I-10 in Louisiana. Now for those readers who have *not* traveled it, we're talkin' *BAD!* My head and body ached for three days after the first section.

Perhaps the beauty of the woods and hills where I walked while recuperating made it all worthwhile. Babbling brooks, clear, fresh streams, and new-born wildlife christened the paths on which I trod. Memories of yesteryear's pet woodchucks, chipmunks, rabbits, and other furry creatures abound as I watched with delight, the more cuddly signs of spring!

Can You Go "Home" Again?

It is disquieting to try to return "home" particularly when one has been away as long as I have. So many memories yet no solid stakes to attach them to. So much has changed, yet much remains the same.

Mostly, it all looks the same! Time has proven me wrong. The things I thought at the time could be better are far better than many can dream. These were wonderful times; my attitude toward some of them could have been better at the time. The people could not have been better. I was remarkably blessed to have had these special people in my personal history.

It seems strange to walk into the home where my parents lived after they retired with its familiar rooms and space yet know it now has become home to another family. It helps to remember the old farmhouse just down the road where I grew up and enjoyed many happy years.

The farmhouse is gone now as are the people. Our dairy farm has become a large and "successful" sod farm where the richness of the land is systematically being depleted by repeat harvestings of topsoil and earth. We used to cross the pastures to get to the beautiful Hudson River where I learned to swim on hot summer evenings after working all day in the fields. The fields have been lowered by several feet now, and I fear, in time, it could become nothing more than a flood plane.

The farm as well as the Hudson River and Valley hold many memories. So, too, does the Saratoga National Battlefield where I literally lived and the unique town of Stillwater, New York, my hometown.

Chapter 20

I wonder as I wander . . .

Traveling in the Northeast

Our unscheduled schedule called for several reunions in New York, New England, Maine and much of the northeast coast. We headed for Boston and it was good that we had decided on a brief stay just outside of the city. Ol' Tex reviewed this decision via sign language with one of the locals once we were on the major interstate. Seems the local didn't think there was enough space for the bus to travel the highway, and Ol' Tex shared a similar opinion about the local's little green car which had snuck in front of him from the right shoulder.

After Tex demonstrated the volume of Dreamcatcher's horn, the "green hornet" decided to show Ol' Tex the agility of his footwork on the braking system of his vehicle by applying the brakes once he arrived directly in front of the coach.

Sign language was used to end the discourse.

Kennebunkport

We stayed in the Old Orchard Beach area. I had visited this same area as a young teenager on summer vacation with friends. I remember Maine rather well considering how very long ago that was. The thing

I remember most, unfortunately, was our sleeping with all our clothes on because it was so cold in July.

This time, we arrived in Maine *before* the middle of May. Talk about cold! The sun was shinning brightly each day as if to compensate for the freezing nights. With gratitude, we welcomed spring which moved in during our visit.

We toured from Wells to Freeport via Jeep in order to see the various towns and cities. One of our favorite spots was Walker Point at Kennebunkport, a favorite of George and Barbara Bush as well. They were not at home when we visited but we did get to see the compound.

LOBSTER, LOBSTER, LOBSTER

The headline for this story was going to be *Boothbay Harbor*, but what we found there seemed more significant than the place.

We parked the Dreamcatcher in magnificent Shore Hills, a campground unlike any we had seen so far in the northeast. The facility was picturesque with large sights, good, clean surroundings, first class accommodations, and even a personal "deck" with dining room table! This was a place we could call "home."

In the afternoon we visited the quaint little shops in Boothbay Harbor and made arrangements with lobsterman Mr. Parkhurst to return at 5 o'clock for the lobster he would prepare for us.

Tex ordered a 2 pounder for himself, and Mark went to the bins and found a lively critter for me. I wanted the biggest lobster he had. So, we climbed up to the next row and he hauled out "Louie." I immediately bonded with him. Those beady eyes staring directly into mine from that beautiful six pound body begged me to turn him down. I did.

Tex kept threatening that I would end up "sick from too much lobster" the first week of our tour. "By the time you get to Nova Scotia, there won't be anything for you to eat."

I told the young man I'd settle for a three-pounder but I didn't want to "meet it" before he cooked it. He accommodated my request. For good measure, Mark threw in a few crabs and even a spider crab--just the legs since the body has something not fit to eat.

We enjoyed visiting with Parkhurst and Sons while we waited for our dinner to boil. We learned that Parkhurst supplies many large grocers around the country as well as restaurants. They presently supply all of Albertson's in Montana and are working at getting the entire chain.

His lobster boat was a beauty--and big! The interior is all teak and mahogany wood. He thought he might like to travel around the country in an RV one day once the boys were through school and the business was paid off. "Get as far away from the water as I can," he said.

But, after telling us about the whales he watched, the tuna he caught, the life at sea, Mr. Parkhurst decided, “I could no sooner leave the ocean than stop breathing.”

We had no trouble understanding. Minutes later, Mark came out with a huge bag filled with lobster and crab for us to take home and enjoy on our personal deck. While the sun warmed us outside, the delicious, fresh seafood warmed us inside.

Inlets, Harbors & Fishing Villages

We felt as if we were living in a movie. Everything was picture perfect! Tiny villages laden with lobster pots, shops filled with handmade crafts, and white church steeples poked gently through the richly treed countryside. Fresh! Crisp! New England at its finest.

We toured Boothbay, Boothbay Harbor, Ocean Point, East Boothbay, South Bristol, and Smugglers Cove. We then took Mariner and Pioneer Trail to Pemaquic Point Light House. While in this area, we felt no trip would be complete without a tour of Christmas Day (1614) at Christmas Cove in John's Bay. You will no doubt recall Captain John Smith and perhaps the Dixie Bull (1632). Okay, maybe I should have said, "History majors, you will enjoy...."

It was difficult to say "so long" to Booth Bay area, especially with Mr. Parkhurst & Sons on the wharf waving lobster at us, but it was time to head for Bangor and another family reunion.

Memories & Maine

Memories of kinship and youth were rekindled by a personal reunion. So, too, did the sights, sounds, and smells of Maine regenerate a sense of the past. Fields of wild, delicate Forget-Me-Nots and purple Violets added a gentleness to the earth while flowering fruit trees filled the air with a fragrance so sweet I wanted to bottle it. The potent scent of fresh, cut grass and thick woods with everything from white birch to northern pine filled my heart as well as my nostrils. Walking became a marriage of yesterday and tomorrow as my mind surfed the future and the past. It was great just to be alive and part of this nomadic existence.

Bar Harbor

More LOBSTER! This time we got serious and bought our own big lobster pot for cooking! We had honestly tried to make-do with what we had on board, but we were in lobster country and could not afford to waist time piddling around with small pots.

The village of Bar Harbor was quaint and filled with traditional gift shops and restaurants each touting the availability of lobster. Lobster cruises were available as were whale watching voyages. I had been on working lobster boats in earlier years, and although I always enjoy the sea, I decided that I would rather sink my money into the pot.

Acadia National Park

Our first rainy day since we began this northeast tour was spent in Acadia National Park. Arcadia is naturally crafted by the ocean's waters and glaciers. Although it is one of the smallest National Parks, it is filled with many gifts and secrets of the sea.

Rain caused us to enjoy much of the tour from our vantage point of the Jeep while we traveled the roads designed and donated by John D. Rockefeller. However, when we got to the sandy beach, we knew we had to get out and walk the shore.

The tour afforded us diversity of islands and mountains, sand and rock, pounding, thundering surf, solitude and silence. These diversities offered opportunities for contemplation and companionship. We were in harmony with nature.

Acadia had experienced a wealthy era with mansions and millionaires. In 1947, fire destroyed the forests and mansions but the beauty and wealth of nature remain for all to experience and enjoy.

Eastport

A small fishing village, Eastport is the most easterly point in the USA.

It was here that we spent the night *right on the coast* with the seagulls and whales. We bundled up, walked the beach, and when the tide was out, we walked the natural jetty to the nearby island in search of treasures from the sea. I was not disappointed when I found small, fragile half-balls filled sea urchins, several small seashells, and dinosaur bones with teeth. *Dinosaur!* Or was it from the Lock Ness Monster???

We drove north through Perry, Robbinston, and Calais to take a peak at the border crossing. Yup! It was there; a tight squeeze, but do-able. In the morning, we would get on the bus and leave the country!

Border Crossing

Not nearly as traumatic as our west-coast crossing, we pulled right up the border guard and declared we were American citizens on vacation.

"You don't sound like you're from Texas," the "Mounty" said to Ol' Tex who was hanging out the front window.

"Livingston, Texas!" Ol' Tex persisted. The guard stared back at him, "Where are you originally from?"

The air filled with silence. I couldn't stand the suspense any longer. "Ft. Wayne," I prompted in a hushed voice.

After what felt like an eternity, Ol' Tex chimed in, "Born and raised in Ft. Wayne, Indiana."

"Any guns?"

"Nope!"

"Guaranteed?"

"Guaranteed!"

"Have a good trip."

"But don't you want to see all my cooked fruit?" I wanted to ask as I re-belted my relieved position in the co-pilot chair. Better safe than sorry.

Author's Note: In various states as well as Canada, there are restrictions for taking fresh fruit (which I almost always have with me) across the borders. I happened to have had a good amount of fruit confiscated on the west coast before learning the rules.

St. Stephen & St. Andrew

First stops on the other side of the border were two quaint little villages along the sea. St. Stephen's claim to fame other than border patrol is the Ganong chocolate factory where the first hand-dipped chocolate was made.

St. Andrew was bustling with holiday tourists in anticipation of the Queen Victoria Day look-alike contest which would take place on Monday. We decided to skip all the excitement, buy our lobsters, and head back to the campground where we had a *primo* view of the sea.

Sometimes less is more.

And Speaking Of....

Less is more when the voltage dropped below acceptable, Ol' Tex had reinforced our inadequate electrical supply by enhancing it with the power booster purchased from Camping World. On low, this barely kept the minimum running. Therefore, by evening, he went out and flipped the switch from low to high. In the morning, the power had returned to sub-normal once again which was enough to blow my electric blanket. "Oh phooey," I said (or something like that!!!). Here we were, stop one on our extended tour of "Antarctica."

Maybe the whale-watchers could feign warmth and don summer shorts, but I want to tell you, it was c-o-l-d! Sharp, cutting, "crisp!"

Understatement of a Lifetime

One day, I was parking the coach on a narrow embankment overlooking the ocean while Tex was directing me into the spot. Suddenly, an irritated voice pierced through my walkie-talkie while I carefully looked through my rear-view mirrors.

"You are seeing a little too much of me are you not?"

Ol' Tex was gritting his teeth in my mirror while our bed was literally hanging off the cliff—several feet above the open sea.

New Brunswick

Victoria Day, a three day national holiday similar to Memorial Day in America, was underway when we arrived in New Brunswick. Holidays in Canada are a marvelous family oriented experience, people enjoying people. Everyone was out and about. I watched through our big picture windows and was reminded of the many summer evenings in Ocean City, Maryland (which has 33 city blocks of boardwalk) where we and other families "walked the boards" at night. What was interesting in New

Brunswick is that there were no shops, restaurants, or amusement parks to draw people out. This was strictly people enjoying people. Didn't Barbara Streisand acknowledge something similar? Ah yes, "People, people who need people are the luckiest people in the world."

We celebrated the holiday in St. Andrews, St. Stephens, and Sussex with *the people!*

Prince Edward Island

Signs warned us that there would be a toll to cross Confederation Bridge which spans the distance from New Brunswick to Prince Edward Island. Our concerns began after the first five minutes of transit at 90 km per hour. Another five minutes later, our concerns were addressed: $44.00 for the privilege.

After parking the bus, we headed out to North Cape to explore. We whipped through the village of Summerside and took the scenic route all the way to Elephant Rock before stopping. Here, we had no choice but to stop. No more road!!!

No Elephant Rock either!

It's on to North Cape where the tides meet and go in different directions. This is also where strong winds threatened to blow me off the farthest point. We watched for whales; we saw birds.

We made the uneventful trek back noting that all the lobster boats were parked in yards adjacent to houses. Not a good sign for lobster-lovers' evening meals. The absence of shanties and markets in route curtailed any remaining hope and we returned to emergency supplies of hot sausage and spaghetti. Life can be difficult.

PEI Perfection

Prince Edward Island is off the coasts of New Brunswick and Nova Scotia. This is where the blue of the sky meets the blue of the sea. Grass is greener and the earth is red. The Islanders are dedicated to farming and fishing. It appears to be an unencumbered life.

Here, the sun shines brighter, the air smells fresher, and the storms are more ferocious. We can attest to all of them. During the course of one day, during two of our exploratory journeys on the Island, a storm moved in and we thought we would be blown to kingdom come.

We hung-on tight in Charlottetown, the capital of PEI.

Charlottetown

The capital of Prince Edward Island, Charlottetown, is the birthplace of Canada. The waterfront is lined with green area and parks while quaint shops and restaurants abound.

To make any visit complete, one must dine on seafood at water's edge and watch the waves' crash against the shoreline. It is a quaint, old city, the hub of Prince Edward Island.

Nova Scotia

Should there ever be doubt in one's mind about the name, the bagpipe player standing on the knoll as you enter the province will convince you that this is New Scotland! Both the land and the sea fill your senses. Words would only serve to encumber the natural beauty. This is nature at its finest!

Halifax

Our first stop on the tour was the capital city, Halifax, NS. It is metropolitan in its traffic and buildings, yet seafaring in its surroundings and livelihood. Our tour included the old downtown as well as the ports which were filled with ships.

Mahone Bay

First stop on the scenic Lighthouse Route was Mahone Bay. The charm of the town is its traditional crafts and creativity displayed in simple shops by local merchants.

The town was founded in 1754 by "Foreign Protestants" who were brought in to create what became a world renowned boat-building industry. Each summer, the town celebrates this heritage with the Wooden Boat Festival. Perhaps the most notable and inspiring sights are the famed "three churches." You will notice them the moment you enter the bay area.

Town of Lunenburg

Founded in 1753 by German, Swiss, and French Protestant settlers, this picturesque, historic town was designated by UNESCO as a World Heritage Site in 1995. Again, a seafaring, ship building village, the people of the town are eager to share the food and the beauty of the area where they live.

Oak Island

From the mist and mystique of the sea we stumbled upon Oak Island known world-wide to both treasure hunters and adventure seekers.

Here, a mysterious system of tunnels and shafts originally discovered on the Island in 1795 have inspired two centuries of seekers to unsuccessfully try to uncover a pirate's booty. We found the island heavily fenced and guarded by dogs. We selectively investigated the area. Our imaginations served us well and the value of the experience surpassed the water-logged treasure buried beneath the sea.

Peggy's Cove

Some call it a "fishing village," but it was truly a *lobstering* village par excellence! It was small enough that this working village appeared to be in miniature, and the simple beauty of the place absolutely delights the soul.

The famous lighthouse is perched atop mounds of rock accessible from land. It is important enough to have its own post office inside! We excitedly climbed the rocks and took the necessary photos. Then we sat and watched the lobster boats as they passed into the nearby cove. This is an experience everyone should have at least once in a lifetime!

Experiencing the Masterpiece

From mainland Nova Scotia, we crossed Canso Causeway onto Cape Breton Island. True to its highly acclaimed reputation, this rugged, raw area of land conjoined with the sea to form the piece de resistance of years of environmental and geological sculpting. It was ours to explore and enjoy.

The drawbridge was up when we arrived at the Causeway affording us ample opportunity to bask in the excitement of our anticipated adventure, drink in the variety of lush greens and blues, and appreciate the breadth of our experiences as we plunged headlong into Nature's Masterpiece.

Surrounded by rich, thick, forests in variegated green, rolling hills, and craggy cliffs which hugged the coastline, we snuggled into a tiny cove at Bras d'Or near Baddeck where the quiet was ethereal.

Cabot Trail

We spent my birthday in the Cape Breton Highlands where we drove the famous Cabot Trail. We explored world-class vistas and the famous and rugged shoreline. The Highlands were a tree-hugger's paradise and a sailor's worst nightmare. Celtic mist forms large clouds of thick, dense fog making pea soup of land adjacent to the shore. It comes and goes. The fact that one is experiencing sunshine and a clear day does not necessarily mean the entire trail will be enjoying the same weather. Regardless, this was Nova Scotia at its finest hour...pristine and uninterrupted by mankind.

We watched for bald headed eagles and sought the company of whales. Moose were everywhere. We saw the evidence. It was a sight to behold and it was all within our grasp.

Once in a life time I pass this way. Let me live each of these days to the fullest. "I shall pass through this world but once. . . ."

Dreamers we once were. Doers we have become. We do live each day to the fullest; and, each day we are remarkably blessed.

Beady-eyed Bad Boys

And, speaking of blessings, somewhere between Maine and Nova Scotia I lost my camaraderie with the lobster and cut to the chase. I could walk up to any lobster tank, point to the biggest, meanest, bad boy waving his claw at me and say, "Weigh him!"

The farther in we went, the bigger our appetites and selections became until one night, we tagged and bagged two so big Ol' Tex said, "Put a saddle on 'em. We'll just ride 'em home."

That evening, for the very first time in our lives, neither of us could eat more than the claws on those bad boys! We backed away from the dinner table with two tails still sitting on our plates. Honest!

Alexander Graham Bell

We visited the Canadian National Historic museum devoted to *Dr. Alexander Graham Bell,* a most complete and educational opportunity.

Artifacts from his life of dedication to human communication and invention were thoroughly displayed in Baddeck near his beloved Beinn Bhreagh at Bras d' Or Lakes.

Canadian Fun Factoid

A one dollar gold piece is a loonie!

Fortress of Louisbourg

Because the Fortresse de Louisbourg had not officially opened for the season, we were offered a private, guided tour of the completely restored French town. We were not disappointed, but were we ever cold!

At the time of our visit, the major portion of the village was occupied by a French film crew making a documentary. We wanted to volunteer as "extras," but all the positions had been filled. So we toured and watched the cast and crew instead.

And so, "What is Louisbourg?" you ask.

It is a heritage, a proud, national heritage complete with folklore, legend, and even African slaves. It is a multi-cultured heritage that boasts ties to all of Europe and the West Indies. It remembers the natives who helped pioneers and early settlers to survive. The same settlers, in turn, fortified and expanded the meager existence of the natives.

It was founded in 1713 for cod fishing during a time when Europeans were establishing prosperous North American colonies while they struggled for continental supremacy. "Louisbourg enjoyed three peaceful decades as a French colonial seaport," and was "France's crown jewel of military strength and commerce in the New World," according to authorities.

Louisbourg was seized by the British during the War between the two countries in 1744 but was returned to the French as a term of the treaty at the end of the war. Again, the town flourished but it was conquered by the British in 1758 and destroyed in 1760.

Today, one fifth of the original village has been restored and the Parks Department immortalized it in the year of 1744. Players in period costumes roam the grounds and live and act as French settlers.

Au - revoir to Nova Scotia

It was difficult to say good bye to the fresh countryside, the pure, clean water, and the warm, welcoming people of this foreign land. We looked longingly out over St. Patrick's Channel as we drove east. We stopped at Glenholme, Masstown, Lower Onslow, Onslow, and Upper Onslow before heading back into New Brunswick.

Nova Scotia is the place for all who enjoy an uncorrupted, rugged, natural environment, who yearn to get back to nature. It is unencumbered by convenience yet affords one opportunity to address all needs. Its beauty is in both its simplicity and abundance.

It has rejuvenated our spirits and taught us to enjoy all that is ours to embrace.

The Beaches of New Brunswick

Along the far east coast of New Brunswick, Detroit de Northumberland Strait, is the French-Canadian summer vacationland. To accommodate us, summer arrived the same day we did with temperatures in the eighties.

We stopped at Parlee Beach in Shediac but had to go to Pointe-du-Chene to purchase our lobsters for dinner. (The lobster factory in Shediac did not have any live lobster left!)

By now, more French was being spoken than English, so we knew that if we were going to be in the Bathurst area the following day, we had better brush up on our French.

Petit-Rocher

Our last stop before heading into Province de Quebec was Petit-Rocher on Baie des Chaleur (Chaleur Bay). We were fortunate to be able to park the Dreamcatcher on the shore while we explored the immediate area. It was a cold, foggy, rainy day and we were unable to enjoy quiet walks on the beach as the sea raged against the shore. It was a magnificent sight defining the strength of nature. By morning, the wind quieted enough to permit further travel.

Crossing La Gaspesie - Le Quebec Maritime

We traveled the coastline from Petit-Rocher to Campleton where we entered the Province of Quebec at Metapedia. From there, we traveled north along the Metapedia River. At many times during this trip across the peninsula, I was reminded of the beautiful Idaho Panhandle particularly along Clear River from Butte, Montana to Kamaih, Idaho.

When we reached the St. Lawrence, we traveled Ouest (that's West in French) right along the Seaway in dense fog and rain until we reached Rimouski where we stopped and stayed for the night. The remainder of our trip along the St. Lawrence was brilliantly sun-filled and awesome. This was truly a gift.

Rimouski

Rimouski is a reasonably good sized city for the region and I began practicing my French in order to ready myself for our stay in Quebec City. I managed a few belated oui (s) and several merci (s), but by the time we arrived in Quebec City, my speaking French still felt woefully inadequate.

Quebec City: An Absolute "Must-See"

We enjoyed a two hour guided Gray Line tour which provided us with the wherewithal to enjoy Quebec City on our own later on. We were delighted to have both opportunities.

We faced a nearly impossible decision when we tried to select a place to have lunch. There are many fine French restaurants available. Once we had decided upon Restaurant le Cavour, however, we were overwhelmed by the caring and concern of the entire staff---from our French waiter to the chef!

After a delightful luncheon, we combined shopping and sight-seeing. I was becoming better and more confident in my use of French although I did notice people convert to English once I responded in French. Finally I asked one of the locals if there was something wrong with my "Bonjour." She assured me my "bonjour" was perfectly fine, "It is your accent that betrays you."

Now Ol' Tex took the other route which he enjoyed immensely.

It went something like this:

"Bonjour Monsieur!"

"How---dy," was his cool, drawn-out response.

"Where are you from?"

"Texas," he would say with a grin reaching from ear to ear (or brim to brim depending on your point of view). I lost him to the French girls several times; and, had I not gone back to pick him up, he would still be standing there, cooing his little cowboy heart out! (Did I mention he would go absolutely nowhere without his ten-gallon, signature cowboy hat!)

While Tex was being entertained by the ladies, I managed to make some chic French clothing purchases chez shoppee.

(You do what you have to!)

Chapter 21

Chuga Chuga . . . WooWoo!

Returning to the US of A

We chose to enter the States through Vermont this time. Jim wanted to revisit some old haunts from his first job out of college which included people and places in Vermont.

Burlington, Middlebury, and Rutland were stops along the route as we worked our way back to the Saratoga, Schuylerville, Stillwater, Mechanicville areas of New York State. Our travels brought on great melancholy as we contemplated our early years. We roamed the familiar yet distant haunts.

This would be our last, great, tour before going "back to work" at the difficult job of finding and deciding on a place to put down roots. In a way, we knew we were "heading home." And yet, we still had no idea where it was going to be. We had mixed emotions.

We had more areas to search............... *"and miles to go before we sleep."*

Saratoga National Historical Park - Saratoga Battlefield

No doubt, the Battle of Saratoga was the "turning point in the American Revolution," but for my Brother Bill and me, the Battlefield was where we grew up. We took advantage of the time we had and went to the Visitor's Center, picked up a guide, and headed out on the park tour to compare our version of what really happened on this land to that of the Feds. After we had grown up and left the old homestead, the National Park Service stepped in and both claimed and changed it.

Some may see General Burgoyne's surrender during the Campaign of 1777 as the thing of greatest significance for these historic lands. We saw the hayfields, the wheat fields, and the cornfields. We saw where the very old block house used to be and the area where towns' people used to come to picnic with friends, families, and church groups. We saw where the ball fields once were, long gone now since the Feds "improved" and made authentic with signage these rolling hills overlooking the Hudson River.

We saw where Mother and Dad planted our family garden on top of the hill each year--where we would go after dinner in the evening and sit on the hilltop eating homegrown water melon while we watched at a distance, yachts and barges going up and down the Hudson.

We saw where our orchard used to be, and where, in the evening, we would follow the hedge-row to the River to take a quick dip after working in the fields during hot summer days. We saw wholeness and goodness. We saw yesterday.

On our way back to the Dreamcatcher that evening, we once again stopped by the cemetery to check on our newly planted flowers, a Mona Lisa lily for Mother and a Star Gazer for Dad, Incarvillea for Mary, Cliff, & Bill. We had raised the gravestone and it was looking much better as were the other flowers we had added to the plot.

Yesterday was a lifetime ago. Yet, for me, the folks of yesterday are a part of who I am today.

Movin' On

Engulfed in nostalgia of yester-year, I noted: Everything was different but nothing had changed. No, that was not true: *I had changed.* My world of yesterdays would always remain. It was me that was *movin' on.*

Maryland, 'Our' Maryland

How would we feel about our Maryland now that two years had elapsed? We had lived in Maryland longer than any of the dozen or so places we had lived during our years together, so it was as much "home" as anywhere we had ever lived.

Surprisingly, there were no strong emotions concerning our old estate and community. More than anything, we were annoyed with the congestion created due to greatly increased population. Mostly, I expect I was more upset to note the absence of emotions.

It was simply another time, another place, another life. Amen.

Ghosts of the Past

A visit to our former home in Forest Hill was a treat in several ways. First, we viewed the property and enjoyed a fabulous visit with former neighbors. Our old homestead and grounds which we sold just before leaving the area were as lush and breathtakingly gorgeous as ever. More importantly, we enjoyed the beauty; we did not miss it.

Our old stomping grounds had changed very little. Pleasantview Farms was as lovely as ever. Downtown Bel Air remained much the same only more congested, and, this time, not from cows crossing Main Street as they had when we first moved to the area.

We left once again with no regrets but a great sense of satisfaction.

Suicide Circle & the Belts

The only way to head south out of the Baltimore area is by leaving early Sunday morning when the beltway, also known as "suicide circle," is not as heavily traveled. From suicide circle, you continue south on I-95 (another test of nerves) around the Washington, D.C. beltway where you cringe and close your eyes (just kidding about the "close your eyes" part, sort of).

As we cruised south thru scandal land, we wondered what Slick Willie was up to now that the wars and impeachment were over. Ol' Tex wanted to "do lunch" with Hillary but at that time, she was spending a lot of time in New York!

A political junkie, I am forever tied to D. C., but until they clean-up the city, I will probably never again be able to stop for even a visit. Our last few trips to the nation's capital were so unnerving that we did not enjoy them. This is, sadly, the murder capital of the nation, a real pity. I still think we should send the troops in to clean up this city before sticking our nose in the affairs of the rest of the world. Selfish, I suppose.

We rounded the curve and crossed the Woodrow Wilson drawbridge over the Potomac then into Alexandria, Virginia. As we looked back, we noted that the District of Columbia was obscured by clouds much as the future of America is metaphorically obscured by the uncertainty of a cloudy, self-absorbed government.

(Some things never change.)

Update

Since that time, we have returned to the area. The traffic is worse, if that is possible, and, of course, it has gotten more dangerous. So much has happened since then to our own country and to the world. I still long to see it all once again, but some things are best achieved through memory.

Carry Me Back to Old Virginie and Colonial Williamsburg

Our years of living in Maryland had afforded us many opportunities to visit and know Williamsburg, Virginia. It is always fun to return and glimpse the excitement of years' past--ours as well as the colonists!

Lush green, deciduous trees mingle with burly evergreens and grow thicker and richer with each mile on the approach as we rolled gently along through the forests of Virginia toward Colonial Williamsburg. I was certain the vegetation could get no prettier when blooming magnolia trees sprung forth and ushered us into colonial gardens filled with colorful perennial blooms.

This is the appetizer to Williamsburg. The main entree, of course, is the Pottery Factory where you literally "shop til' you drop." Miles and miles of warehouses on hundreds of acres have become the meat and potatoes of this familiar destination. We shopped and looked longingly at fountains, brass, baskets, silk flowers, linen----you name it--but alas, we realized we could not buy. We had no place to put these material delights.

The dessert of Williamsburg is the College of William and Mary, one of the oldest, most reputable, and certainly, most beautiful campuses in the country. Colonial red brick fencing surrounds the red brick buildings that house the classrooms, lecture halls, and auditoriums. Red brick sidewalks route you to and from the buildings and offices. Light green moss was growing from the thick brick fencing.

Colonial Williamsburg is always a pleasant place to spend time.

Note: On a visit approximately a decade later, the area was much the same except for the Pottery Factory which was on a noticeable decline since the owner's death. It was sad to see considering the many wonderful memories we have of this former decorating mecca.

All Aboard?

We said our good-byes to Williamsburg knowing that it would be awhile before we found time to visit this enchanting area again. It was time to continue the *search for our personal paradise*, a place to settle down, a community where we could put down roots.

Eventually, I came to realize that what I was searching for was "Utopia." ***Utopia is everywhere and nowhere.*** It took me a few more years to accept the fact that Utopia is merely a state of mind.

Pinehurst Area

Again, finding an adequate place to park the Dreamcatcher in North Carolina is a bear! We rejected three losers before going way out of our way and settling for a "not-so-hotsy" campground which was nearly out of the state. We parked the motor home and climbed into the Jeep the next morning to head out for the day.

Pinehurst, Southern Pines, Aberdeen, Laurinburg.

Amid the massive pine trees there was *golf, golf, golf, and golf!!!* We spent a day looking--a whole day in the car. By the end of the day, we hated it and we hated each other. This was no place like home! This was definitely not Utopia!

On to the beaches.

Coastal East

We decided to get a new perspective on the Carolinas from the coast. So, we put the bus in gear and pointed it toward the Atlantic.

We headed for the Wilmington area and saw beaches: Holden, Sunset, Ocean Isle, Kure, Carolina, etc. We saw plantations (with a capital "P"): St. James, Winding River, Magnolia, etc. You get the picture. We saw congestion; we saw beach shacks; we saw T-shirt factories such as Wings and Waves. This was the view from the beach perspective.

It seemed that we were staunchly and obviously making comparisons. The question was to what? There had to be an "elsewhere" which we had seen that was a better choice to put down roots.

My patience was waning. We existed running from one bad campground to the next which we categorized as bad or, "God forbid," even worse! During this particular North Carolina coastal tour, we could find but one campground and it was what we referred to as "end of the road" at best!

Vacation season in full swing with the 4th of July weekend rapidly approaching, we couldn't get into campgrounds at Myrtle, Charlestown, Hilton Head, or Savannah.

"It doesn't get much worse than that," to coin a phrase, and I was not fairing it well. I *had* suspended criticism, judgment, and complaining in general, but I want to tell you, I was ready to *burst at the seams*. This had become one great opportunity to practice "an attitude of gratitude."

I turned to politics, always distracting if not satisfying. I was not disappointed. There was "dead duck" Willie at the podium trying to look like a hero dragging a news conference on and on, avoiding good questions, crowing about war stories. "What about Saddam?" I wondered. God only knows what he has been mixing up in his bath tub while we play footsie with Slovadon Milosivitch! Maybe watching Slick Willie was not the answer either.

Myrtle Beach - Ready or Not

The campground hosts were not sure whether they could accommodate us but they were willing to consider. So off we headed for Myrtle Beach. Anything had to be better.

Home Is Where You Park It!

After booking ourselves into a "spendy" campground on the coast for three days and paying the big bucks, we realized that a half a day would have been quite enough, thank-you! But, we had fun. Ol' Tex bought a T-shirt that said, "I survived Myrtle Beach," and I bought one that said, "Myrtle Beach ain't 'the place'."

We never had to turn on any music of our own but boogied to the beat of Urban ethnic wrap, Latin American sounds, and tantalizing, trendy rhythms of today's tempo. Yup, we were "cruizin'."

Weekend warriors, out in full force, were burning burgers on the bar-be while we battled bugs. This was livin' *"and the livin' is easy,"* or so the song says.

"Fish are jumpin...." Yeah! Right!!" Ol' Tex never took one of his dozen or so new lures out of the box. "Too shallow," he admonished after a stroll along the beach. (We're looking at the Atlantic Ocean here, folks!)

Oh well, we seemed to enjoy it all or perhaps it was the fact that we wouldn't have to move the bus again in Pirateland until Tuesday.

"What's that you ask, mate-ee?"

You mean I didn't mention the coop de` trauma?

Pirateland

We called ahead to reserve a spot at Pirateland thinking nothing of their friendly response, "We'll work you in." Our supposed challenge was to arrive after 11:00 a.m. This we did.

"Your *balance* is $118.62 and spot 1264 on Captain Ahab Way is yours for three nights."

"Look out mate-ees," and off we blindly went. After all, according to the Trailer Life Directory, the camper's bible, this was a very highly rated 8.5/9/9 campground.

"They gotta be kidding," I shrieked. "We're going back for another assignment."

Undeterred, Mr. "No-Sweat," replied in a disgustingly cool, calm demeanor, "Now, they did the best they could. This will do."

He brought the bus in, missed the post and bird bath by a quarter of an inch while the awning kissed the trees and I cried into my walkie-talkie, *"It can't be done!"* We weren't even within eye-sight of #1264.

Fellow RVers gawked nervously as panicked onlookers ran to the side and held their breaths in unison as Ol' Tex forged ahead.

Sight #1264

We arrived at Sight #1264. I quickly stashed the Jeep out of the way and shut my eyes as the driver began backing up. I opened one eye in time to note in horror there was no way we could possibly hook the sewer, electric, and water from the present position and as far as I was concerned, there was no other position.

I raced to the door of the bus trembling all over and shouted, *"You get out and look!!"*

He did.

With great wisdom, Ol' Tex reasons, "Won't work. We're gonna have to move it around."

I raced to the door again and shouted, "You direct! I'll park it."

We wiggled and inched forward, then backward. "Hard right! Hard left!" he barked into the walkie-talkie. Then we did it all over again and again and again.

Perspiration dripped from my over-worked, over-stressed brow. I put the big machine in neutral and pulled the emergency brake.

"No," Ol' Tex reasoned, "I don't like it here. We're gonna have to park it catty-whomp across the spot."

"CATTY-WHOMP???"

"Forward, hard right, hard left. . . ." Those were the words that locked out my next personal opinion on the matter.

There you have it. My sweat and stress; Texas's wisdom. We parked the Dreamcatcher catty-whomp on #1264.

When I think back on it, that's pretty much how life on the road was: sweat, stress, wisdom. We managed to share them equally.

Gifts by the Sea

During our stay along the coast, we were entertained by a Mama and Papa duck plus four wee ones. They moved with the Mama through land and water as if they were appendages. We also enjoyed watching two very colorful Peckers of the Wood. Their full maroon head dresses and formal tuxedo style body suits of black with white made these feathered friends much more than common red headed woodpeckers.

We also enjoyed watching a furry friend carefully remove peanut butter from the sandwiches we fed him and leave the bread for an interesting variety of reddish brown and tan stripped road-runners, southern cousins to Pecos Pete of Ft. Stockton, Texas.

Our short stay on Myrtle Beach turned out to be rather entertaining after all.

Return to Charleston

Hot, sultry, lazy days filled our stay in historic old Charleston, SC. We meandered around the town enjoying the sights and smells, shopping in the famous old city market place. We watched the black women craft sweet grass baskets. The work of Celestine Wilson caught our eye and we were so impressed with it that Ol' Tex said, "We can't leave here without one of these baskets for our new home."

We asked Ms. Wilson about her work. She told us the historic baskets. "They are made of long leaf pine needles, Sweet grass, Palmetto leaves, and Bull Rush." According to Wilson, “It is craftsmanship handed down from generation to generation by slaves from West Africa."

"Though the art is hundreds of years old, it has never changed and is found only in this part of the U.S.A."

Content to Settle

Coming down the East Coast again was a God blessed opportunity. I did not feel frustrated or irritated by the congestion, over-population, heat, rain, road-rage, and bugs. I was content in knowing that at one point in my life I would have been willing to put up with all of it in order to be "in the thick of things." Today, I am not. I am content to settle on a place that is not in the "thick" but filled with friendly people living in a gated enclave with heated pools, fitness center, golf courses, a billiard room, library, classrooms, auditorium, stage, banquet facilities for holiday and gala events, and medical facilities with an airport reasonably nearby for destinations beyond the USA.

The possibility that loomed large in front of us at the time was Del Webb's Sun City Hilton Head. Our visit there is only a short commute to Savannah.

Del Webb Hilton Head

We were pleasantly surprised to be able to put this community on our "possibility" list. Tucked safely away on the mainland, this community has everything to offer in the lifestyle we want. Savannah is a half hour away and Hilton Head Island with all of its amenities is less than fifteen minutes away. There are ample fishing and boating opportunities available for Ol' Tex.

Directly adjacent to the gated community is the land where the University of South Carolina at New River did build its new campus. At the time of the original visit, we had been told that there would be a golf cart path for an easy commute to and from class. Over time, this proved to be a good idea that did not come to fruition.

Note: *We were not totally convinced at the time that this was the place. We did, however come back several years later to rent and live in Sun City Hilton Head for a year while waiting for our home to be built in the Charlotte area.*

Historic Savannah

No visit to the area is complete without walking the old cobblestone streets of the historic river front at the Cotton Exchange in Savannah where shops and restaurants are plentiful.

It was a fire-cracker hot 4th of July, crowded with people enjoying a stroll along the lovely Savannah River. What better way to celebrate our nation's birthday?

B-Beep! B-Beep!!

The bus rolled west--Macon, Opelika, Auburn, Montgomery, Selma, Demopolis, Meridian, Vicksburg.

Yup! We're rolling and relieved to be heading west where campgrounds and campers are friendly. We had a successful visit to Hilton Head providing us pause and at least one eastern possibility as far as putting down roots. Now, we were ready to relax. "Heading home" was just the ticket.

Mississippi

One of my favorite *fun* places to *visit* is Mississippi. Laid-back, unassuming, detached from the dog-eat-dog world, it is the first friendly place west of the frenzied East Coast. Perhaps that's why I like it so much--you can *feel* the difference.

Mississippi is green and lush with forest-rich land throughout. In July, foliage is as green and lush as it is in the springtime. I-20 is lined so profusely with tall, green trees that you have the feeling you are traveling through a tunnel created by nature. While the thermometer displayed a solid 95 degrees, the ambiance was cool and soothing.

There's a sense of romance about Mississippi. Maybe it is because this is where the land meets the mighty Mississippi. You simply can't cross this land or thematic river without a dozen or so songs and stories haunting your heart and soul.

Shreveport, Louisiana

Friendly! A good place to stop for a respite.

Put the Peddle To the Metal

I recently learned one sorry lesson in motor coach technology. When you depress the throttle, (push the go peddle) from the driver's seat, the "mechanics" are really a series of electronic inputs that run some 40 feet to the device under my bed pillow called a King Control box, named for the manufacturing company who built what we now know to be a *defective* unit. This device *should* tell the motor coach to "go" and "how fast to go."

Yup, this expensive little baby was defective from the "get-go" and a cause for major corporate pow-wows between Monaco and King Control.

It's a long, irritating story, but the reason we knew there was potential for disaster was that someone inadvertently sent us a letter advising us that attention was needed in that area. When we made an appointment and went into the Monaco factory to have it fixed, they, in effect, told us, "If it works, don't fix it."

But Ol' Tex with his keen mind and a disposition for perfection could not seem to accept this resolution. King Controls had said, "We sent Monaco new boards for a reason."

Tex tackled the problem while we were waiting for yet another over-due parts delivery from Monaco at Livingston. Seeing major discoloration on said equipment, he dutifully called King. "Don't take that coach on the road," the service tech told him. You have a serious problem. You were lucky you weren't stranded."

So, we sent the "go power" back to Minnesota and held our collective breath until it was returned and then re-installed by non other than our own mechanical wiz, Ol' Tex.

Chapter 22

Homecoming Edition

The L-O-N-G Wait

With no choice, we waited for our package from Monaco which should have been in Livingston, Texas two to three weeks earlier.

Of course we called! The response, much like the cliché check, "It's in the mail."

Although we always enjoyed our stay at home base Livingston, after a week anywhere, we itch to travel. So a week really begins to push my comfort zone. I had done enough maintenance chores, cleaned enough crannies, reorganized enough closets, and found enough "good" in small things to last me until the next go-round.

Observations from…Another Thing I like About Texas

Texas friendly!

Indeed. There is nothing quite like Texas friendly.

Another thing, people ask to help you when you go into a store or any other place of business. At first, you sense that someone is *invading your space* as the employee moves quietly in on you. As customers and consumers, we have become accustomed to fending for ourselves in this day and age of "self service" when businesses feel "inconvenienced" by customers. But once you realize this sincere, smiling, real person is doing his/her job and is happy to do it, you begin to enjoy this now novel idea of caring called "waiting on you."

Then there is the conviviality between co-workers like the employees in the parts department of Bounds Chevrolet/Ford/Jeep (well you get the idea) Dealer in Livingston who hung a sign under the clock that reads, "This clock will never be stolen because Joe and Scottie are always watching it."

How about the dentist who doesn't bother to tell you that your appointment is on his regular day off---just so he can accommodate ***your*** schedule! That would be our Dr. Woody Reese along with his right-hand Mrs. Reese of Livingston both sacrificing their personal time to see us.

Texas is rich with nature's rewards. The sky is vivid blue with whiter than white puffy clouds. Occasionally, some of the white clouds turn to a dark grey/blue warning of the potential for storm. Then a rainbow will appear out of nowhere without a drop of rain appearing.

When rains do come, we're talking *real* rain, Texas style. We used to call them "belly-washers," when the heavens open up and water teems down for hours clearing in time for evening. Then, there's the breathtaking solitude of eventide.

Evenings glow pink and warm with the setting sun, promising an even better tomorrow.

Wally World Revisited

Earlier I wrote about Livingston Walmart. It deserves an encore mention.

Going to Livingston Walmart is an event, a real happening! You sample freely the good-sized servings from the bakery, foods, produce, and deli. Actually, you are wise if you shop around lunch time accomplishing two things at once-- addressing your shopping needs as well as eating lunch out. *Who said, "There's no such thing as a free lunch."*

It is a Super Wally, open 24 hours a day; and, if that is not enough, during the weeks we were there, they were preparing for the *new* grand opening (whatever that is) since it had been open at this location ever since we had been traveling through East Texas.

Regardless, the employees who worked there were plenty exited about the upcoming event. I talked to some of the folks about the planned affair.

"It's going to start at 8 in the morning and gonna last all day into night!"

"My granddaughter is gonna perform."

"My neighbor is one of the performers."

Mostly, however, it is a place to mingle with the masses. Originally, I called it a lesson in ethnic diversity but that explanation or definition is too restrictive. The Livingston Walmart experience transcends even those explanations. Livingston Walmart is a cultural extravaganza.

Windmills

Not so unlike Don Quixote, Ol' Tex has been chasing air conditioner leaks to the point of obsession. (I was tempted to use the word 'madness' but at this point, he was becoming paranoid about what I wrote about him.) Anyway, he had added so much Freon to the motor coach that I was tempted to buy stock in the company. Not one single connection had been lost to his scrutiny or tightening. He had studied, researched, searched, and tested the system engaging every iota of his mechanical/ electrical genius and education.

The last I saw of him, he was in his nightshirt and cap, with flashlight in hand, headed out into the night to watch the last installment leak out!

Deep in the HOT of Texas

We wanted to see Texas in July and August. **NO!** *We had not been drinking loco water.* Since Texas remained on our list of potential home base areas, we wanted to see it at its hottest. We were not disappointed.

The consoling part of the heat-filled experience was that most of the rest of the country was even hotter that year, and certainly dryer. New York, Maryland, New Jersey, Pennsylvania, Indiana, Kentucky... basically everywhere but the absolute Northwest coast was consistently as hot and usually worse from weather reports we watched and referenced.

That did not make it any easier to experience, but one obvious difference in Texas is that no one ever mentions it. As a matter of fact, one particularly scorching day, Ol' Tex engaged in a casual exchange of pleasantries with a fellow Texan who inquired about his well-being.

"HOT!" Tex responded to his query.

"I hadn't noticed," said the straight-faced gentlemen who walked away leaving Ol' Tex a tad dismayed.

Moving On

Finally, parts arrived and we were "on the road again."

It took some maneuvering, but we headed as directly west as possible from Livingston to Old Settlers RV Park in Round Rock, Texas which is located about half way between Austin and Georgetown, Texas on the old Chisholm Trail. We were eager to see if the Del Webb's Sun City at Georgetown, Texas was as magnificent and we remembered it to be. We both had grave concerns that our memories may have exceeded reality.

Our "plan," which even I must admit, was an extremely intelligent one. First, we were going to completely survey the surrounding areas of not only Georgetown but Austin, San Marcos, New Branfels, Temple, Waco, and even on up to Dallas, Ft. Worth. *BUT. . .*

The Call...

As soon as we parked the Dreamcatcher in what would turn out to be its home for the next month and a half, we got a phone call from a fellow by the name of Tim Dugan. We had met Tim during our first visit to Sun City Texas and he was the dearest sales associate we had met during our national tour in search of a place to call home. Ol' Tex answered the phone.

"We're in the Austin area. Mmmm. I guess we could come on up and take another look...."

Talk about psychic!

And, with that exchange, we abandoned the intelligent plan of visiting the surrounding area and headed straight for Sun City in Georgetown the following morning. Keep in mind that we had not heard from Tim or Sun City Texas since our first visit, quite some time earlier. He had no way of actually knowing that we were only a few miles away in Round Rock. Further, he called within the first few minutes that we were there!

Eerie and serendipitous things would continue to happen.

The homes turned out to be what I had envisioned when I had mentally designed my ideal. In case you have never tried "visualizations," I endorse them fully.

The community was everything we had remembered *and more*! Emotions combined with intelligence and counsel from a higher source kept us returning day after day. Regular folks on the model home tour communicated exactly what we needed to hear at that point in time. I felt as if we were in a dream. None the less, I continued to pray, "Send me a sign...."

Send Me a Sign

We looked tirelessly without success of finding the perfect home. Finally, we decided to look at building lots, *maybe* even consider putting down a small sum to hold a lot until we were more certain and ready. Then, out of nowhere, our perfect home suddenly appeared. There it was sitting right on the sixth green! Talk about a sign!!!

"Could we be dreaming?" was our first question.

Obviously, it was *"meant to be"* or it would not have been sitting there. An award winning architecturally designed fountain on the front of the house was overwhelmingly beautiful. Along with that, there was the most fantastic golf view ever in the back and it could be seen from all sides of the house and every window. We agreed to purchase 102 Holly Springs Court--without hesitation the day we saw it!!!

Can you believe that one? "Without hesitation." It was everything we ever wanted, and more. BUT...***we*** don't do things like that! We evaluate, we sleep on it, we discuss the pros and cons; we spend time making major decisions—about everything. Not this time!!!

So after a full day of searching, and we returned to Tim's office he asked, "What do you think?"

I said, ***"We'll take it!"***

Tim literally fell right off his chair and Ol' Tex's mouth fell wide open. This was not me. I had been taken over by . . . . We'll never know, but it was one of our best decisions.

The landscape architects had been competing in a contest, and our fountain design had won first place. Because of whatever in-house reasons, the house was designed and built with tons of wonderful upgrades that we would never have felt were "cost effective" or whatever practicality we could conjure up. They were all there and included in the home. There was no debating, deciding, torment; the upgrades were to be ours.

There was a lake for Ol' Tex and college in town for me. There was a Senior University in community, plus classrooms for every possible learning experience one would ever want.

There would be opportunities to return to the stage—right there within the gates of the community, and a computer lab with classes by experienced teachers and other professionals.

Beyond that, there was a first class fitness center with indoor and outdoor pools, a woodshop and an interdenominational worship center. Plus, there were three golf courses and two restaurants. The Village Center within offered opportunities to shop, eat, and buy golf carts and equipment and service. Parking was abundant.

Pink Cloud

At that point, I jumped on one of the soft, puffy clouds that start pink in the early a.m. and return to pink at night. Ol' Tex was happier than I had *ever* seen him. We had three days and four nights of this frivolous behavior before we went in to apply for a mortgage. This was of no concern or worry to us because we were financially capable of this purchase. This was the point where logic ends and lunacy begins.

Knowing full well our entire situation, the financial institutions wanted a "source of monthly income." There was no explaining that we take out only what we *need* from our financial portfolio. The banks, in their infinite wisdom, wanted us to hire a financial manager to send a check each month to pay our bills and expenses.

There was no explaining that Ol' Tex is the best "financial manager" on the planet. There is no one on earth who knows more about managing our money!

We had researched financial matters from "sea to shining sea." I can remember spending Sunday afternoons in Law libraries at both the County Courthouse and the University of Maryland School of Law, researching financial matters. We had flown into Chicago for money management seminars with the pros that only served to confirm our own findings!

This is Jim's passion; he *loves* finance! And, he is *good.* We are both good, but he has made it his avocation. Actually, more. It is his life!! And to think that some young whippersnapper, with red ink still drying behind his ears might manage our money is like leaving money on a door step for a burglar so he wouldn't have to be bothered breaking in to steal it.

This issue became sheer "Mickey Mouse" nonsense. In the end, the mice won---sort of. First, the chief writer in the family created a document which said "a program had been established..." and we presented this official paper, hot off the Dell laptop's printer, to the mortgage company. Then....

You remember the kid with the "red ink" stains behind his ears we mentioned? Well, he had to write a letter, send it to our mail forwarding company who sent it priority mail to the Georgetown Post Office which in turn gave it to us where upon we took it to the mortgage company confirming that the investment company would send us a check until such time as we rescinded the agreement. The mortgage company was happy. We continued to bang our heads on the wall and rant and rave for a couple more days until we realized we were the only people being hurt by this *brouhaha!* So we quit and went shopping.

Need Everything

Day after day, we shopped. We measured. We shopped some more. We needed everything. We had nothing for the new home.

We had spent the final five years before we quit working, getting rid of *all our stuff.* Now we needed it all back!!

Somehow, after being constantly together for twelve hundred sixty-three days, fourteen hours and thirty-two minutes in three hundred and twenty square feet of space, we decided we would be happy in a very large home with two separate wings. Well, that's what we ended up buying anyway.

Sticker Shock

It took us a few days to get used to the prices on home furnishings. It had been a while since we bought furniture, appliances, and window treatments. Then, we needed to adjust to style. Finally, we arrived at a point of "anything at any price." *Let us be done with it.*

The problem was compounded by many factors. We had never been in Austin or the surrounding area before. We had no clue of how to get around this busy metropolitan city or where to go.

The good news was folks in Texas are very helpful. The bad news was, we couldn't tell them what it was we were looking for because we really didn't know. So much had changed since we had been in the market for these things.

Consequently, we muddled along until we began to get a handle on things. This was a challenge in 105-108 degree temperature.

Really HOT

Make no mistake, it is *HOT* in Texas. The good news is, as your blood thins, you get used to it. The bad news is it takes 3 to 4 years!

What is so remarkable about Texans, both native and immigrants, is that no one complains (except for Ol' Tex and Lady Bev) at this point in our Texas history. We were figuring by the following summer, we would be enjoying the hot of the day in the pool or in Colorado—perhaps even the mountains of New Mexico.

Armadillo

It wasn't long before I experienced my first armadillo. Early one morning while I was out walking at first light in an attempt to beat the real heat of the day, I climbed the hill at Old Settler's Park and noted something on the roadway several feet in front of me. *It was staring back.* Could it be an attack rat forging for his breakfast?

He was the cutest little critter--round little ball for a nose on a petite snout with whiskers that twitched with delight in appreciation of his latest find. As he turned to leave the area, I noted he had a quaint little armor-plated house on his back.

Talk about self-sufficient Texans!

Wiley Coyote

Speaking of self-sufficient...my early morning walks are going to get me in trouble yet!

Same time, same place, different critter. I froze when I looked into the eyes of this furry beauty. I couldn't remember. "Do you run, stand your ground, or walk on by?"

Slowly, I put my Nikes in reverse and backed down the hill. Then, when I felt I was within running distance of the motorcoach, "Slowly I turned," put one foot in front of the other, jumped into high gear, and never looked back until I could peer from the window of my Monaco Dynasty.

It would be a few days before I would do the "same time, same place" thing again.

Show Me the Money

We shopped 'til we dropped, spending money like "drunken sailors." Then I would freeze and scare the both of us--me in particular. At that point, we would have to take a morning, sit down, and *recalculate.* Where are we going? And, where have we been?

This financial review was a necessary part of starting from scratch with thousands of dollars going out daily. We called this ritual meeting, "Show me the money!" Ol' Tex, the mutually appointed Financial Advisor, and me, the willing financial spender. We have enjoyed this successful joint financial adventure for many years.

Long Hot Summer

Although the summer of 1999 was long and hot, we did enjoy every minute of it. We spent a lot of evenings returning to the home we were purchasing with any excuse to be there. We measured, we planned and we dreamed.

The developer's quality control inspector and team checked and worked tirelessly to make certain the house was perfection.

Finally, the day came and both the house and the new residents were ready.

Home on the Sixth Green!

We moved into the ***"home on the sixth green,"*** as it was officially called, on the Legacy Hills Golf course at Sun City Texas and lived there happily for five years. We parked the Dreamcatcher in a covered garage nearby. Although we did take it out on a road trip once in a while, truth is, we were too busy to spend much time away from home. In this community, we knew if we were gone, we would miss something!

We lived there for five years before we decided it was time to move back East before it was too late. We had never lived in the southeast and it was time to give it a try.

Just before we sold our home, we sold the Dreamcatcher. It was difficult to do so since it was now part of our psyches. We also sold the Jeep Grand Cherokee which served us so well during our years on the road. It was time to leave the "good old days" behind and begin a new adventure.

Another Prophetic Sign or Omen

For starters, we moved to Venice, Florida right on the Gulf of Mexico where we muddled through and anxiously survived eight (8) hurricanes. We were moving out of Florida the day that Hurricane Katrina roared up the West Coast of Florida before hitting New Orleans.

From Hurricanes to Hilton Head

Whatever were we thinking???

Someone had to ask that question, so I thought I'd do it for you. We were being guided to a new venture just outside of Charlotte, North Carolina. It was in Indian Land, South Carolina that we began a remarkable new adventure.

Home on the First Green!

A new beginning from "scratch" was begun at Carolina Lakes. We took a number to purchase long before the entrance to the community was even cut through.

We moved into our "***home on the first green"*** in June, 2006. Homebase became Indian Land, South Carolina where we began to write for three (3) newspapers. This time, the "Beautiful Bev" became

"Bev the Reporter," while Ol' Tex became "Jim the Photographer." Both hold independent positions and work together as a team. And, no, it doesn't get any better than that—at least not yet! Of course, from their point of view, as long as they are together, it is always "the best."

Happy Trails!

In the RV World, when friends are separating for any length of time, they never say "good-bye" but rather, "Happy Trails!" Implied, if you recall the lyrics, is 'til we meet again.

No matter where you are, each day is a new adventure. Each moment has something remarkable to offer. Our lives are filled with opportunities. Our minds may be filled with memories, yet we know in our hearts we have "miles to go before we sleep."

Happy trails . . . .

Epilogue

It's just stuff!

I embrace the idea that we are on earth for a reason. We are here to learn lessons from this life. If ever there was a lesson to be learned about life, it's about *stuff.* Me and my partner, Jim, were fortunate to learn this lesson before it was too late. It came early in our decision-making process when we entertained the idea of traveling full-time in a motor home.

Age-wise, we were both close to clearing the half century mark in our lives and, as so many of us do, we managed to accumulate a lifetime of material goods which we carted with us from city to city, town to town, house to house as we were promoted and transferred around the country.

During the process of decision making and preparation to pursue "the road less traveled," we often shared our dreams and thoughts with friends. They listened politely even enthusiastically to our plans. They asked many questions, but, perhaps the most pointed, demanding question of all was, "What about your beautiful stuff? What will you do with all your *stuff?*"

Between ourselves, we agreed we would keep whatever we wanted. Neither of us would ever *have to* give up anything we felt we wanted to keep--no matter the reason. At the time, we owned and lived in a home with four bedrooms, four baths, two family rooms, two offices, living room, dining room, country kitchen, entertainment center, screened in summer extension with deck, two car garage, plus several storage rooms. It was truly an estate. It was literally filled to the rafters with lovely, albeit *stuff*.

What would we do with all of our stuff?

It was not an easy decision. We investigated storage facilities. We researched the idea of finding a home base. We thought about keeping the home that we had which housed all the *stuff*. Fortunately, we had plenty of time to process and make the right decision for us. We, independently, and in partnership, decided to get rid of *all our stuff*.

One of us lost sleep over how we would achieve this Herculean goal. The other, the one who couldn't stand to see the mate so wrought with stress, began to literally work the stuff out of the house. With each load, the process became easier and easier as far as letting go. There was a freedom neither of us could have imagined. The process was so revitalizing, that we became excited each time we found a new home for some of the *stuff*.

Lessons of Stuff

We did pack up a few cardboard boxes with items we felt we needed and carted them in a very tiny trailer to Indiana for storage in a small corner of an attic. Some boxes would continue on with us when we made the final journey west to pick up our motor home; some would stay in an attic until such time as they were needed.

We were down to bare essentials when we sold the home and moved to temporary quarters to live out the next few months. All the *stuff* had been successfully disbursed.

So, what were the lessons?

LESSON ONE: The first lesson was a spiritual awakening of sorts. The only things I saved were some professional books. Our marriage was beautiful because we had separate careers and lived independent lives. When we came together on the weekends, we shared our experiences and supported each other in our professions.

By choosing this new lifestyle, we were going to be melding together as one. We never gave that much thought until one day I realized what this choice meant to me. I would be giving up my independence, my strength as a person. This was not a problem as long as we were together. However, it was the big "what if" question I couldn't bring myself to think of in realistic terms. "What if" something happened to my mate and I was alone?

It seems I had a subconscious fear that by melding together, I would lose myself, my identity, and I would not remember who I am. By keeping the boxes of books which represented to me who I was, I could go back and find myself.

LESSON TWO: The second lesson is that we don't really need *stuff* to be happy. It weights us down and makes us assume a responsibility for having it that is not necessary. There is a great sense of freedom when one does not have it. Today, we could close the door wherever we are, walk away with our wonderful memories, and revel in the fact that we have each other.

LESSON THREE: Today, we are two different people. We have *stuff*. More importantly, each day we begin anew and care nothing about *stuff* while cherishing the moment—and each other.

ABOUT THE AUTHOR and HER PHOTOGRAPHER

Beverly Lane Lorenz is a professional writer, columnist, reporter, and author. She writes for magazines, newspapers, and has authored books and other publications. Her career began as a dream in elementary school but her guidance counselor and parents said, "Newspaper reporting is too difficult a job for a woman."

In the meantime, she became a University Professor teaching speech, theory, law, writing and many other communication subjects to college juniors and seniors while counseling their career choices. During that time, she was asked to write a novel. This was when she realized that writing is her passion.

Beverly has worked for private Advertising Agencies and Public Relations Departments for major corporations as well as educational facilities. She has held seminars in the art of persuasion and marketing. She has taught and evaluated public speakers and political candidates. She is a consultant in the communication industry.

James Paul Lorenz began his professional career as an engineer in the bearings industry but soon moved into the oil industry where he became an executive for a major oil company. During his career, he traveled and was a liaison to many major industries.

In his free time, Jim enjoyed using his photography skills. He often traveled with his camera and enjoyed capturing scenes and people. Eventually, they joined forces as writer and photographer and have enjoyed many exciting assignments together.

Bev and Jim find new adventures as they continue their journey. May their dreaming never end.